110668611

# Battle for the Big Sky

*To Hilary—*

*Without you, the Montana sky would be smaller and this place last,
and most certainly not best.*

# Battle for the Big Sky

## Representation and the Politics of Place in the Race for the U.S. Senate

**David C.W. Parker**
*Montana State University*

Los Angeles | London | New Delhi
Singapore | Washington DC

Los Angeles | London | New Delhi
Singapore | Washington DC

FOR INFORMATION:

CQ Press

An Imprint of SAGE Publications, Inc

2455 Teller Road

Thousand Oaks, California 91320

E-mail: order@sagepub.com

SAGE Publications Ltd.

1 Oliver's Yard

55 City Road

London EC1Y 1SP

United Kingdom

SAGE Publications India Pvt. Ltd.

B 1/I 1 Mohan Cooperative Industrial Area

Mathura Road, New Delhi 110 044

India

SAGE Publications Asia-Pacific Pte. Ltd.

3 Church Street

#10-04 Samsung Hub

Singapore 049483

Copyright © 2015 by CQ Press, an Imprint of SAGE Publications, Inc. CQ Press is a registered trademark of Congressional Quarterly Inc.

All rights reserved. No part of this book may be reproduced or utilized in any form or by any means, electronic or mechanical, including photocopying, recording, or by any information storage and retrieval system, without permission in writing from the publisher.

Printed in the United States of America.

A catalog record of this book is available from the Library of Congress.

ISBN 978-1-4833-6863-4 (pbk)

This book is printed on acid-free paper.

Acquisitions: Sarah Calabi

Editorial Assistant: Raquel Christie

Production Editor: Bennie Clark Allen

Copy Editor: Michelle Ponce

Typesetter: C&M Digitals (P) Ltd.

Proofreader: Laura Webb

Indexer: Terri Corry

Cover Designer: Gail Buschman

Marketing Manager: Amy Whitaker

14 15 16 17 18 10 9 8 7 6 5 4 3 2 1

# Contents

# Tables and Figures

## TABLES

## FIGURES

# Preface

There are many reasons to write a book on a competitive Senate campaign and congressional representation. Mine boil down to three: to show the real consequences of representational activities undertaken by members of Congress, to demonstrate how campaigns can matter, and because I could. As a political scientist, I study how members of Congress interact with their constituents and—through that research—have come to believe that member interactions with constituents have clear electoral consequences. Trips home, electronic newsletters sent, press releases issued, and casework undertaken on behalf of constituents attempting to navigate a complicated federal bureaucracy are essential to building a lasting and trusting relationship with the folks back home. The 2012 Montana Senate race provided an interesting test of the proposition that these interactions matter because the two candidates were incumbents representing the same geographic space. Both had served Montanans in Congress during the same period, and both had access to similar tools with which to build trust with their constituents. How did Republican Congressman Denny Rehberg and Democratic Senator Jon Tester engage with Montanans in their official capacities, and which interactions generated a deeper and more effective connection? Finally, would the disparity in official resources between a House member representing a state alone and a United States senator affect how Montanans perceived the two candidates? This book shows how the home styles first documented by political scientist Richard Fenno nearly four decades ago still matter in a very different political era dominated by polarized political parties and social media.

If representational activities matter and generate impressions among constituents, the campaigns undertaken by members of Congress bolster and solidify those impressions in the minds of voters. Candidates raise millions of dollars in Senate races because they believe that efforts to communicate with voters about their records and those of their opponents have consequences for election outcomes. Political science, however, has not been so sure that campaigns affect election outcomes. In fact, much of the existing scholarship suggests that campaigns do not matter much at all. What matters most are the fundamentals underlying each congressional race, including whether there is an incumbent (who usually wins), the state of the economy, the popularity of the president, whether the incumbent shares the president's party, the partisan leanings of individual voters, and the existence of a presidential campaign. I argue that while campaigns very often don't matter because many House and Senate races are simply not competitive in the first place, in competitive elections they absolutely can make the difference between winning and losing. In this book, I show how.

Ever since I read Fenno's pioneering work as an undergraduate, I hoped I would have the opportunity in my career to soak and poke my way through a campaign as he did. Doing research like Fenno's carries risks: It is time intensive and requires extensive travel and considerable effort sorting through voluminous materials. In a discipline increasingly measuring research productivity by methodologically heavy peer-reviewed articles, it seemed too much of a gamble for junior faculty. A prominent scholar reviewing the impact of Fenno's collective work notes, "Everyone cites Fenno, but very few people do that kind of work. There was remarkably little follow through."[1] Compounding the problem of replicating his method is the changing nature of a political landscape that is less trusting and more polarized.

Serendipity played no small role in the emergence of this project. I moved to Montana two years after Senator Jon Tester had beaten a scandal-tarnished incumbent in the closest Senate race of 2006. Political forecasters anticipated that Tester's 2012 reelection would be competitive and close. As a newly minted Montanan, I discovered how small and intimate the state really is. Republican Congressman Denny Rehberg's eldest daughter, Katie, was a student in some of my classes at Montana State. I met the congressman in 2008, and he spoke to my classes on occasion. I got to know him a bit and enjoyed learning from him.

In late January of 2011, I heard the rumors about Rehberg challenging Tester.

Participant observation still had a chance in this small state where access was the norm. Better yet, I would try to do something Fenno had not: watch the campaign from both sides as it unfolded. My career was well-positioned so that tenure was not at risk. Right place, right time, right race, right person, and right . . . method. The stars had aligned.

Like Fenno, I spent a lot of time dipping in and out of the lives of Senator Tester and Congressman Rehberg on the campaign trail. I enjoyed unprecedented access to both campaigns, and—in addition to my visits with the candidates—interviewed nearly 50 people involved in the campaign and Montana politics. To better understand the political careers of Congressman Rehberg and Senator Tester, I closely examined the bills they sponsored, the earmarks they obtained, and the press releases both issued from their Washington offices between 2007 and 2010.

To get a solid fix on the impressions Montanans had of both candidates before and during the campaign, I relied both on polls and focus groups. I reviewed public polls released throughout the race (including exit polls), private polls commissioned by Senator Conrad Burns and Congressman Rehberg, and conducted three focus groups of Montana voters in Gallatin County, the state's fastest growing. I also obtained copies of television advertisements aired by the campaigns, outside groups, and the parties, as well as advertising contracts and invoices from Montana's six media markets. This information allowed me to understand how each side framed the choice for Montanans and when and where each side had the informational advantage on television. Finally, I poured over election returns to explain why the fundamentals, which favored a Republican victory, failed to behave as anticipated by election forecasters and political prognosticators. The end result is a project using a variety of information, both qualitative and quantitative, to support my conclusions about representation and campaigning in the 21st century.

This book is divided into two parts. Part I provides the background necessary to understand Montana politics, the cast of characters, and the representational relationships established by Senator Tester and Congressman Rehberg prior to their 2012 campaign. Part II is an account of that campaign and how Jon Tester overcame substantial barriers to win reelection. I provide evidence throughout that the representational actions of candidates and campaign choices affect the outcomes of elections.

Part I, Chapter 2 focuses on Montana and its land, which is central to the politics of Montana and the West more generally. This chapter contextualizes the paradoxes of modern politics in Montana, drawing upon recent scholarship about the state's political history as well as a series of interviews with thoughtful Montanans who celebrate the state in their words, their deeds, and their industry.

The final three chapters of Part I discuss the prepolitical and political careers of Tester and his 2012 rival, Rehberg. I weave a theoretical argument throughout that the governing styles of both Tester and Rehberg are central to how they build relationships and constituencies within Montana. It is their home styles that ground their respective campaign narratives in 2012 and are central to the campaign's eventual outcome.

Part II opens in the winter of 2011—the early days of the campaign. Chapter 6 examines how both candidates primed and framed particular issues for voters at the very beginning of the campaign, showing how these decisions reflected the key electoral constituencies each candidate had built as well as their political experiences. I focus on two issues central to the race: the federal debt and the Affordable Care Act. Finally, I show how early spending by outside organizations on television, courtesy of *Citizens United*, created both opportunities and frustrations for Rehberg and Tester.

Chapter 7 looks at voters through the lenses of polls and focus groups. I demonstrate how the reputational styles of both Rehberg and Tester left clear impressions on Montanans and how this shaped the ensuing narratives the campaigns developed. I pay particular attention to how voters viewed Tester and Rehberg personally and the decision by Senator Tester to launch a series of biographical spots beginning mid-March 2012. This decision created an informational advantage for Tester that had important repercussions for how the race unfolded.

Millions of dollars were spent by the parties, candidates, and outside groups on television advertising during the 2012 race. Chapter 8 looks at the literature on how campaign advertisements affect the decisions of voters—focusing in particular on the importance of developing an informational advantage in television advertising spots. Given that the literature stresses that information advantages are important to affecting voter perceptions, I explore why the Republican informational advantage in the closing days of the race does not yield the anticipated benefits for Rehberg. I again demonstrate how Tester's considerable advantages as an incumbent senator provided an additional bonus in the earned media he received.

The penultimate chapter opens on Election Night 2012 in Great Falls, where I watched the results trickle in at Jon Tester's campaign headquarters. I pick up with both the candidates and their staff members in the weeks and months following the campaign, explaining how Tester found a path to victory in a Republican-leaning state. In particular, I debunk some theories as to why Tester won that have gained favor in the months following the campaign's close. In addition to interviews with the candidates and staff members, I examine exit polls, precinct returns, and voter turnout data to stress the importance of the campaign message, grassroots mobilization, and voter perceptions of the economy on the final outcome.

Chapter 10 concludes by taking a 30,000 foot view of congressional elections to apply the lessons of Montana's 2012 Senate campaign to our collective knowledge of electioneering and congressional representation. Specifically, I consider the unexpected consequences of *Citizens United*, how the development of representational relationships matters more than ever, and how campaigns can affect election outcomes even if many outcomes can be predicted well in advance.

Hillary Clinton once said it takes a village to raise children. Although this book has my name on the cover, it took a village to help me research and write it. My first debt is to Richard Fenno who provided the intellectual inspiration for the project. He also generously agreed to read a draft of the project. I hope that, even as I fall short of his standard, these pages remain true to his scholarship and those of his many students—most especially Barbara Sinclair and Wendy Schiller, whose work is cited in these pages.

If one person provided the intellectual spark, a slew of others stoked the flames during the twenty months I followed the Montana Senate race intently. And, I can't thank Senator Jon Tester and Congressman Denny Rehberg enough for generously allowing me to step into their campaign lives and travel with them in cars and planes throughout Montana. And I want to thank their families—especially Sharla Tester and Jan Rehberg. I appreciate you letting me come along for the ride and entrusting me with your stories.

But as important as the central characters are to this tale, I could never have told it without their respective supporting casts in Montana and in Washington. In particular, I'd like to acknowledge Tom Lopach, Bill Lombardi, Randy Vogel, Andrea Helling, Jed Link, Aaron Murphy, Erik Iverson, Kathy Weber, and Jake Eaton. Without your support and help, this book would be less interesting, less insightful, and still just a dream. I spent so many hours of your time during and after the campaign that I'll spend the next twenty years trying to repay each of you.

I spent a lot of time travelling to Montana's television stations to get copies of advertising contracts and invoices. This was essential to analyzing all the outside spending in the campaign. Everyone was courteous as I spent hours digitally photographing thousands of pages of records. A few people stand out for going above and beyond the call of duty: Tim Keating at KTVQ in Billings, Leslie Stoll O'Neill at Montana Max Media in Missoula, and Patricia King at KSVI/KHMT in Billings. Tim helped me understand the process of buying television time and mysterious rate schedules. Leslie and Tim also provided me with electronic summaries of television advertising on their stations by group and by month which was very useful in compiling my spending numbers. And Pat, thanks for the "invoice."

Several Montanans helped me understand their state and the early careers of Senator Tester and Congressman Rehberg. Without them, the first half of the book would have been impossible. Congressman Pat Williams, Secretary of State Bob Brown, Governor Stan Stephens, State Senators Dennis Iverson, Carolyn Squires, Bob Marks, Dan Weinberg, Jon Ellingson, Royal Johnson, John Cobb, Trudi Schmidt, and Mike Halligan graciously met with me to share their love of Montana and their political experiences. Bill Wyckoff, Bob Swartout, Dan Kemmis, Dorothy Eck, Harry Fritz, Jim Murry, Ken Toole, Ray Rasker, Todd Wilkinson, Henry Kriegel, and Archie and Nina Alexander provided their thoughts about Montana, which gave me labor, business, environmental, cultural, and historical perspectives. I spent a memorable afternoon with former Senator Conrad Burns, who gave me two-plus hours of his time after which he gave me a bunch of memorabilia. I'm particularly grateful for him granting access to his polls from the 2006 race. A few others provided me information but needed to do so on background. You know who you are, and I thank you.

My colleagues at Montana State provided much needed inspiration and research support without which this book could not have been written. Research funds paid for travel and time off from teaching allowed me to follow the campaign unimpeded. Jerry Johnson, department head when I was hired and when this project began, didn't at all think my idea harebrained. He sent me to Mark Young, head of Experimental Program to Stimulate Competitive Research (EPSCoR) on campus, and my dean at the time, Paula Lutz, to get the financial support and teaching buyout necessary to follow the campaigns in the fall of 2012. I am particularly grateful to Paula for agreeing to grant me leave in the fall of 2012 and a new computer—both of which were instrumental to the project. My colleagues, Liz Shanahan, Sara Rushing, Eric Austin, Franke Wilmer, and Linda Young graciously tolerated my absence from the office throughout much of the summer and fall of 2012.

Colleagues beyond Montana State helped, too. Sean Kelly and Scott Frisch at California State University Channel Islands, whose extraordinary work doesn't receive the attention it deserves, have helped me find publishers while providing moral support. Justin Grimmer at Stanford and Craig Goodman at the University of Houston-Victoria, both co-authors and friends, never grew tired of my stories and Facebook posts about the race. Sean Theriault and Wendy Schiller cheered me on, always knowing when I needed kind words.

The project also owes a lot to my students at Montana State. All of them endured my stories from the trail. Simply sharing my experiences and getting their feedback has helped as I've worked to match observation to theory. Students of my Congressional Campaign class in the spring of 2014 assisted by reading a complete draft. Five students, in particular, deserve mention because they engaged in some arduous coding of press releases and newspaper articles—some for the experience, others for their capstone projects. Thanks especially to Steaphan Clement, Hannah Walhert, Samantha Olson, Cassidy Geoghegan, and David Swedman. Your late nights and early mornings with Excel live on in Chapters 5 and beyond.

Chuck Johnson, longtime bureau chief for Lee Newspapers in Helena, read a complete draft as did Craig Goodman. Chuck's niece, Jane, was one of my top students at Montana State. She went on to work for Senators Baucus and Walsh, reading the first five chapters along with Pavielle Haines, now ABD in political science at Princeton. Mary Murphy and her husband Dale Martin, colleagues in the Department of History, read the history of Montana presented in Chapter 2. I am immensely grateful for their thoughts and observations, which made the book better.

Steve Turkiewicz, President and CEO of the Montana Bankers Association, also bears mention. He has helped in countless ways as I have worked on this project. He was an early supporter, he helped me meet a variety of folks important to Montana's industry, and offered me a variety of venues with which to share my insights on state and national politics. I truly appreciate our friendship and look forward to our early morning political coffees.

The focus groups I conducted and which were critical to understanding Montana voters could not have been undertaken if it weren't for the selfless efforts of three Bozemanites: Chris Mehl, Anders Lewendal, and David Yearous. These guys not only recruited friends to spend ninety minutes chatting about the Senate race during the summer of 2012, they generously opened their homes and provided some great food and drink at their expense (despite my repeated efforts to reimburse them). Your willingness to pitch in and help this researcher is emblematic of the community spirit that helps make Montana the "Last, Best Place."

To the Montanans I have come to know, love, and respect, thank you for sharing your beautiful state with me. It is a privilege to live among you and to educate your sons and daughters. In these pages, I hope to surprise and delight you. I may, occasionally, annoy. I only ask that you treat what I write as advice from a good and well-intentioned friend, much as K. Ross Toole asked so many years ago. You may not agree with everything in these pages, but I do hope you respect what I have to say. I certainly respect you.

I've saved the most important person for last: my wife Hilary, to whom I've dedicated the book. Words do not convey what she has done for me during our partnership together. Throughout everything we have shared, the ups and the downs, she has been my biggest fan, my most trusted editor, my muse, and my copilot. I have a lifetime to thank her, but that just won't be enough. She has always believed in me, but more importantly, she helped me to believe in myself.

---

# NOTE

1. Richard F. Fenno, Jr, *The Challenge of Congressional Representation*, (Cambridge, MA: Harvard University Press, 2013), 2.

# About the Author

**David C.W. Parker** is an associate professor of political science at Montana State University. He is the author of *The Power of Money in Congressional Campaigns, 1880–2006* (Norman: University of Oklahoma Press), as well as articles on the consequences of divided government and how members of Congress build reputations with their constituents. His article, "Making a Good Impression: Resource Allocations, Home Styles, and Washington Work," won the 2010 Alan Rosenthal Award from the American Political Science Association. His co-edited volume on archival research methodology, *Doing Archival Work in Political Science,* was published by Cambria press. As a respected nonpartisan analyst of politics, he frequently provides media commentary for local, state, and national news outlets — including *The New York Times,* the *Los Angeles Times, Washington Post, The Wall Street Journal, USA Today,* the *Associated Press, The Guardian,* the *Billings Gazette* and the *Bozeman Daily Chronicle.* His research on the Montana Senate race was featured in the PBS *Frontline* documentary "Big Sky, Big Money." Prior to entering the academy, Dr. Parker worked as a field representative, communications director, and campaign manager for a presidential, mayoral, and two Senate campaigns. He also writes a blog entitled "Big Sky Political Analysis."

# Why What Happened in Montana Won't Stay in Montana

**M**ontana witnessed a Senate campaign for the ages in 2012. That race itself was a singular event and the state certainly is unique. But the record of that campaign, and the insights it provides, are applicable to other competitive races, whether for House or Senate seats and irrespective of location. Through careful study of this campaign, we gain a better understanding of the politics of the American West and of the substantial political clout it has gained. And, we can see more clearly how members of Congress understand the process of representation and its electoral consequences.

Incumbent Senator Jon Tester was elected by a razor-thin margin in 2006 and was considered to be one of the most vulnerable Democrats running for reelection. Although characterizing Montana as a Republican state is overly simplistic, voters frequently cast their ballots for Republican presidential candidates. In 2008, Barack Obama may have had the best showing of a Democratic presidential nominee since Bill Clinton, who eked out a win in 1992, but the newly elected president quickly became unpopular among Montanans.[1] The Republican nominee was expected to win the state by double digits in 2012. The Tea Party-fueled midterms in 2010 that brought Republicans a stunning 60-seat gain and a majority in the House of Representatives coincided with similar gains for Montana Republicans. Democrats lost 18 seats in the lower house of the state legislature, becoming a tiny minority in the chamber.

Two years before Election Day 2012, internal Tester polls showed the senator losing to Congressman Denny Rehberg—the widely anticipated Republican nominee—by more than eight points.[2] Tester was in trouble—and if Tester fell, the Democratic majority in the U.S. Senate likely would follow. In February 2011, Rehberg, who had served as the state's lone congressman since 2001, announced his candidacy. This prompted respected national political prognosticators Charlie Cook, Larry Sabato, and Stu Rothenberg to rate Tester as "extremely vulnerable." All considered the race a toss-up.[3] Many months later, in his final election prediction for the *New York Times,* election forecasting guru Nate Silver gave a 66 percent chance of a Republican Senate victory in Montana.

But Silver would be wrong. Jon Tester defied nearly everyone's expectations and beat Republican Denny Rehberg by nearly four percentage points while Republican presidential candidate Mitt Romney handily carried the state by thirteen. Out of

1

the thirty-three Senate races in the 2012 cycle, Montana was only one of two that Silver predicted incorrectly. Why were Silver and so many other prognosticators wrong? How did Tester survive? Finding an answer to that puzzle is one of the reasons I wrote this book.

It is not the only reason. Through an in-depth analysis of the Montana Senate race, we learn a lot about congressional campaigns, elections, and the process of representation. One might ask whether we can learn anything generalizable from one race unfolding in such a distinctive place. Admittedly, Montana is unusual, as any Montanan will proudly tell you. While it is the fourth-largest state geographically, it is sparsely populated (and only one of seven states with just one member serving in the House of Representatives). Montana also is one of the poorest states in the country and has little ethnic or racial diversity. The two largest minority groups in the country—Latinos and African-Americans—together make up a mere fraction of the state's population. In many ways, Montana appears to be an outlier from which one could not make broad, sweeping conclusions about political phenomena.

But as unique as Montana is, the state—and this particular campaign—is exactly the place a student of politics should study to look for widely applicable conclusions about electioneering and representation at the dawn of the 21st century for four reasons. First, because the race was competitive from start to finish, the 2012 Montana Senate campaign sheds light on whether and under what conditions campaigns affect electoral outcomes. Second, the rise of the West politically throughout the 20th century has made the region critical to the balance of political power nationally while simultaneously altering the content of the national political debate. Third, Montana is no different when it comes to how members of Congress craft and communicate representational styles to constituents—representational styles which are central in the campaign narratives of all congressional campaigns (and especially meaningful in competitive campaign environments). Finally, because I enjoyed unprecedented access to both candidates during the campaigns, I saw campaigns in a way few political scientists do. I travelled with the candidates, watched them interact with constituents, interviewed their staff members after the campaign, and had access to some of their internal data. As a result, we get an up-close-and-personal look at the campaign and its issues.

## DO CAMPAIGNS MATTER? MONTANA VOTES "YES"

Let's begin by acknowledging a larger debate among political scientists that has beset the discipline since its very beginnings: Do campaigns matter? Some of the earliest research suggested "no." These studies of voter behavior indicated that casting a ballot was mostly a function of a person's partisan identification and socioeconomic status.[4] Given that these characteristics are immutable, campaigns really didn't matter much because voting was a reflexive act. Add more recent scholarship indicating that partisanship actually acts as an information filter—individuals seek information conforming to their preexisting views and discard information contracting those beliefs[5]—and some political scientists quickly conclude that campaigns are full of sound and fury, signifying nothing.

Alternatively, the authors of *The American Voter,* who identified partisanship as a critical determinant of voter behavior, addressed a puzzle contradicting this theory. In 1952 and 1956, the electorate was overwhelmingly Democratic, and yet Republican Dwight Eisenhower won two presidential races decisively. Something about Eisenhower caused Democrats to abandon their party—at least in the short term—for someone carrying the other party's banner. The authors attribute Eisenhower's appeal to his "projecting a strong personal image and stressing the foreign policy concerns of voters. This allowed less attached and less interested Democratic adherents to overcome their predispositions and cast a vote for Eisenhower."[6] In short, the Republican campaign for Eisenhower mattered. Other scholars have found important campaign effects on the ability of voters to identify and recall candidates, the ways in which candidates and parties are evaluated, increasing voter turnout, and how accurately voters recall the ideology and issue positions of a candidate.[7] This book sheds light on this larger debate among political scientists about campaign effects, concluding that campaigns matter.

A related reason to look at one Senate race in one state—even if that state may not be representative—is that if we believe that campaigns can matter, they should matter the most in a competitive race. The fact is that campaigns often do not matter in many congressional elections because most congressional races are no longer competitive. A singular feature of the modern electoral landscape is the disappearance of so-called marginal congressional districts, a phenomenon first noted by David Mayhew in the early 1970s. Mayhew wrote that between 1956 and 1972, the number of contested House seats with incumbents running for reelection—where the Democratic Party vote share is between 45 percent and 55 percent—declined by roughly half.[8] He argues that one factor for the decline is the increasing value of incumbency; political scientists spent the next two decades measuring incumbency's precise electoral value.[9] When a House incumbent chooses to run for reelection, they win 95 percent of the time throughout the postwar period. According *The Cook Political Report,* the number of swing congressional districts declined 45 percent between 1998 and 2013, from 164 to just 90.[10] A substantial minority of House members run uncontested each cycle, while another sizeable percentage never face a quality, well-funded challenger (defined as a candidate who has successfully run for and served in an elected office before running for Congress).

But Senate incumbents are not as well-protected as House members. They represent states, not districts, so they are not subject to the redistricting that increases electoral security. Senators are also more likely to draw a quality challenger to run against them. Even so, they enjoy a substantial incumbency advantage. From 1946 through 2012, Senate incumbents choosing to run for reelection who reached the general election won reelection 82 percent of the time. On average, those incumbents won with 63 percent of the vote; only 37 percent of Senate incumbents received less than 55 percent of the vote in the previous election. Forty-five percent of Senate incumbents in the postwar era do not even draw a quality challenger.[11]

In noncompetitive congressional races, voter partisanship and the incumbent's greater name recognition yield the almost universal outcome of the incumbent winning reelection regardless of the campaign effort the incumbent undertakes. But these situations are not a true test of the hypothesis that campaigns matter, because the incumbent dominates the information environment. To better test the proposition that campaigns affect election outcomes, we must look at races where the information environment is up for grabs, such as open seat races or races where the incumbent faces a competitive challenge from a quality candidate.

Congressional incumbents actively discourage the emergence of competitive challengers, so races where they are at an informational disadvantage are rare. Incumbents establish a veneer of invulnerability by constructing massive financial war chests and winning elections by substantial margins. These two factors signal to would-be candidates that most challenges would be costly and unsuccessful. The best candidates—those who have run and won a campaign for elected office—often chose not to run against incumbents because the costs of entry are high, and the return on investment low. Open seats represent the obverse scenario: a lower cost of entry with a higher potential payoff. As a result, the best quality candidates often choose not to challenge incumbents, waiting instead for the incumbent to retire. The end result is that most incumbents breeze easily to reelection while open seats are often expensive, hard-fought affairs where either party's nominee could win. Campaigns can and often do matter in open seat races.[12]

But incumbents can and do lose, and they are much more likely to do so when they present a target of opportunity for a strategically minded challenger. Incumbents embroiled in scandal, as well as those who are perceived as out of touch with constituents, have health problems, or simply have not created a large reelection constituency shatter the cloak of invulnerability. These situations draw quality challengers to run against weakened incumbents. One way to systematically identify incumbent vulnerability is to classify incumbent campaigns as competitive or not by using three factors: the incumbent's previous vote share, whether the challenger they face in the general election is "quality," and whether the incumbent represents a state that was won by their party's presidential candidate in the last presidential election.

I examined each Senate election featuring an incumbent between 2000 and 2012 and coded a race as "competitive" if the incumbent won the previous election with less than 55 percent of the vote and faced a quality challenger. I also coded a race as competitive if the incumbent's presidential party did not win the state in the most recent presidential election prior to the incumbent's reelection bid. This yielded 79 competitive Senate races with an incumbent candidate running for reelection out of a total of 186. Of the 107 races defined as noncompetitive, the incumbent only lost three times—a reelection rate of 97 percent. In competitive races, 23 incumbents lost for a reelection rate of 71 percent—11 percentage points less than the postwar average of 82 percent.[13]

The Montana Senate race between Jon Tester and Denny Rehberg in 2012 was, by this definition, a competitive race. Rehberg, as the state's lone congressman, was certainly a "quality" challenger. Democrat Tester won his initial campaign in 2006 with only 49 percent of the vote—and, in fact, beat incumbent Senator Conrad Burns by less than 3,600 votes. Finally, Republican presidential nominee John McCain won the popular vote in Montana by a little more than two percentage points in 2008. The most important question for our purposes, however, is whether the Montana Senate race as a case is representative of the larger population of competitive Senate races. If so, it is much more likely that we can apply the lessons learned from this single case to competitive Senate races (and to the bigger question of whether campaigns matter). If it is not, then we have an interesting story to share but not much else.

In three important respects, the 2012 Montana Senate race is a typical example of a competitive Senate campaign. The average Senate incumbent spent $9.2 million dollars in competitive races between 2000 and 2012. The average challenger? $5.4 million. In Montana, incumbent Tester spent a little more than $13 million. His challenger, Rehberg, spent slightly more than $9 million. In both cases, these amounts are above the mean by less than one standard deviation. In other words, the spending by both the incumbent and challenger is about what one would expect in a typical, competitive Senate campaign. The average Republican presidential share of the vote in competitive Senate elections was 58 percent; in Montana, Mitt Romney won with 55 percent of the vote in 2012. Finally, competitive Senate seats are more likely to be found in more sparsely populated states: Competitive Senate races averaged 850,792 in population compared to 2.5 million in noncompetitive campaigns. Montana—population one million, distinctive and different in so many ways—is precisely the place to understand the dynamics of a competitive Senate race because it is not terribly distinctive from other places hosting competitive Senate elections. The 2012 Montana Senate race matters to an audience beyond Montana because it is a case from which generalizable conclusions can be drawn about competitive Senate races.

## THE RISE OF THE WEST

To understand the second reason why the 2012 Montana Senate race is important to the study of campaigns and elections, it helps to think about the larger social forces sweeping across the American landscape over the past 100 years. One of the most prominent changes across the 20th and early 21st centuries is the nation's demographic march westward.

At the turn of the 20th century, the West was literally empty. According to a report of the United States Census Bureau, only 5.4 percent of Americans lived in the 13 western states in 1900.[14] The most populated region? The Midwest, which nearly 35 percent of Americans called home. A century later, 23 percent of Americans live in the West—well eclipsing the nine eastern states at 19 percent. And the percentage of Americans living in the Midwest has fallen considerably to just 22.9 percent. The South grew, too, but at a much slower pace. In fact, the report notes that the West grew faster than any other region in every decade during the 20th century—and at twice the rate of every other region in every decade save during the 1930s.

The shift of America's population southward and westward is perhaps best expressed by the movement of the mean demographic center of the country. In 1900, that center was in Bartholomew County, Indiana, to the south and east of Indianapolis.[15] In 2000, the center had gravitated all the way to Phelps County, Missouri—324 miles west but only 101 miles south. Americans were moving to sunnier and more temperate climates in droves, but the shift westward was more dramatic than it was to the old Confederacy. The West has been the engine of demographic growth and change in modern America. As Horace Greeley exhorted famously "Go West, young man!"—we have.

The West was becoming less isolated culturally and politically. The diffusion of innovation and ideas was challenging in a region with few navigable rivers, often impenetrable mountains, and nearly no urban centers. In 1900, only San Francisco—with a population of 342,000—was ranked as one of America's ten largest cities (and it was tenth). Both Cleveland and Buffalo had more people. Fast forward to 2010: Now four of America's largest cities—Los Angeles, Phoenix, San Diego, and San Jose—are in the West and each has a population of 900,000 or more.[16] The creation of the federal highway system allowed Americans to spread beyond the crowded cities north and east of the Mississippi. Some moved to suburbs, but still more moved to the open spaces of the West. The establishment of reliable water supplies has been critical for urbanization and population growth. Reliable water came courtesy of federally funded irrigation and hydroelectric projects built by the U.S. Bureau of Reclamation, which was established by the Newlands Reclamation Act of 1902.[17] As the West overcame isolation and water scarcity, it became a more attractive place for Americans to live.

As Americans moved west, political ramifications followed.[18] This massive demographic movement drained the East and especially the Midwest of political clout in the House of Representatives. In 1900, 40 percent of House seats belonged to the Midwest—more than any other region and fully ten percentage points more than the South and the West combined. The West only had five percent of those seats.[19] If population growth trends continue as estimated, the West will receive 105 House seats by 2020—or 24 percent of available seats, beating the Midwest by 2 seats.[20] The West already surpassed the East in congressional seats during the 1990s apportionment and will be second only to the South politically in 2020.

Unlike the South or the East, the West remains a politically contestable region. During the last decade, more than two-thirds of all House and Senate seats were controlled by the Democratic and Republican Parties in the East and the South, respectively. In the West, 51 percent of Senate seats were held by Republicans during the same period. In the House, Republicans controlled 43 percent of House seats. The Midwest also remains quite competitive between the parties, with Democrats controlling 58 percent of Senate and 47 percent of House seats, respectively.[21]

As political power shifts to the competitive West, the influence of the region on the nation's politics increases. This means that specifically Western issues—public land use, water law, the management of endangered species, and environmental management more generally—will take up a greater portion of the national political conversation. If we want to understand where American politics is going, we must study the region gaining political prominence and examine the congressional elections there, such as Montana's Senate race between Congressman Rehberg and Senator Tester.

## BUILDING CONSTITUENT CONNECTIONS

Finally, the reason why the 2012 Montana Senate campaign may be applicable to other elections centered on the art of connecting with constituents. Richard Fenno's pioneering studies of members of Congress, which spanned more than a dozen books across four decades of scholarship, advanced a simple but powerful observation: To understand how members of Congress represent their constituents, one must observe them as they spend time at home. Fenno argues that members of Congress develop "home styles" reflecting relationships with constituents, their allocation of official resources, and their Washington work.

All members of Congress cultivate distinctive home styles in dealing with their constituents. Although it is true that particular home styles are more widely used by House members than by senators, and while there is clear evidence that state size affects how members choose to represent constituencies and allocate their representational resources, the cultivation of a home style is fundamental to understanding how members of Congress do their jobs.[22] It is also fundamental to the reputations they craft and communicate on the campaign trail. Significantly, Members of Congress themselves behave as if those representational relationships matter in terms of how their constituents perceive them. This belief is grounded empirically.[23] To witness how these relationships are forged requires an in-depth case study such as the one that unfolds in these pages. And while the representational styles Jon Tester and Denny Rehberg chose to adopt are a function of the state they represent, the fact that each chose different styles in the same geographic constituency is further evidence that what is witnessed in Montana is not unique to Montana. That a diversity of home styles exists within a place that is, by most measures, not terribly diverse is powerful evidence that the routines and relationships observed in Montana are applicable elsewhere.

To show the importance of each candidate's relationship with constituents to the outcome of the 2012 Senate election, I documented their home styles—the interactions both Congressman Rehberg and Senator Tester had individually with the folks back home in Montana. To do this, I relied not only on their communications with constituents but also their legislative accomplishments. I also repeatedly travelled with and interviewed them as they engaged in the process of representation while their campaigns for the United States Senate unfolded in 2011 and 2012. Although events dictated many of my questions, I began with their perceptions of representation and often went back to those perceptions. Did they see themselves as primarily constituent servants, looking for and solving constituent problems? Was their primary responsibility as representatives to take positions on the key issues of the day? What about bringing pork back to the state? Or did their conception of representation defy such categorization? How did they define Montana and the value of its citizens? I wanted to know how each communicated his work in Washington to Montanans and how his conceptualization served as a rationale for why he should either be reelected (Tester) or sent to the Senate instead (Rehberg).

Who they believed they represented within Montana was as important as each of their individual conceptualizations of representation. In Fenno's words, who were their primary constituents, and who were their intimates? To which groups did each pay the most attention, and why? And, last but not least, how did they work to communicate that message to Montanans when they travelled throughout the state? Just as important as their answers to these questions are the interactions I observed between them and Montanans. By travelling with both the senator and the congressman, I could see clearly not only how each *did* the job of representation but how that representation was *perceived*. The difference in the styles each demonstrated and their reception by Montanans explains in part why Tester was able to prevail despite facing fundamentals on the ground favoring his erstwhile challenger.

## A RINGSIDE SEAT

The stakes were high in Montana in 2012. The Senate majority was up for grabs, and the path to that majority ran straight through the Big Sky. The low cost of media in Montana, the successful recruitment of Montana's lone congressman, Denny Rehberg, to run, and first-term Senator Jon Tester's low margin of victory made this an attractive pickup opportunity for Republicans. Democrats absolutely had to retain this seat or risk losing their recently achieved competitive edge in the Rocky Mountain West. The two men vying for the seat had deep roots in Montana agriculture but represented very different political philosophies. Both could readily claim a connection to Montana's unique and somewhat contradictory political traditions. Most importantly, the story that unfolds here illustrates the process of congressional representation in an era of polarized parties and social media while providing a window into the elusive world of modern electioneering that so far is absent from much scholarship on congressional elections and campaigns. And, as I had access to and cooperation from both candidates throughout the campaign, I am uniquely positioned to understand and evaluate the actions and responses of both sides as events unfolded to a grand conclusion—one that was never pre-ordained or certain. I had a ringside seat. And now, so do you.

## NOTES

1. Clinton's victory was likely because Ross Perot's third party candidacy pulled 26 percent of the vote, well above the 19 percent he received nationally in the popular vote.

2. Tom Lopach, interview with author, January 7, 2013.

3. Jeremy P. Jacobs, "Starting Lineup: Rehberg Running," *Hotline on Call*, February 1, 2011, http://www.nationaljournal.com/blogs/hotlineoncall/2011/02/starting-lineup-rehberg-running-01; "Montana Senate: Rehberg Moves Race to Toss-up." *Rothenberg*

*Political Report,* February 1, 2011; Larry J. Sabato. "The Crystal Ball's 2012 Roll-Out, Part One," *Sabato's Crystal Ball,* January 6, 2011, http://www.centerforpolitics.org/crystalball/articles/ljs2011010601/.

4. Bernard R. Berelson, Paul F. Lazarsfeld, and William N. McPhee, *Voting,* (Chicago: University of Chicago Press, 1954); Angus Campbell, Philip E. Converse, Warren E. Miller, and Donald E. Stokes, *The American Voter,* (Ann Arbor: University of Michigan Press, 1960).

5. Leon Festinger, *A Theory on Cognitive Dissonance.* (Evanston, IL.: Row, Peterson, 1957); Susanna Dilliplane, "All the News You Want to Hear: The Impact of Partisan News Exposure on Political Participation," *The Public Opinion Quarterly* 75, no. 2 (2011), 287–316; Natalie J. Stroud, "Polarization and Partisan Selective Exposure," *Journal of Communication* 60, no. 3 (2010), 556–576.

6. David C.W. Parker, *The Power of Money in Congressional Campaigns, 1880–2006.* (Norman: University of Oklahoma Press, 2008), 5n, 245n.

7. Parker, *The Power of Money in Congressional Campaigns;* Richard Johnston, Andre Blais, Henry E. Brady, and Jean Crete, *Letting the People Decide: Dynamics of a Canadian Election* (Stanford: Stanford University Press, 1992); Larry M. Bartels, *Presidential Primaries and the Dynamics of Public Choice* (Princeton: Princeton University Press, 1988); Samuel L. Popkin, *The Reasoning Voter.* 2nd edition (Chicago: University of Chicago Press, 1994); John Zaller, *The Nature and Origins of Mass Opinion* (New York, NY: Cambridge University Press, 1992); Geoffrey C. Layman and Thomas M. Carsey, "Party Polarization and 'Conflict Extension' in the American Electorate," *American Journal of Political Science* 46 (2002): 786–802; Constantine J. Spiliotes and Lynn Vavreck, "Campaign Advertising: Partisan Convergence or Divergence?" *Journal of Politics* 64 (2002): 249–61; John R. Petrocik, "Issue Ownership in Presidential Elections, with a 1980 Case Study," *American Journal of Political Science* 40 (1996): 825–50; Steven E. Finkel and John G. Geer, "A Spot Check: Casting Doubt on the Demobilizing Effect of Attack Advertising," *American Journal of Political Science* 42 (1998): 573–95; Paul Freedman and Kenneth M. Goldstein, "Measuring Media Exposure and the Effects of Negative Campaign Ads," *American Journal of Political Science* 43 (1999): 1189–1208; Richard R. Lau and Lee Sigelman, "Effectiveness of Political Advertising," in *Crowded Airwaves: Campaign Advertising in Elections,* eds. James A. Thurber, Candice J. Nelson, and David A. Dulio, 10–43, (Washington, DC: Brookings Institution Press, 2000); Kenneth S. Goldstein and Paul Freedman, "New Evidence for New Arguments: Money and Advertising in the 1996 Senate Elections," *Journal of Politics* 62 (2000): 1087–1108; Kenneth M. Goldstein and Paul Freedman, "Campaign Advertising and Voter Turnout: New Evidence for a Stimulation Effect," *Journal of Politics* 64 (2002): 721–40; Kim Fridkin Kahn and Patrick J. Kenney, "How Negative Campaigning Enhances Knowledge of Senate Elections," in *Crowded Airwaves: Campaign Advertising in Elections,* eds. James A. Thurber, Candice J. Nelson, and David A Dulio, 65–95 (Washington, DC: Brookings Institution Press, 2000); Travis N. Ridout and Michael M. Franz, *The Persuasive Power of Campaign Advertising,* Kindle Edition, (Philadelphia, PA: Temple University Press, 2011); James E. Campbell, *The American Campaign: U.S. Presidential Campaigns and the National Vote,* (College Station, TX: Texas A & M Press, 2000); Donald P. Green and Alan S. Gerber, *Get Out the Vote: How to Increase Voter Turnout,* 2nd Edition, (Washington, DC: Brookings

Institution Press, 2008); D. Sunshine Hillygus and Todd G. Shields, *The Persuadable Voter in Presidential Campaigns,* (Princeton, NJ: Princeton University Press, 2009); Thomas M. Holbrook, *Do Campaigns Matter?* (Thousand Oaks, CA: Sage Publications, 1996).

8. David R. Mayhew, "Congressional Elections: The Case of the Vanishing Marginals," *Polity* 6 (1974), 295–317.

9. See Morris Fiorina, *Congress: The Keystone of the Washington Establishment,* Revised Edition. (New Haven, CT: Yale University Press, 1989); Bruce Cain, John Ferejohn, and Morris Fiorina, *The Personal Vote and Electoral Independence,* (Cambridge, MA: Harvard University Press, 1987).

10. David Wasserman, "Introducing the 2014 Cook Political Report Partisan Voter Index," *Cook Political Report,* April 4, 2013, http://cookpolitical.com/story/5604. A great debate in political science concerns the causes of polarization and the decline of competitive House seats. See Sean M. Theriault, *Party Polarization in Congress,* (Cambridge, UK: Cambridge University Press, 2008).

11. Analysis available upon request.

12. Gary C. Jacobson and Samuel Kernell, *Strategy and Choice in Congressional Elections,* (New Haven, CT: Yale University Press, 1982).

13. Analysis available upon request.

14. Frank Hobbs and Nicole Stoops, *Demographic Trends in the 20th Century,* United States Census Bureau Special Report, November 2002, 19, http://www.census.gov/prod/2002pubs/censr-4.pdf. The Census Bureau defines the American West as Montana, Wyoming, Idaho, Colorado, Arizona, New Mexico, Utah, California, Washington, Oregon, Nevada, Alaska, and Hawaii. The Midwest includes Illinois, Indiana, Iowa, Kansas, Michigan, Minnesota, Missouri, Nebraska, North Dakota, Ohio, South Dakota, and Wisconsin. The Eastern states are New England plus New York, New Jersey, and Pennsylvania.

15. Ibid., 17.

16. United States Department of Commerce, Census Bureau, "Highest Ranking Cities, 1790–2010," http://www.census.gov/dataviz/visualizations/007/508.php, accessed September 26, 2013.

17. Marc Reisner, *Cadillac Desert: The American West and Its Disappearing Water,* Revised Kindle Edition, (New York, NY: Penguin Books, 1993).

18. Political scientists have spent more time focused on the South's political development than on the West's.

19. I used Keith Poole and Howard Rosenthal's NOMINATE data for congressional membership and coded members of Congress by region. Analysis available from author. NOMINATE data can be downloaded at http://www.voteview.com.

20. Sean Trende, "What 2010 Census Tells Us About 2020," *Real Clear Politics,* December 28, 2011, http://www.realclearpolitics.com/articles/2011/12/28/what_2010_census_tells_us_about_2020_reapportionment.html

21. Calculated from Poole and Rosenthal's NOMINATE data. See footnote 18 above.

22. David C.W. Parker and Craig Goodman, "Our State's Never Had Better Friends: Resource Allocation, Home Styles, and Dual Representation in the Senate," *Political*

*Research Quarterly* 66, no. 2 (2013), 370–384; Frances E. Lee and Bruce I. Oppenheimer, *Sizing up the Senate: The Unequal Consequences of Equal Representation,* (Chicago: University of Chicago Press, 1999).

23. Ibid.; Wendy J. Schiller, *Partners and Rivals: Representation in U.S. Senate Delegations,* (Princeton: Princeton University Press, 2000); David C.W. Parker and Craig Goodman, "Making a Good Impression: Resource Allocation, Home Styles, and Washington Work," *Legislative Studies Quarterly* 34, no. 4 (2009), 493–524.

# Montana: The Last, Best Place?

To understand politics in Montana and the process of representation, one does not begin with people or politicians. One begins with *place*, because without place the rest does not—cannot—be made to make sense. How Montanans understand themselves, their representatives, their history, and their relationship to others—including the federal government—begins and ends with place. It is also place that presents Montanans with their greatest challenges and opportunities. To use Richard Fenno's terminology, we must begin with the geographic constituency—not only as a physical space and place, but as a shared idea and experience. To understand Montana and Montanans, we must start with the land known variously as the Treasure State, Big Sky Country, or perhaps the most evocative: The Last, Best Place.

In this chapter, I provide the reader with a short history of Montana's relationship to the land, its historical development, the complicated relationship it has with the federal government, and the challenges the state faces as it transitions from a resource-intensive economy to a more diverse one based upon tourism and hi-tech industries. I claim that the deep connection Montanans have with their physical surroundings shapes how they view politics, the cleavages which exist among them, and the representatives they choose to represent them. Place also dictates the representational choices members of Congress make to build trust with their constituents. In particular, members of Congress are careful to cultivate a representational style known as "one of us" with their constituents. Without a keen sense of place, it is impossible for the observer to understand and interpret governing and campaigning in Montana specifically and the West more generally.

## PLACE-BASED CONNECTIONS

Late April of 2012, I drove 200 miles north to Choteau, population 1,620. Choteau sits along the Rocky Mountain front where the rolling Great Plains crash into craggy peaks. A predominately agricultural community, Choteau has witnessed the clash of cultures driven by wealthy out-of-staters moving in to enjoy access to public lands and Montana's legendary scenery. The purpose of my trip was to witness one of the last town hall meetings Congressman Denny Rehberg conducted during the election year. The subject of the meeting was the

Rocky Mountain Heritage Act. This bill, sponsored by Senator Max Baucus and cosponsored by Rehberg's campaign opponent, Senator Jon Tester, proposed protecting public land along the front—defined as where the plains meet the mountains—from mineral development.[1] Rehberg had criticized the proposal and held the meeting to hear from constituents.[2] The meeting drew a large crowd, nearly filling the high school auditorium. Rehberg took comments for about ninety minutes; opinion was mixed. The meeting was generally cordial despite the intense emotions displayed.

The most interesting aspect of the meeting, and the one most telling about Montana, was the understood introductory protocol: Before addressing the Rocky Mountain Heritage Act, speakers prefaced their remarks with their family's genealogy. "Hi, Denny, I'm a fourth-generation Montanan," the native-born would say. Those not born in Montana apologized for it and struggled to make some meaningful connection. "I've only been here fifteen years" someone might say, "but my kids are both native Montanans." Bill Wyckoff, a cultural geographer at Montana State would say that it was a classic display of place identity, an expression of an historical relationship to Montana signifying that the opinions following ought to carry additional weight: "I'm deeply rooted in this place; you can trust my judgment."[3] By contrast, the newcomer's opinion about Montana is, and should be, suspect.

I asked Ken Toole, himself a fifth-generation Montanan, a former state senator, and a son of the great Montana historian K. Ross Toole, about trotting out the Montana-born credential and its meaning. "I think part of it is fear and lack of security, and a desire to have a place and a spot and slot," Toole began. "But I think part of it is being proud. I mean, part of it is a positive thing. You feel like . . . you know . . . if you can make a living here, you're doing pretty well . . . I think it helps them self-identify with that Western, Marlboro Man thing."[4]

Dan Kemmis, former mayor of Missoula, author, and a native of Montana, has a slightly different take, suggesting that "it reflects an awareness that we are in fact shaped by our place, and the longer a family stays intact in a particular place, the more likely it genuinely is to have been shaped by that place."[5] Many who have lived here all their lives feel that, like tea, Montana values and connection to place must steep into a person's soul and bones. Until that process is completed over generations, it is impossible—and imprudent—to understand and speak for Montana.

As a political scientist (and nonnative), the experience immediately reminded me of the process of representation and how members of Congress work to establish trust with constituents. In this instance, constituents signaled to their member why he, Rehberg, should trust them and their opinions. Conversely, Rehberg and Tester often signaled to Montanans that they could place trust in them because of their own family histories and deep connection to the state. Rehberg often describes himself as a fifth-generation Montanan who is a rancher from Billings, and Tester calls himself a "third-generation Montana dirt farmer" from Big Sandy. The people of Choteau were telling Rehberg that "we" are one of "you"—the "you" being "Montana." And because they were "Montana" as demonstrated by their lineage, what they had to say mattered.

## "ONE OF US"

Political scientists often think of representation simply as a member of Congress demonstrating issue congruence with constituents.[6] But representation is more complicated than position taking and voting on legislation; in fact, sometimes that is not even the most important piece of the representational equation. Richard Fenno reminds us that "we should not start our studies of representation by assuming [issues] are the only basis for a representational relationship. They are not."[7] Fenno continues, writing that "though voters want to know the policy positions of their representatives, they are equally or more interested in using issue presentations as an opportunity to judge their representative as a person."[8] The Choteau experience indicates the utmost importance of place in how Montanans think about representation, and the expectation that elected representatives demonstrate a connection to place through what Fenno calls their "presentations of self." In particular, Montanans want representatives who are extensions of themselves—who present themselves as "one of us."

The notion of "one of us" is basically an effort by members of Congress to display their connectivity to a place and a group—and through that connection, demonstrate trustworthiness. In terms of representation, a member of Congress validates the trust constituents place in him by evoking that connection to a people and a place, and in so doing "convey . . . a sense of empathy with his constituents. Contextually and verbally, he gives them the impression that 'I understand your situation and I care about it'; 'I can put myself in your shoes'; and 'I can see the world the way you do.'"[9] "One of us" is an intimate representational style because it invites constituents to trust a representative the most completely. What could be better than to have someone who is a spitting image of them, making the same decision they would when confronted with exactly the same information?

Visually, "one of us" can include the way a member dresses. Rarely, if ever, does one see a Montana politician decked out in a sharp suit and tie, sporting polished shoes. More often, they are wearing a pair of cowboy boots, a comfortable button-down oxford, and a pair of jeans. On more formal occasions, a jacket makes an appearance, but a tie? Only if it's a bolo. In this way, "one of us" evokes another political science concept: descriptive representation. Political scientists usually reserve this representational style to describe ethnic or gender-based representation, but the concept applies here.[10] Montanans want someone reflecting them in terms of shared experience and history—and this sometimes trumps a representative who is substantively more reflective of their interests. Members may have their own ideas of how to best represent a place, but constituents impose behavioral expectations upon them; expectations which reflect the political culture and shared experiences of a common place. Place creates expectations, and in Montana, the expectation in turn doubles back to demonstrating connection to Montana and the experience of the American West.

Although representation begins in a legally constituted and bounded place, it does not end there. All members of Congress have geographical entities they represent, both a district and a state. In the case of Congressman Rehberg, Senator Tester, and Senator Baucus, together they represent the same geographic entity, Montana, on Capitol Hill. And although it is true that Montana's congressional delegation represents different groups and interests within Montana, all three work to build trust with constituents through repeated and meaningful connections to the space they share. Centrality of place lies at the heart of representation and politics in Montana, and in the American West more broadly, because it constitutes a shared meaning or understanding. Once that is understood, it makes it easier to understand the foundation for the representational choices facing Rehberg and Tester as they campaigned for reelection in 2012.

## MONTANA: THE PLACE

Montana is physically imposing, remote, and beautiful. Its unofficial motto, the "Big Sky," captures the state's immensity. The western third of the state is studded with mountains. Although not as high as the mountains in Colorado, these towering walls of granite and limestone still serve as both a physical barrier to life in the rugged West and a lifeline to everyday living. While the wonders of modern engineering have built railroads and interstate highways up seemingly impossible grades, or when necessary, blasted pathways through tunnels, the often intemperate Montana weather can make these outlets to the world impassable with wind and snow even in summer. Yet those same mountains slowly and inexorably release snowmelt that sustains life in the Treasure State. In addition to the water, the mountains contain other riches: gold, silver, platinum, copper, coal, and timber. Montana's mountains—the very word *Montana* means mountains in Spanish—have long provided both opportunities and limitations for those settling here.

The eastern two-thirds of the state is covered by the high prairie grasslands of America's Great Plains. Here one starts grasping the notion of Montana's "Big

Sky." There are no sight lines in Jordan, Plentywood, or Big Sandy. You might see the Rocky Mountains looming far off in the distance, but more likely you will see miles of undulating grassland broken only by high, dry buttes. "High, wide, and handsome" is how journalist and historian Joseph Kinsey Howard described Montana.[11] The east is both high, wide, and, although some might disagree, handsome in its ruggedness and (seeming) vegetative simplicity.

It is hard to capture the state's sheer size. Statistically, it is the fourth-largest state in the country, with more than 145,500 square miles. But what does that mean? "When you take Montana out of a map of the United States and you set one corner of Montana around Chicago, the other corner of Montana reaches almost to the Atlantic Ocean," said former Congressman Pat Williams.[12] The drive from Montana's eastern border, near Beach, North Dakota along Interstate 94, to Lookout Pass at the far western end of the state on Interstate 90, is almost 700 miles and takes nearly ten hours.

Montana is not the least densely populated state in the union, but it's pretty close. According to the most recent census, there are 6.8 persons per square mile in Montana.[13] In fact, Montana has more cows than people, with 2.6 head of cattle as of January 2013 for every person.[14] But the metric best capturing Montana's sparseness is the miles of paved roads per Montanan. At 0.15 miles per person, only North and South Dakota maintain a higher ratio.[15] Montana is thinly populated, and most Montanans like it that way. When Montana reached a major demographic milestone of one million residents between November and December 2011, the Associated Press published a story about the possible psychological effects on a state that has prided itself on its lack of crowds and traffic.[16]

Montana is dry. "Most sectors of the West, even the high desert land of Nevada, can support agriculture, but water must be brought in: Beyond the 100th meridian (the north-south 'dry line' running through the middle of the Dakotas and then through Nebraska, Kansas, Oklahoma, and Texas), annual rainfall by itself is insufficient to grow crops," writes Charles Wilkinson, a leading scholar of natural resource policy in the American West.[17] In fact, Montana is the 5th driest state.[18] On the Great Plains, home of the state's grain crops, most areas receive just 10 to 18 inches per year on average—and a few even less.[19] Compare this to Indiana, blessed with some of the nation's most agriculturally productive land, which averages more than 40 inches of precipitation. The lack of rain makes growing crops challenging and forces residents to rely upon the highly variable annual snowpack to survive through the summer and fall.

Montana's topography has historically meant isolation. That isolation was undoubtedly mitigated to some degree by the arrival of the railroads in the 19th century, the completion of Interstate 90 in 1978, and the recent growth of regional airports with direct flights. And yet it is still more than 500 miles from

Billings, the state's largest city, to Denver. Distance from markets has added tremendous transportation costs to goods leaving the state and has historically discouraged the development of manufacturing. The first McDonald's opened for business in 1969, and while Starbucks might be a ubiquitous part of the American landscape, it has hardly made a dent here.[20] The first one appeared in 2003 in Billings, and another finally made its way to Bozeman in the winter of 2013.[21] This isolation traditionally has served as an impediment to economic growth, but this view has begun to change. All places are shaped by their geography. But if the deterministic effects of geography were to be placed on a continuum from least to greatest impact on the collective fortunes of a people, Montana would exist at the extreme end. It is the land that determined both the why and the who of Montana's first settlers. The rich abundance of wildlife provided sustenance to Montana's first Native American tribes, estimated to have reached the territory more than 13,000 years ago.[22] The first European settlers were brought by wildlife, too, specifically to trap beavers in the 18th and 19th centuries.[23] The next wave of immigrants sought the riches of Montana's mountains, coming in the 1860s after news of gold strikes along Grasshopper Creek and Alder Gulch made its way eastward.[24] The miners kept coming after silver was found in the 1870s, but it was King Copper that put Montana on the mining map. Finally, so-called "honyockers"[25]—mostly German and Scandinavian families—followed the promises of railroad promoters and dreams inspired by the Enlarged Homestead Act of 1909 in hopes of claiming their 320 dry acres in eastern Montana during the second decade of the 20th century.[26]

What tied each of these migration events together was the necessity of living off what could be hunted, mined, pulled, or grown from the land. And what came from the land was shipped elsewhere to be consumed. In Montana, it was a daily struggle to survive. Out of that struggle came an image and an identity that Montanans still venerate—the rugged individual who moved West to make his fortune with only his grit and the clothes on his back. The rugged land created rugged men and women who, through their ceaseless toils with the land became, metaphorically, one with that very land. Those who survived were to be revered because not everyone survived and not everyone stayed. "In Ireland, they have two terms for the people who come in with the high hopes the way some people come to Montana," relayed Congressman Williams over coffee. "The people who come into Ireland [and leave because they can't handle the weather], the Irish call them 'blow-ins.' The ones that stay more than five years, the Irish call them 'stickers.' Montanans have a lot more blow-ins than we have stickers."[27] This was especially true after severe drought and the agricultural crash of the late teens and the early 1920s. As Carroll College historian Bob Swartout reminded me, Montana "is the only state in the union—there were 48 states then—that had a smaller population in 1930 than it did in 1920."[28] The blow-ins blew out, making the stickers who stayed behind especially proud of having survived. It is a pride—and an obstinacy—that still shapes the stickers and their politics today.

## MONTANA AND THE FEDS: A LOVE-HATE RELATIONSHIP

The mythos of the rugged individual, the cowboy on his steed that was popularized by those Marlboro Man ads in magazines, is still very much alive in the minds of Montanans. It is he who settled the West with a rope, a gun, and steely determination. But as much as Montana history is populated with colorful characters who worked their will on our destinies (and that part of history has certainly bled into the present), the federal government is the proverbial elephant in the room that is just as important to Montana's present-day situation. Specifically, it is the incentives and disincentives the federal government creates through policy. The Marlboro Man was not as independent and self-reliant as one might believe—even if we can agree that he was gritty and tough. He was helped, encouraged, and pushed by the federal government's policies concerning Western expansion and settlement. It is these policies, combined with the federal government's response to the Great Depression, which forever altered Montana. What's more, these policies determined the economic choices and decisions Montanans *can* make—whether fifth or first generation—today.

The federal government's role in the formation of Montana and the West begins with a fact: that most of the West was—and is—owned by the federal government. Unlike the states east of the Mississippi, the great swaths of land constituting the West had been obtained by the federal government through treaties with foreign countries. And because Congress required most states admitted after the original thirteen to adopt a disclaimer clause which would renounce any state claims to federally owned lands within its boundaries, the federal government retained much of that Western land when states gained admission.[29]

Today, a substantial portion of the eleven Western states still is owned and controlled by the federal government (see Table 2.1). Montana is actually on the lower end with less than 29 percent of land owned by the federal government. Nevada sits at the other end of the spectrum with 81 percent of the land under federal control.[30] This pattern of widespread federal ownership in the West exists in contrast to the Eastern states. For example, less than one-half of one percent of Connecticut is under federal supervision. In fact, east of the Mississippi, the federal government owns no more than thirteen and a half percent of the land in *any* state.[31] Federal land policy looms large in how the West was cultivated and it remains a major source of contention among those living in the West today.

## TABLE 2.1
*Federal Control of State Lands in America's West*

| State | Federal Land Acreage | Total Acreage | Percentage of State Land |
|---|---|---|---|
| Arizona | 30,741,287 | 72,688,000 | 42.3% |
| California | 47,797,533 | 100,206,720 | 47.7% |
| Colorado | 24,086,075 | 66,485,760 | 36.2% |
| Idaho | 32,635,835 | 52,933,120 | 61.7% |
| Montana | 26,921,861 | 93,271,040 | 28.9% |
| Nevada | 56,961,861 | 70,264,320 | 81.1% |
| New Mexico | 27,001,583 | 77,766,400 | 34.7% |
| Oregon | 32,665,430 | 61,598,720 | 53.0% |
| Utah | 35,033,603 | 52,696,690 | 66.5% |
| Washington | 12,173,813 | 42,693,760 | 28.5% |
| Wyoming | 30,043,513 | 62,343,040 | 48.2% |
| Western State Average | | | 48.1% |
| Eastern State Average | | | 5.0% |

*Note*: Data obtained from Table 1: Federal Land by State, 2010. Ross W. Gorte and Carol Vincent. "CRS Federal Land Ownership: Overview and Data," Congressional Research Service, February 8, 2012.

If the bounty of the land in the form of furs, minerals, timber, grasslands, and soil initially drew immigrants and Easterners to Montana and the West, the federal government sweetened the pot—first by taking a hands-off approach and later by aiding their movement with "the most extensive program of subsidies ever adopted by any government."[32] Most central were the policies established first by custom and then enshrined in statute by the federal government beginning in the late 19th century, which still play a central role in contemporary politics today. Wilkinson calls these policies the "Lords of Yesterday." Four of the five "Lords of Yesterday" are particularly important to understanding Montana. They include the Hardrock Mining Law of 1872, the Rancher's Code, the Forest Service's Organic Act of 1897, and the doctrine of prior appropriation governing water usage and rights.[33]

Generally speaking, these policies encouraged individuals and corporations to use public lands for private resource extraction. To this day, individuals may submit mining claims on most public lands for gold, silver, uranium, copper, molybdenum, iron, lead, aluminum, and gemstones.[34] A claim includes property rights and royalty-free hardrock elements. The claimant is only required to work the claim annually with a minimal financial commitment.[35] Much the same can be said about grazing on public lands. The federal government in the 19th century did not have a legal structure in place to deal with the use of public lands for private grazing, so in its absence, individual ranchers simply had their cattle help themselves to public grasslands.[36] The use of public lands became expected and customary; some states even created legal protections for those who grazed these lands without the federal government's permission. Federal forests were no different, essentially open for the taking through the 1880s.[37] Even water policy, as byzantine as it is today, was simple as to its purpose: to encourage land improvement and development with an eye toward resource extraction of agriculture, mining, or livestock.

It was the presence of gold in creek gravels that first brought miners to Montana, but the Hardrock Mining Act brought large-scale mining to Butte. As easy pickings in creek beds played out, "work focused increasingly on the more labor-intensive lode deposits—minerals embedded in quartz or other rock. . . . The higher capital requirements for lode mining, which usually required deep tunnels, brought in eastern and foreign investors, and these sophisticated capitalists held concerns about the security of their operations."[38] That security required clear legal title to claims that would allow investors peace of mind as they poured money in to support the necessary infrastructure. Security is what the federal government provided via the Hardrock Mining Act.

The large veins of copper running beneath Butte set Montana's destiny apart economically, politically, and demographically from its neighbors. The tale of the copper barons and the conflict between Marcus Daly and William Clark has been told elsewhere.[39] What is important here is the emergence of one company, the Anaconda Copper Mining Company, which dominated the mining of copper in Butte, smelting in Anaconda, and refining in Great Falls from 1910 through the early 1970s. Anaconda became one of the largest industrial corporations in the world, and it exhibited nothing short of a stranglehold on the state politically.[40] It owned many newspapers, held substantial sway in the legislature, and dominated the state's economy.[41] The presence of Anaconda and its mining operations also created one of the most dynamic urban centers in the West: Butte. The mines attracted Cornish, Irish, Scandinavians, and Slavic immigrants, among others, to work them. "Almost every immigrant group from around the world could be found in Montana" recalls historian Bob Swartout.[42]

The miners of Butte were among the best-paid industrial workers in the world. Because of the mining and the need for timber and electricity, Montana had a relatively large blue collar population, one that joined labor unions and voted Democratic. All of these things were unusual in the context of the broader West, according to Swartout. It is "very rare that a western state would have the kind of company that would wield the kind of influence that ACM would have in the state for three quarters of a century. And that has an important impact on how politics would evolve in the state, the kind of love-hate relationship Montanans have with a company the size of ACM."[43] The industrialization and increasing urbanization of the western portion of the state stood in stark contrast to Eastern Montana, which—at the turn of the century—was still thinly populated by Euro-Americans and dominated by big ranches.

The major impediment to settling the West, generally, and Eastern Montana in particular, is its aridity. According to Montana historians Michael Malone, Richard Roeder, and William Lang, three factors came together to populate one of the last open frontiers in the West: "the dry farming system of agriculture, the availability of large tracts of land either free or at low prices, and the mammoth promotional campaign that cranked up around 1900."[44] These elements together made moving to wide open, dry, and tough land plausible. The Enlarged Homestead Act offered the land for free provided it was developed for five years (modified to three years in 1912).[45] But how would settlers farm without a steady supply of water? Dry land agriculture provided the answer.[46] The Campbell system, as it was called, was prefaced by preserving as much moisture as possible in a climate with little rain and by cropping the land every other year. As described by Malone and his colleagues, "Campbell's famous subsurface packer tamped the subsoil while loosening the topsoil. In order to maintain a fine surface mulch that would hold down evaporation, his system then called for constant discing and harrowing, especially after each rain."[47] His system seemed to make the impossible—agriculture in a land of sagebrush and rattlesnakes—possible. For Europeans unable to obtain ownership of land and lacking opportunity in heavily stratified societies, moving to Montana was suddenly attractive.

Then the railroads came along to give newcomers another push. The railroads wanted more goods to ship to market because more goods meant more profits. Three railways dominated by James J. Hill and the Milwaukee Railroad began a promotional campaign throughout the eastern states and Europe "to publicize the fertility of the northern Great Plains and to lure farmers there."[48] Pamphlets were scattered across Europe extolling the wonders of the Great Plains and the endless agriculture riches to be made easily. Many native-born Americans, as well as German and Scandinavian immigrants, were sold. What could go wrong?

The federal government's policy of westward expansion fit within the larger national objective of building a robust industrial economy. Seen through this lens, the West was viewed as an endless bounty of land crucial to feeding a growing and increasingly urbanizing Eastern population, which in turn was necessary for the new factories churning out an array of consumer goods. These factories not only needed food for workers but also materials to fashion into shovels, phonographs, carriages, and cars. They needed copper to transmit electricity for larger and more powerful generators. The West had the resources to spare. It merely needed the people to remove them and the transportation infrastructure to send them to Eastern factories.

In short, the American West served as a colonial economy of the East. Settlers stripped the land of resources, processed some, and sent most away to be finished into products. Transportation, intense labor requirements, and ready access to global markets made locating manufacturing concerns in the West prohibitively expensive, which served only to reinforce the reliance upon nature's bounty by the newly settled inhabitants of the West. Federal land policy in the West, such as it was, centered on securing the raw materials essential for economic growth and industrialization.

Federal policy concerning Native Americans grew within this broader economic picture. Native American reverence and respect for the land is anathema to resource extraction and was seen as inherently wasteful because valuable resources were left untouched and underutilized.[49] They were seen as an impediment to civilized economic development based on John Locke's labor theory of value. The legacy of this resource-based culture in all its forms, particularly the immediate and residual effects on Native Americans housed on reservations, is one with which Montana still wrestles.

As the 19th century turned into the 20th, it became clear that laissez-faire land policies had consequences which threatened the long-term sustainability of the Western economy. The land was becoming scarred and less productive in a "tragedy of the commons" *writ large*. Forests were clear cut and fires raged throughout the West. Rangeland was overgrazed and water wasted. The Progressive Era heralded productivity through management. And, as the federal government became increasingly professionalized, Congress and the bureaucracy began developing policies to manage federal land to ensure its perpetual productivity. In many ways, the Forest Service became emblematic of this movement; its founder, Gifford Pinchot, provides the clearest articulation of what later became known as "traditional conservation." According to one scholar:

> The first principle of conservation is development, the use of the natural resources now existing on this continent for the benefit of the people who live here now. . . . In the second place conservation stands for the prevention of waste. . . . In addition to the principles of development and preservation [prevention of waste] of our resources there is a third principle. . . . The natural resources must be developed and preserved for the benefit of the many, and not merely for the profit of the few.[50]

The progressive-inspired regulation of federal land was not to preserve wilderness in an unaltered state as desired by John Muir and his Sierra Club. It was, instead, to ensure that natural resources could be employed sustainably by industrial markets for the widest possible benefit. Pinchot, for example, felt that that preservation for its own sake was not the purpose of scientific management of forest lands: "There may be just as much waste in neglecting the development and use of certain natural resources as there is in their destruction," he wrote.[51] The Forest Service, through Pinchot and the professionalization of forest rangers, saw fundamental to their mission as managers of public lands the protection of forests and grasslands to provide timber for loggers and grass for cattle in perpetuity. The notion that "wilderness is a necessity" for John Muir's "thousands of tired, nerve-shaken, over-civilized people" was neither a part of Pinchot's vision nor the rationale for federal land management in the early 20th century.[52]

The boundless possibilities of Westward expansion and industrialization collapsed, however. The bountiful rains that had come to the Great Plains and Eastern Montana in the early 20th century were an aberration. A series of droughts wracked the region throughout the late teens, twenties, and thirties. Worse, the Campbell system's deep and regular plowing tore up the native grasses that had for centuries developed and protected the rich topsoil. Exposed to the high winds, much of this rich, fertile loam blew away when the rains stopped. Many of the homesteaders who had blown in blew out again in the 1920s.

The eastern portion of Montana lost population throughout the 1920s; this demographic bleeding more or less continues today save for the counties surrounding the oil development of the Bakken formation. The western portion of the state was not spared from the economic chaos, either. The collapse of copper prices worldwide precipitated layoffs in the copper mines, the smelters, and sawmills.[53] Montana, like the rest of the nation, fell into an economic malaise. The Great Depression had arrived.

Much of the New Deal was designed to save the resource-based market economy of the West by extending the scientific management principles laid down by Pinchot and by the progressive presidential administrations of Theodore Roosevelt and Woodrow Wilson. The collapse of Wall Street in 1929 and the emergence of the Dust Bowl in the 1930s resulted in part from untrammeled individualism pursuing short-term profit. The solutions promulgated by FDR's administration sought to bring markets under tighter federal regulation. This extended to land policy. Overconsumption, overproduction, and an overabundance of short-term thinking at the expense of long-term planning had pushed families and the nation to the brink.

At first, the New Deal aimed to reform the resource extractive system by making it more sustainable. Emblematic is the Taylor Grazing Act passed by Congress in 1934. The overgrazing of the plains had terrible consequences in Montana and the West in the late 1880s. The Taylor Grazing Act created local grazing districts populated with resident ranchers and overseen by the newly formed Grazing Service.[54] Grazing fees also were established and assessed along with the requirement of permits for range use. Although range management perpetually was underfunded and grazing fees kept low, the Taylor Grazing Act was an attempt—however feeble—to conserve scientifically the grasslands as a resource.[55] Just as important, the act was justified in the language of traditional conservation as it "specifically identified livestock grazing as the dominant use" of the lands subject to its regulations and management.[56] Other policies, such as the Agricultural Adjustment Act, used a program of subsidies both to "reduc[e] the huge crop surpluses that glutted the market" and to allow for heavily plowed land to recover by making "direct cash benefit payments to farmers who agreed to restrict crop acreages."[57] In both cases, Pinchot's principles of waste prevention and the development of resources to benefit the most lay at the heart of these reform efforts.

The New Deal also helped Montana build an infrastructure to sustain a modern economy while providing jobs to needy families. Ostensibly, the goal was again to encourage and perpetuate the resource-intensiveness of Montana's economy. Millions of dollars poured in to build roads, irrigation, and flood control projects. The Works Progress Administration (WPA) "employed over 14,000 local workers" by the middle of 1939 and "directly benefit[ed] more Montanans than any of its counterparts." The WPA alone built "7,239 miles of highway, 1,366 bridges, 301 school buildings, [and] 31 outdoors stadiums."[58] The Rural Electrification Administration increased by 116 percent in four years the number of farms powered by electricity.[59] Between 1933 and 1939, the federal government loaned to and spent in Montana more than $525 million. This represented $974 in federal loans and spending for every Montanan, the second-highest per-capita rate in federal investments in the period.[60] Clearly, Montana benefited mightily from the New Deal.

And yet, while the New Deal provided both a safety net for Montana's resource extraction economy and built an infrastructure to maintain it into the future, it also sowed the seeds of change. The Civilian Conservation Corps (CCC), in particular, hinted at a different path forward. The CCC enhanced national parks and forests, building access roads, fighting forest fires, creating visitor centers, and planting vegetation.[61] While these projects created short-term jobs for young unemployed men, they also created an infrastructure centered on Montana's scenic landscape. Montanans could more easily access public lands not only for resource extraction but for recreation. Improved highways provided better access to global markets for Montana's resources as well as tourists seeking dramatic landscapes and outdoor recreation opportunities.

Montana's relationship to the land thus far had been based upon taking for subsistence, a policy encouraged by the federal government. The New Deal, in some respects, opened another door for Montanans: living from and off the bounty of the land without taking from it. The bounty was no longer mineral, animal, or plant but rather the value of the undisturbed landscape. The possibility of a different relationship to the land also laid the groundwork for a new relationship with the federal government.

The seeds sown by the CCC began to sprout in the 1950s. After World War II, returning GIs came home to start families, build homes, and to take advantage of America's economic predominance globally. Families that had sacrificed during the War now had the time to spend and relax. Leisure time increased, and America looked for new adventures. Many found travelling America's byways became easier after the construction of the Interstate Highway system. "Outdoor recreation on federally-owned lands had exploded after World War II," according to a recent history of the Bureau of Land Management.[62] "By the mid-1950s there was growing public concern that [the Forest Service and the National Park Service] did not have the land or resources to meet all of the future recreation demand. Visits to the national park system went from 33 million in 1950 to 79 million in 1960, and visits to the national forest system rose from 27 million to 93 million in the same period."[63] Many visits were to the West, which not only contained the vast majority of public land in the United States but also had landscapes dramatically different from the everyday surroundings of most Americans.

Families did more than visit the West: They moved there. Earlier migrations had been fueled by the resource economies that provided jobs. But as manufacturing and financial jobs moved West and South, reliance upon what was in the earth became less central to the economic opportunity structures. In-migration to the West brought people who loved the land because of the vistas and took advantage of the opportunity to spend their leisure hours there.[64] The land remained an asset but for what it was rather than what was in it. People, industries, and companies could now more easily move to beautiful places. As former Montana Governor Brian Schweitzer recently noted on *Late Night with David Letterman*, they were left as God removed His hand.[65]

Federal land policy began incorporating this new vision of public space in the 1950s, a vision that there was value in leaving the land alone. Congress acted in 1958 by creating "the Outdoor Recreation Resources Review Commission to (1) complete a comprehensive inventory of recreational resources and demand, (2) estimate future recreational demands, and (3) propose new strategies for dealing with outdoor recreation."[66] The recognition that recreation had value and was a legitimate use of public lands immediately brought into conflict those wedded to the traditional vision of conservation. The old clash of visions reemerged. The preservationists now demanded inclusion in federal land decisions. The rise of the environmental movement and its early successes made that demand a reality.[67]

The 1960s was the watershed decade for federal land policy. No longer was resource extraction to be the sole purpose. Now federal agencies had to consider the needs of recreationalists, who demanded preservation, as well the health of the environment and the well-being of wildlife stock. These changes began under the guidance of Interior Secretary Stewart Udall and eventually were codified in a series of laws, including the Federal Land Policy and Management Act, the National Environmental Policy Act, the Multiple Use Sustained Yield Act, and the Wilderness Act.[68] Collectively, these policies institutionalized the shift of power away from resource extraction toward other environmental considerations. In Montana specifically, the move toward a new relationship with the land and possibly a new identity can be witnessed in the preamble to the new state Constitution adopted in 1972: "We the people of Montana grateful to God for the quiet beauty of our state, the grandeur of our mountains, the vastness of our rolling plains, and desiring to improve the quality of life, equality of opportunity and secure the blessings of liberty for this and future generations do ordain and establish this constitution."[69]

The rugged individualist, wedded to traditionally defined conservation and supportive of a federal policy giving institutionalized power to resource extractive endeavors, did not go quietly into the Western night. Wilkinson's Lords of Yesterday, which fundamentally tipped the balance in favor of commoditization of the land earlier in the century, were threatened. Testifying in front of the congressional committee considering the Federal Land Policy and Management Act, Utah state legislator Calvin Black spoke for many frustrated westerners: "We plead with you to leave the public land laws as they are and . . . reestablish the original intent of these old, proven public land laws . . . and allow the private citizens the opportunity to acquire a more reasonable percentage in their rightful inheritance in their State and counties than they have now."[70] Two themes emerge: first, the wish to keep the traditional Pinchot-based definition of conservation in place, protecting and managing public land for its resource extractive qualities; and second, the desire to keep the bounty of that land closer to those extracting the wealth. The colonial relationship of the West with the rest of the country is admitted, but the frustration is with the wealth generated there going elsewhere.

Calvin Black taps into the old populist resentment that rocked the Plains and the West in the 1880s and 1890s, focused then on wealthy Midwestern railroads and corporations like the Anaconda Copper Mining Company that wrested the land's profitable bounty from the West and sent it elsewhere. Populist resentment was now squarely focused on a federal government seen to be curbing traditional extraction activities on public lands with environmental impact statements, or by halting it altogether with land withdrawals, such as in the Wilderness Act, which was seen as an "all-purpose tool for stopping economic activity."[71] The environmental movement had "succeeded in politicizing the notion that commodity production represented the primary national purpose served by public lands," and this is exactly what Westerners like Black feared.[72] In response, Westerners wishing to protect the old way of doing business launched what became known as the Sagebrush Rebellion, a states' rights, anti-federal government movement that still shapes politics in the American West.

The Sagebrush Rebellion first erupted in Nevada in 1979 but spread throughout much of the Rocky Mountain West—including Montana. The specific event triggering the rebellion was the passage by the Nevada Legislature of a bill to establish state control over "national public lands under the administration of the Bureau of Land Management." But the heart of the rebellion concerned the national push concerning how to satisfy the nation's increased energy needs. The East wanted more clean domestic energy sources—abundant in the West—while imposing a regulatory environment making extraction more difficult and less profitable. Worse, the arrogant East protested when Western states sought higher severance taxes for their efforts. In the mid-1970s, Montana passed a 30 percent severance tax on coal, the highest in the nation.[73]

Generally speaking, the Sagebrush rebels believed that the federal government—and the rest of the nation for that matter—did not understand the West. These new, top-down regulations impeding progress were imposed by "heavy-handed bureaucrats" who undermined states' rights and stifled Western self-determination.[74]

Ronald Reagan's election diffused the rebellion as his administration pursued resource-extraction-friendly policies and eased federal regulations concerning the use of public lands. But the perception of an assault on both the Western way of life and the traditional livelihoods of Westerners smolders just beneath the political surface, ready to be reignited by the right circumstances. The most recent spark was the ascendency of Barack Obama to the presidency and the passage of a new series of federal laws, including a massive overhaul of healthcare that reawakened Western resentment in the form of the Tea Party. Like the Sagebrush Rebellion, the Tea Party responded with the doctrine of nullification, pushing for state laws to block a whole host of federal regulations after they won state legislative victories throughout the West.[75]

In addition, new economic opportunities deepened Montana's identity crisis. Distance from markets, the great barrier to economic diversification bewitching Montana historically, is no longer an issue with blazing fast Internet connections that flatten the economic landscape. High-tech entrepreneurs can live anywhere now; why not move to Montana, especially when you can take advantage of the state's expanded airline connections to jump on a direct flight to Los Angeles, San Francisco, Seattle, Salt Lake City, Chicago, Denver, or New York to meet with clients? One of Bozeman's largest employers, RightNow Technologies, formed in Bozeman precisely for those reasons. The idea economy driven by what Richard Florida calls the "creative class," now can be a part of the Montana economic landscape.[76] And guess what? The creative class moves to Montana not to extract wealth from the land but to recreate and commune with it. This conflict of identity, centered on what it means to have a relationship with the land, will become more contentious as Montana's economy diversifies beyond resource extraction. Significantly, that conflict of identity no longer pits Montana against the federal government alone. Now it is a conflict between Montanans living together but sharing different visions for Montana's future.

## MONTANA: THE PEOPLE

Demographically, Montana is overwhelmingly White; nearly 90 percent claim European ancestry.[77] Compared to other regions of the West, there is a substantial Catholic population—much of it the product of the mines in the western third of the state which drew heavily on immigrants from Catholic Europe for labor.[78] Although Latinos are the fastest-growing minority group nationally and constitute the largest minority group in many states, only three percent of Montanans claim Hispanic roots. The largest minority group, at more than six percent of the population, is Native American—many of whom are concentrated on reservations in the northern and eastern parts of the state. Relative to the rest of the nation, Montanans are older, poorer, and more likely to have served in the military. More than 16 percent of Montanans are 65 or older, making the state's population the fifth oldest in the country.[79] A very high percentage served in the military; as of the 2010 census, more than ten percent of Montanans are veterans. This high proportion of veterans may be explained by the relative lack of economic opportunities and relatively low wages paid to Montanans. With the median household income around $40,000 in 2011, Montana is well below the national median.[80]

Yet Montanans do not necessarily consider themselves poor. I asked a wide array of prominent Montanans if Montana was a poor state. Pat Williams said it was and largely blamed Montana's companies for refusing to pay good wages. "Our incomes are way too low. Particularly for the work that's done. It's hard work out here. Our employers don't pay well. It's the truth of it."[81] At the other extreme is Headwaters economist Ray Rasker, who flatly disagreed:

> When we compare Montana, they'll have some statistic—per capita income or whatever—and we'll rank somewhere above Louisiana. OK, but we don't have a big metropolis. We don't have a Seattle, a Portland, a Denver. We don't have a big city. Our biggest city isn't a big city. It's small. It's like a medium-sized city in most states. So, what I did is (say), "Let's look at the economic statistics in Montana, and let's compare ourselves to our peers." So I looked at Colorado, but pulled Denver out of it. I looked at Utah, but pulled Salt Lake City out of it. And took Portland out of Oregon. We're actually doing better, on all measures, than our peers. . . . As a rural state, we're doing quite well."[82]

Others argue that Montana's land and identity create a wealth beyond wages. Mike Halligan, the executive director of the Dennis and Phyllis Washington Foundation and former president of the Montana Senate, argued that "poor isn't measured by incomes in Montana. . . . because you can't . . . monetize the amenities from the fishing to the scenic values to just the ability to recreate."[83] Dan Kemmis, the former Missoula mayor, agreed. "If the only way you measure well-being is by average individual income, then yes, we're a relatively poor state. But we all know that's not all there is to well-being and in fact it's not all there is to prosperity and if we add in some things that make it really worth being here and that bring people here and keep people here—the physical surroundings, the strength of our communities, and so on—if you factor that into the sense of well-being, we're not a poor state. We're a very fortunate and, I would say, a prosperous state."[84]

Montanans are prideful. "If Montana were a nation," said Williams, "it would be one of the most nationalistic nations on earth."[85] That pride begins with the land. Montanans know they live someplace special and do not take it for granted. In 1988, writers William Kittridge and Annick Smith published an anthology featuring some of Montana's best literary talent entitled *The Last Best Place*.[86] The title became synonymous with the state itself; in fact, Montana's congressional delegation led by former Senator Max Baucus protected the phrase for the state and its people with a trademark.[87]

Recall that Montanans view themselves somewhat wistfully as rugged individualists in part because they survive such an unyielding place. They believe it makes them distinctive. I asked Congressman Rehberg how to describe Montana to a New Yorker during our first trip together. He went straight to "rugged individualist."[88] He came back to it when talking about Montana values, saying that

Montanans believe in a "value system where the individual still matters."[89] Rehberg's answer stressed toughness and the value of each person's own contribution. Former Republican Secretary of State Bob Brown, who served for decades in the state legislature and taught high school social studies, also mentioned individualism. But his emphasis was different: "Montana was kind of one of the last places to be settled of the adjacent forty-eight states at least. So, my thinking is, perhaps Montanans have in our genes at least a kind of a wanderlust. . . . maybe a little more of . . . an individualistic [attitude], maybe people that just don't want to conform and settle down."[90] The freedom to be left alone, to be nonconformist, seemed to be a right Montanans particularly prized. Perhaps this leave me alone attitude was the perceived benefit of surviving where few else dared to even try; my ruggedness tamed this place, but I won't be tamed in return.

But that is still an incomplete portrayal. Montanans are not a bunch of misanthropes despite the belief among some that the state is populated by a bunch of Ted Kaczynskis.[91] When I asked Wyckoff what Montana meant to him, he went straight to community: "The . . . distinctive thing about Montana is the sense of community and the sense of traditional values and that kind of connection to tradition in towns. . . . You kind of get a sense of how important that identity with place is."[92] What are those traditional values? One is a sense of togetherness which belies the simplistic notion of Montanans as rugged loners. I asked Mike Halligan about the apparent contradiction. "I just think that the internal ethic that drives the rugged individualism also is one that is broad enough to kind of pull in the ethic that we are part of a community that we all have the responsibility to protect this place" he explained. Montana is "a working ranch, and in a working ranch, everybody—the owner, the family, the ranch hands, everybody—works together to make it all happen.[93] It is clear that Montanans believe strongly in a communal responsibility to each other in this cold and often harsh landscape. "If you get in a tough spot," says Wyckoff, Montanans will "help you out."[94] Part of the rugged individual mystique is also a reliance on neighbors to lend a helping hand because Montana is one big family in "a town with long streets."[95]

The threats to this community and place are many: fiscal profligacy, in-migration of folks with different values who build gated communities and drive up land prices, and the graying of the generation that knew Montana before Starbucks, the Internet, and the interstate. But perhaps the two most dangerous threats to the values Montanans claim to share also have had the greatest impact on Montana's historic development: the federal government and corporations. Both are a source of fear because they are viewed as distant and "other," meaning they are incapable of understanding Montana's unique historical place or its people's connection to the land and their traditional values based upon rugged individualism. Resentment of the federal government is spread throughout Montana despite—or perhaps because of—the federal government's looming presence in Montana financially.

The federal government plays an outsized role in the Montana economy; Montana wins the federal spending game. According to a recently published analysis, Montana received $1.50 in federal dollars for every dollar sent in taxes to Washington, DC in 2008.[96] *The Economist* looked at federal transfers over a longer period, from 1990 through 2009. Federal spending accounted for 184 percent of Montana's gross domestic product during the 20-year period examined. In other words, federal spending in Montana for the period was almost twice the economic output of the state's domestic industry. Only four states performed better at the federal trough. Montana's economy is, in essence, sustained by outsiders and non-Montanans—especially taxpayers in the blue states of Delaware, Minnesota, New Jersey, Illinois, and Connecticut.[97] This directly contradicts Montana's image as rugged individualists and breeds resentment.

The resentment goes beyond shame in appearing dependent. It is an anger rooted, perhaps, in the federal government's complicity in selling Montanans, particularly those in the East, on a false dream founded on dubious premises. It was the federal government that opened the West with the promise of free land. And while the drought and the financial collapse may not have been the fault of the feds, those who remained pride themselves on their own wits, ingenuity, and spirit in surviving the catastrophe of the 1920s and 1930s. The federal government did help, and many of those struck by the disaster of the drought and the Great Depression appealed for that help and were glad to have it.[98] But others were too ashamed or stubborn to ask for it, and over time, the federal government that continues to help Montana with large sums of transfer payments, agricultural subsidies, and federal highway dollars became to be seen by some as much a cause of suffering as the solution to it. Certainly, the distrust of the federal government has only grown post-Sagebrush Rebellion as every government program and initiative is seen as a potential threat to the resource-based livelihoods of Montanans—livelihoods, one might add, that were once subsidized and encouraged by the same federal government that seemed to change the rules midstream.

The other fear—the other "other"—are large corporations. While the federal government established the structures and policies encouraging western settlement, it was corporations that often bent the rules to their advantage. Federal policy made land available to Westerners, but as Bob Swartout reminded me, James J. Hill's railroad was "the real villain" that advertised the wonders of dry land agriculture in eastern cities and throughout Europe.[99] It was the Anaconda Copper Mining Company with the help of Montana Power—both in this case

Western-grown corporations—that pulled the strings of Montana's legislature for decades. Asbestos mining in Libby by W. R. Grace and the cyanide leaching from the Zortman-Landusky gold mine have left behind a sad environmental legacy. And then there are the riches that have migrated elsewhere. The effects of Montana's legacy as a one-company state echo in the Constitution and its political practice laws which, until recently, prohibited corporate and labor union money in campaigns and placed tight restrictions on the contributions candidates for office could accept. Montanans are wary of the federal government and corporations from afar because they see them as false prophets carrying tidings which, invariably, break down community, hurt the land, and ultimately serve to make Montana like every other subdivision and street corner in America. They threaten Montana's distinctiveness, and Montanans are justifiably leery.

## CONCLUSION

Montana is the Last Best Place, but by being last Montana is, by definition, endangered from without. Montanans have an array of choices to make as they move forward into the 21st century, but those choices depend first on how they understand their past. They can choose to move boldly forward, confident in a promising future by drawing energy from a shared past. Or they can move timidly, fearing that same past and—instead of learning from it—become enslaved by it. Pat Williams summed it up succinctly: "Montana can be that lyrical place where a river runs through it and a kind and generous people populate it. Or it can be the place of the Freeman where anger and isolation set our tomorrows."[100] Montanans must be ever vigilant against the threats facing their state and communities, but that vigilance can either be tempered by optimism or by fear.

It would be up to the electorate to begin answering that question more clearly. Montana's Senate race in 2012, at its core, was about two men shaped by the contractions swirling about the meaning of Montana and the American West. Each is rooted in different experiences in the land and philosophies about the federal government. How Montanans would decide the shape and tenor of their tomorrows boiled down to the choice between two native sons deeply of the land: Denny Rehberg and Jon Tester. Both represented Montana together in Congress and had similar representational styles. Their "presentations of self" focused on their connection to place and demonstrating how they were "one of us." Each had the appropriate credentials allowing them to speak for the land. But they embodied different traditions in that increasingly contested place. As important and distinctive as their ensuing campaign would be for a greater understanding of representation, the role of campaigns in explaining election outcomes, and the consequences of *Citizens United,* it also signified for Montana the end of the most recent and long chapter in Montana's effort to bring her tomorrows into greater focus.

Fenno is right: Members of Congress do not think of their geographic constituency as an undifferentiated mass. As we will see, Tester and Rehberg pay close attention to different constituencies within Montana. But sometimes a place dictates a particular representational style, a presentation of self, reflecting that place. Both Rehberg and Tester tried to capture Montana and the ability to speak for it by evoking their relationship to the land through their generational lineage, their styles of dress, and their work as agriculturalists. Without this connection, without hinting at how each understood the shared story of Montana, constituents would have trouble giving their trust. In many ways, the campaign that unfolded was as much about who could claim the mantle of "one of us" as it was about policy and partisanship.

## NOTES

1.  See "Rocky Mountain Front Heritage Act: Resource Guide," http://www.baucus.senate.gov/?p=general&id=86, accessed June 10, 2013.

2.  Tim Leeds, "Rehberg Sets Listening Session on Baucus' Rocky Mountain Front Act," *Havre Daily News,* April 19, 2012.

3.  Bill Wyckoff, interview with author, May 18, 2012.

4.  Ken Toole, interview with author, May 18, 2012.

5.  Dan Kemmis, interview with author, June 1, 2012.

6.  Fenno, *Home Style,* 240.

7.  Ibid., 241.

8.  Ibid.

9.  Ibid., 59.

10.  David T. Canon, *Race, Redistricting, and Representation.* (Chicago, IL: University of Chicago Press, 1999), 52–55.

11.  Joseph Kinsey Howard, *Montana: High, Wide, and Handsome,* revised edition, (Lincoln, NE: Bison Books, 2003).

12.  Congressman Pat Williams, interview with author, February 21, 2012.

13.  United States Department of Commerce, Census Bureau, "Table 14: State Population—Rank, Percent Change, and Population Density: 1980 to 2010," http://www.census.gov/compendia/statab/2012/tables/12s0014.pdf.

14.  Data obtained from the United States Department of Agriculture National Agricultural Statistic Service Monthly Livestock Inventory surveys, http://www.nass.usda.gov/. Only North Dakota, Nebraska, and South Dakota have a higher cow per person ratio.

15. United States Department of Transportation, Federal Highway Administration, "Public Road Length-2011," *Office of Highway Policy Information, Highway Statistics Series,* http://www.fhwa.dot.gov/policyinformation/statistics/2011/hm20.cfm.

16. Nicholas K. Geranios, "'Big Sky' State Getting Crowded as Montana Population nears 1M," KATU.com, July 4, 2011, http://www.katu.com/news/local/124970069.html; "Montana reaches 1 million in population," *Helena Independent Record,* January 3, 2012.

17. Charles F. Wilkinson, *Crossing the Next Meridian: Land, Water, and the Future of the West.* (Washington, DC: Island Press, 1993), 12.

18. "Average Annual Precipitation by State," *Current Results: Research News and Science Facts,* http://www.currentresults.com/Weather/US/average-annual-state-precipitation.php.

19. Western Regional Climate Center, "PRISM Precipitation Maps: 1961-90," http://www.wrcc.dri.edu/precip.html.

20. Garcia Lainey, McDonald's Press Office, correspondence with author, May 8, 2013.

21. Jan Falstad, "Montana Avenue Gets State's First Starbucks," *Billings Gazette,* June 6, 2003.

22. Michael P. Malone, Richard B. Roeder, and William L. Lang, *Montana: A History of Two Centuries,* revised edition, (Seattle: University of Washington Press, 1991), 9-10.

23. Ibid., 41-60.

24. Ibid., 65.

25. According to the great Montana historian K. Ross Toole, "The origin of the word honyocker is obscure. It was apparently an offshoot of the word Hunyak, meaning an immigrant from Central Europe. It was a term of derision applied to all 'outlanders.'" K. Ross Toole, *Twentieth Century Montana: A State of Extremes,* (Norman: The University of Oklahoma Press, 1972), 25, fn. 1.

26. Ibid., 237-238.

27. Congressman Williams, interview.

28. Bob Swartout, interview with author, May 30, 2012.

29. Wilkinson, *Crossing the Next Meridian,* 120; R. McGregor Cawley, *Federal Land, Western Anger: The Sagebrush Rebellion and Environment Politics.* (Lawrence: University Press of Kansas, 1993), 96-111.

30. U.S. Congressional Research Service, "Federal Land Ownership: Overview and Data." (R42346; February 8, 2012), by Ross W. Gorte, Carol Hardy Vincent, Laura A. Hanson, and Marc R. Rosenblum.

31. New Hampshire is the eastern state with the most federal land.

32. Wilkinson, *Crossing the Next Meridian,* 18.

33. Ibid., 20-21.

34. Ibid., 44. Fuel minerals and other common minerals are subject to leasing and sale under the provisions of the Mineral Leasing Act established in 1920. See Ibid., 54.

35. Ibid., 44-47.

36. Ibid., 87.

37. Ibid., 120.

38. Ibid.,40.

39. See Malone, Roeder, and Lang, *Montana;* K. Ross Toole, *Montana: An Uncommon Land* (Norman: University of Oklahoma Press, 1959); Michael P. Malone, *The Battle for Butte: Mining and Politics on the Northern Frontier, 1864–1906.* (Seattle: University of Washington Press, 1981).

40. Swartout, interview.

41. Williams, interview.

42. Swartout, interview.

43. Swartout, interview.

44. Malone, Roeder, and Lang, *Montana,* 236

45. Malone, Roeder, and Lang, *Montana,* 238; Jonathan Raban, *Bad Land: An American Romance,* Kindle edition, (New York, NY: Vintage Press, 1997), 20.

46. Malone, Roeder, and Lang, *Montana,* 236-237; Raban, *Bad Land,* 25 and 28-34.

47. Malone, Roeder, and Lang, *Montana,* 236.

48. Ibid., 240.

49. For the role of the yeoman farmer and its relationship to Native American dispossession, see Wade M. Cole, *Uncommon Schools: The Global Rise of Postsecondary Institutions for Indigenous Peoples,* (Palo Alto, CA: Stanford University Press, 2011), 33-44.

50. Cawley, *Federal Land, Western Anger,* 17.

51. Ibid., 24.

52. John Muir, *Our National Parks,* (Boston, MA: Houghton, Mifflin, and Company, 1901), http://www.sierraclub.org/john_muir_exhibit/writings/our_national_parks/.

53. Malone, Roeder, and Lang, *Montana,* 295.

54. Ibid., 93.

55. Ibid., 94.

56. Cawley, *Federal Land, Western Anger,* 21.

57. Malone, Roeder, and Lang, *Montana,* 297.

58. Ibid., 300.

59. Ibid., 297.

60. Ibid., 296.

61. Ibid., 299.

62. James R. Skillen, *The Nation's Largest Landlord: The Bureau of Land Management in the American West,* (Lawrence: University Press of Kansas, 2009), 43.

63. Ibid.

64. Historian Harry Fritz notes that the population explosion in the 1990s through the present was fueled by "recreation, education, privacy, and security" not the extractive industries. Fritz, "Montana in the Twenty-first Century," 348.

65. The segment aired April 26, 2012.

66. Skillen, *The Nation's Largest Land Landlord,* 43.

67. Generally, see Cawley, *Federal Land, Western Anger,* Chapter 2.

68. Ibid., Chapters 2 and 3, and Chapter 3 of Skillen, *The Nation's Largest Landlord.*

69. The Constitution of the State of Montana, http://courts.mt.gov/content/library/docs/72constit.pdf.

70. Cawley, *Federal Land, Western Anger,* 39.

71. Ibid., 33.

72. Ibid., 69.

73. Chuck Johnson helpfully reminded me of this fact.

74. Ibid., 90.

75. Alex Altman, "In Tea Party Montana, An Old Idea Finds New Life," *Time Magazine*, June 17, 2011.

76. Richard Florida, *The Rise of the Creative Class: And How It's Transforming Work, Leisure, Community, and Everyday Life*, (New York, NY: Basic Books, 2004).

77. United States Department of Commerce. Census Bureau, "Montana: Quick Facts," http://quickfacts.census.gov/qfd/states/30000.html.

78. Swartout, interview.

79. "Montana: Quick Facts"; U.S. Department of Commerce, Census Bureau, "Population Estimates: State Characteristics, Vintage 2011," http://www.census.gov/popest/data/state/asrh/2011/index.html.

80. U.S. Department of Commerce, Census Bureau, "Median Household Income by State—Single Year Estimates," http://www.census.gov/hhes/www/income/data/statemedian/.

81. Williams, interview.

82. Ray Rasker, interview with author, May 17, 2012.

83. Mike Halligan, interview with author, June 1, 2012.

84. Kemmis, interview.

85. Williams, interview.

86. William Kittridge and Anna K. Smith, eds., *Montana: The Last Best Place*, (Pullman: Washington State University Press, 1988); Jim Robbins, "In Montana, a Popular Expression is Taken Off the Endangered List," *The New York Times*, August 17, 2008.

87. "Last Best Place Slogan Protected from Trademark," *Flathead Beacon*, May 4, 2012.

88. Congressman Denny Rehberg, interview with author, August 22, 2011.

89. Ibid.

90. Bob Brown, interview with author, August 9, 2012.

91. Ted Kaczynski, of course, is the infamous "Unabomber" who was found living in a remote cabin in Lincoln, Montana.

92. Wyckoff, interview.

93. Halligan, interview.

94. Wyckoff, interview.

95. Tom Lopach, interview with author, November 30, 2012.

96. Scott McMillion, "How the Money Flows," *Montana Quarterly*, Summer 2011, 23–27.

97. "The Red and Black," *The Economist Online*, August 1, 2011, http://www.economist.com/blogs/dailychart/2011/08/americas-fiscal-union.

98. Many homesteaders wrote to the federal government for help, even those suspicious of government and reluctant to ask. See Mary Murphy, *Hope in Hard Times: New Deal Photographs of Montana, 1936–1942*, (Helena: Montana Historical Society Press, 2003).

99. Swartout, interview.

100. Williams, interview.

# Jon Tester's Creating a Buzz

To understand the role of campaigns in election outcomes, you must begin with place and then move to the stories of the players shaped by that place: the candidates and the voters. Congressional campaigns begin and end in a particular geographic space that shapes the issue concerns, the shared experiences, and the representational expectations of the voters. This is a truism in any campaign. And it is why campaign plans begin by analyzing the stage upon which an election is contested. Place shapes the narratives of campaigns, much as it shapes the life experiences of the candidates running for office. As public policy scholars Shanahan, McBeth, and Hathaway have written, "Narratives are lifeblood of politics. These strategically constructed 'stories' contain predictable elements and strategies whose aim is to influence public opinion."[1]

In this chapter and the next, I delve into the important personal and political events that shaped Jon Tester and Denny Rehberg. To aid the reader, I include a timeline listing important milestones in the careers of Senator Tester and Congressman Rehberg.

## TABLE 3.1

*The Political Careers of Senator Jon Tester and Congressman Denny Rehberg*

| | Important Dates in the Political Careers of Jon Tester and Denny Rehberg |
|---|---|
| 1983 | Jon Tester elected to Big Sandy School Board. He served for a decade. |
| Jun-1984 | Denny Rehberg beats incumbent Fagg in primary for Montana House seat. |
| Nov-1984 | Rehberg wins election to the Montana House. |
| 1986 | Rehberg reelected to MT House and runs Congressman Ron Marlenee's campaign. |
| 1988 | Montana's Senior U.S. Senator, John Melcher, loses to Conrad Burns. |
| 1991 | Rehberg appointed by Governor Stephens to fill open Lt. Governor position. |
| 1992 | Rehberg runs and wins as Lt. Governor with Marc Racicot. |
| 1996 | Rehberg loses to incumbent U.S. Senator Max Baucus. |
| 1998 | Tester runs for and wins seat in Montana Senate. |

*(Continued)*

(Continued)

| | Important Dates in the Political Careers of Jon Tester and Denny Rehberg |
|---|---|
| 2000 | Rehberg wins open race for U.S. House. |
| 2002 | Rehberg reelected with wide margin to the U.S. House and serves for next decade. |
| 2003 | Tester named Minority Leader of the Montana Senate after winning reelection. |
| 2004 | Tester elected as Montana Senate President; Democrats enjoy unified control in Helena. |
| Jan-2005 | Rehberg appointed to coveted position on House Appropriations Committee. |
| Spring 2005 | Tester announces his bid against Republican U.S. Senator Conrad Burns. |
| Jun-2006 | Tester crushes Morrison in the Democratic primary to win Senate nomination. |
| Nov-2006 | Tester declared winner by 3,562 votes over incumbent Conrad Burns. |
| Jul-2008 | Wildfire flares up at Rehberg's Billings Ranch. |
| Jul-2009 | Tester introduces SB1470, his Forest Jobs and Recreation Act. |
| Nov-2010 | Republicans retake the U.S. House of Representatives in landslide. |
| Jan-2011 | Rehberg takes gavel as House Appropriations Subcommittee chair. |
| Feb-2011 | Rehberg announces his bid for the United States Senate. |
| Mar-2011 | Rehberg introduces HR845, The Montana Land Sovereignty Act. |

The circumstances of their pre-Congressional careers affected their view of Montana, public service, and government more generally. Using their experiences, I show how their careers provide analytical leverage to understand the governing choices both Tester and Rehberg made in the House and Senate respectively. In many ways, the die for the 2012 Senate campaign was cast long ago in Big Sandy and in Billings, after maturating in the two different but equally successful pre-Congressional careers making both attractive and strong Senate candidates. Both had prepolitical careers grounded in the most traditional of Montana enterprises: agriculture. But the lessons each drew from working the land differed, leading each to serve distinct primary constituencies and approach representation differently.

## PREPOLITICAL CAREERS AND REPRESENTATIONAL STYLE

The life experiences and personalities of candidates matter because they provide the building blocks for the narratives campaigners construct to remind and persuade voters. "Stories" continue Shanahan, McBeth, and Hathaway, "are more powerful than scientific evidence in persuading individuals and in shaping beliefs."[2] The tales told by campaigns in earned media and paid advertisements hope to build connections to voters. Sometimes these stories simply activate partisan predispositions, as many voters make decisions based on party affiliation. But other times, these stories seek a more personal connection with voters—a connection that might belie partisanship. Voters can cast ballots for candidates they feel are more empathetic, more attractive, or have more experience even if those candidates may not share their partisan affiliation.

People vote for a person and a party at the ballot box. Sometimes the partisan and individual brand reputations coincide in the minds in the voters; at other times, party pulls the voter in one direction and the person in the other. Sometimes party trumps personality, sometimes the reverse. In Montana, the town with long streets, personal connection might even matter more than partisanship. In the 2012 Senate race, it likely made the difference.

The personality and life experiences of congressional candidates are shaped by their prepolitical careers. "Much of what the campaigning candidate is thinking and doing depends on what he or she has thought and done before you got there—sometimes long before," writes Fenno. "Candidates are recognized, remembered, and evaluated by their career milestones—by the path and content of their careers."[3] The stories campaigns can tell about candidates begin with where they are and what it took to get there. In the language of those who write about political development, the careers of candidates are path-dependent—they build upon previous decisions, experiences, and choices that, once made, foreclose other paths going forward. Where a candidate is and can go depends on where they have been and what they have learned. This means that even the choices made by the candidate and his or her staff during today's campaign depend on the outcome of previous decisions made in earlier campaigns or in other related career contexts. Careers affect the stories that can be told and the strategic choices candidates make on the campaign trail.

Much of what I heard and learned throughout eighteen months on the campaign trail boiled down to the career patterns of the two candidates and how these shaped the representational choices each made in Congress for Montana. Both candidates share what Joseph Schlesinger calls "progressive ambition."[4] Both Tester and Rehberg aspired to ever-higher offices in their political careers, and the paths to those offices and the lessons learned left indelible marks on them personally and professionally. Fenno treats "a career as a developmental phenomenon . . . And careers get shaped by the learning, the growth, the adaptation to changing circumstances by individuals over time."[5] Careers also take place in a strategic context—the opportunities available for advancement and how politicians respond to those opportunities. In that light, both Tester and Rehberg exhibited classic traits of "strategic politicians," carefully weighing context when making major prepolitical and political decisions about their careers. Neither Tester nor Rehberg were political amateurs in how their paths unfolded; rather, they made choices based upon cost-benefit analysis and their own particular political assets.

## THE DIRT FARMER FROM BIG SANDY

Jon Tester is a big man in every sense of the word. He's tall—six feet and a few inches by my estimation. And his girth is ample. Tester must weigh at least 300 pounds, but he's not self-conscious about it. In fact, he often jokes about his size. He often refers to his belly as a "shelf for his drinks."[6] Even his hands are beefy—at least what's left of them. They swallow yours in a tight handshake. His haircut is still the buzz-cut flattop that went out with the 1980s, and he still visits the same Great Falls barber. Tester dresses casually and often wears cowboy boots, but his clothes never fit quite right. Ties often don't match sports coats, of course, that's when he's on official business working as a senator. At the farm, it's jeans and an ancient white Oxford often smeared with dirt and grime. When I visited with Tester at his family's farm in Big Sandy in August 2011, the man was covered in grease and dust as he and Sharla wrestled an uncooperative header onto their combine during the late summer harvest. Afterward, we literally sat in his machine shop to talk about the Senate and representation. Tester often refers to himself as the only working farmer in the Senate because not only is it true but the depiction gets at the core of who he is and the values he holds dear.[7] It may sound trite, but Jon Tester evokes the image of the yeoman farmer celebrated by Thomas Jefferson.

Tester grows organic wheat, barley, and peas on about 1,800 acres (small by Western standards) outside of Big Sandy in the so-called Golden Triangle, an area of the state with near-perfect conditions for grains and the largest wheat producing area in the state. It also yields a significant portion of the state's barley crop. The Triangle is hot and dry in the summer, and cold—brutally so—in the winter. Temperatures can drop to minus 40, and the snow often is measured in feet rather than inches. Big Sandy is rural, remote, and clearing out.

Chouteau County, the home of Big Sandy, registered more than 7,300 people in the 1960 census. In 2010, only 5,600 or so remained. Big Sandy, Jon Tester's hometown, went from 703 to 598 between 2000 and 2010—a loss of nearly 15 percent.[8] Jon Tester's part of Montana is getting quieter, increasingly lonely, and faces a whole different set of policy concerns and challenges from the rapidly urbanizing and growing communities along the Rocky Mountain Front.

Tester's family came to Montana in the last wave of homesteading in the early part of the 20th century. His maternal grandparents had roots in Sweden and first settled in the Red River Valley of North Dakota. Eventually, they made their way to Montana in about 1915—when Montana was still wet. As Tester tells the tale, "the grass was as tall as a belly on a horse . . . and they went back and got all the brothers and cousins [in North Dakota]."[9] They, like many Montanans, came by James J. Hill's railroad, enticed likely both by the fancy marketing materials heralding the land's agricultural riches and the government's aggressive homesteading policies. Tester's grandparents, Fred and Christine, didn't last long. As with so many other families who settled in Eastern Montana on a whim, a prayer, and the promise of rain, the weather broke them once the wet years disappeared and drought settled in. Fred stayed and "did some horse swapping," but much of the Pearson clan decamped to North Dakota where Tester's mother Helen was born in 1920.[10] Unlike so many families whose dreams broke on the harsh Montana plains, the Pearsons apparently could not get Montana out of their bones. They moved back for another go. They were "stickers" this time, and Fred and Christine Pearson homesteaded the land of Henry Pearson, Tester's great uncle, until 1943 when Jon's parents took over the farm.[11]

Tester's dad, David, left his family in Utah when he was 16, during the depths of the Great Depression. The Testers were "starving to death" and like many young men, David Tester took advantage of FDR's New Deal by joining the Civilian Conservation Corps (CCC). He sent his earnings back to his family and learned how to butcher meat. Eventually working for the CCC took Tester's father to Montana where he met Helen Pearson. They married in 1943 and took over the homestead, which is the land Jon Tester cultivates today.

Jon Tester always knew he wanted to farm, and he told his family so at the tender age of eight. Jon's two older brothers never seemed to consider the profession, leaving Big Sandy and agriculture behind. Tester would have the farm to himself, and that proved fortunate. Supporting a family on 1,800 acres is hard enough but doing so on only a third of the acreage would have been nearly impossible.[12] Both Tester and Rehberg had formative experiences stemming from the land that shaped them as individuals and as politicians. Tester's experience came much earlier than Rehberg's—only a year after Jon pledged himself to agriculture. Like many farmers, Tester's parents turned to other income streams to pay the bills. Cutting meat for neighboring families was one way they made ends meet. And young Jon, like most kids in farm families, knew the drill: You pitch in, help out. And, it was in the act of helping that Tester's life changed permanently.

Tester told the story to *Esquire Magazine* in 2010: "I was helping my mom grind meat at our butcher shop, and it just hypnotized me. I don't remember sticking my hand in, but it sheared off the three middle fingers and left me with a pinkie and a thumb."[13] One immediate consequence of losing his fingers on his left hand was Tester, a lover of music, had to forego learning the saxophone in favor of the trumpet—an instrument where three absent fingers did not present much of an obstacle.

Tester's missing fingers are a constant reminder to him of the importance of community and compassion. Right after describing the accident, Tester immediately draws a connection to community: "I was raised in a small school and graduated high school with the kids that I started first grade with. They never cut me a break, and thank God for that."[14] The community did not treat him differently. They did not make exceptions for the seven fingered kid. Tester was expected to pull his own weight and contribute to the community—perhaps even more now that he was differently abled.

Community is central to Tester's world view. Listen when he talks: He rarely says *I* or *me*. It is invariably *we*. When I asked him what Montana values are, Tester went first to honesty because of its centrality to community. "It's neighbors working together. People working together," relates Tester as he picked soiled fingers in his workshop. "My grandfather would not have been able to homestead this place if it wouldn't have been him working with his neighbors. Them helping him, him helping them. The community of Big Sandy and all the other communities in the state of Montana would never have been built if it hadn't been for people working together."[15] The community of Big Sandy put his accident in perspective. It may have made him different, but it did not change his community obligations one whit.

Jon Tester experienced dramatically how chance can change a life. But losing one's fingers is only an extreme example of the vicissitudes constantly facing farmers and ranchers. The basic uncertainty of agriculture affects perceptions of community and government. Jon Ellingson, a former state senator who served as Tester's majority leader, told me how uncertainty shaped Tester. "My father's father was a farmer on the banks of the Snake River," said Ellingson, whose father was a Westerner but moved east to Rochester, New York. Ellingson, who fell in love with Montana while in college, always wondered why his father had left. "I asked my dad, who loved to grow things, who loved to garden, why didn't he want to be a farmer? And he said that he would be damned if he would have his success be determined by the whims of the weather. Unlike my father, Jon has had to deal with success or failure in part being determined by forces that are beyond his control. I think those kinds of experiences give him a sense of what can and should be done on the part of the government to . . . to help citizens lead more productive lives."[16] Farming gave Jon Tester an appreciation for the power of community and the positive role it plays in individual lives. Government—an extension of community—can help provide some certainty in a life filled with unexpected calamities.

It is hard not to notice the fingers missing from Tester's left hand. People stare, sometimes past the point of uncomfortableness. But beyond the stares and jokes, there is something deeper in what those missing fingers represent, beyond the physical. That experience generated a compassion, a sensitivity, and an empathy in Jon Tester for those who struggle. Perhaps it was always there, but the loss of his fingers surely reinforced and strengthened it. Doris Kearns Goodwin writes that Franklin Roosevelt's polio "expanded his mind and his sensibilities. . . . He seemed less arrogant, less smug, less superficial, more focused, more complex, more interesting" after he was struck down.[17] Tester may never have been arrogant and smug like Roosevelt, but his sensibilities are clearly different—more sensitive—than the average person's. When a young boy born without three fingers had difficulty adjusting, Tester heard about it and specifically made a trip to meet the boy. After reading to the first graders at his school and answering some questions, he sat down with seven-year-old Ethan MacPherson in the hallway to compare left hands. "With a smile on his face, Tester looked straight into Ethan's eyes and told the youngster that his disability doesn't change a thing about where his life might take him," wrote a reporter for the *Ravalli Republic*.[18] It is a lesson that Tester has applied in his own life. And it was a compassion typical of Tester.

After graduating from high school in 1974, Tester studied music education at the University of Great Falls, encouraged to do so by his own teachers back in Big Sandy. While in college, Tester met Sharla Bitz at church back home. They married during his senior year, and upon graduation, they together took over the family farm in Big Sandy.[19]

Jon and Sharla, like Jon's parents, could not make ends meet just farming. For two years, Tester taught music part time in the Big Sandy School district and managed to negotiate healthcare coverage. This was one of the few periods during Tester's life that he could afford healthcare. It was a lucky thing. In 1980, the Tester's first child—Christine—was born with jaundice. Without insurance, the family would have been wiped out financially. It "saved our bacon" Tester told me.[20] When he and Sharla could scrape together enough money to get healthcare, it was expensive and with high deductibles. The first quality healthcare Jon Tester had after that brief moment in the seventies was when he later served in the state legislature. He tells the story often on the campaign trail. Not surprisingly, it created an interest in health policy that later became a cornerstone of his legislative efforts in Montana and nationally.

After Tester left teaching, he and Sharla opened the family meat shop full-time. It was during this period that the Testers switched to organic farming—both to make additional money and for health reasons. *New West* reported that "a woman had visited the [Tester] farm from Eden Foods in Minnesota and told the Testers if they could grow her some organic Durham, she'd give them $7 a bushel. On top of that, the herbicide sprays were making them sick."[21] Both Jon and Sharla told me of how they would be laid up for weeks after applying pesticides to their cereal crops, looking green and feeling worse. Even though the switch to organic crops required extensive changes in their business, the additional cash and not having to deal with toxic chemicals made the switch a no-brainer, they told me.

The decision to quit teaching did not mean Tester left the world of education behind. It was too important to him. It had been a part of his life for twenty-five years, and as a person invested in the community, he had a stake in Big Sandy's school system. He ran for and won a seat on the Big Sandy School Board—a position he held for more than a decade. It was also Jon's introduction to politics and one that shaped his approach to policymaking and governance more generally.

Serving on a school board is a thankless task; lots of work, no remuneration, and scant recognition. Increasingly, school boards have also become the front line for some of the most contentious controversies in the culture wars. In Tester's case, the work was tough from the get-go because most of the school board turned over during the first year of Tester's service, to be followed shortly by the District Superintendent announcing his retirement. As Tester succinctly stated, "We lost a lot of institutional memory. It was a problem."[22]

Why would anyone do such thankless work for a decade? Tester described it this way: "I wanted to do it because I thought there was some opportunity to effect change for the better. I knew that business pretty well. And that's why I wanted to do it. I thought it was a place where we could have some success and help kids." Work needed to be done. A problem needed to be solved. If you avoided work on the farm, your family didn't get fed. If you don't help your community in its time of need, who will be there when you need to raise your barn? He did it because he could and because he knew education. And maybe he thought it was a way to pay it forward, much the same way Big Sandy had paid it forward for him.

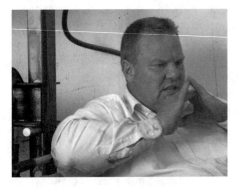

Senator Jon Tester in his machine shop on his farm outside of Big Sandy in August of 2011.

Photo Credit: Hilary MW Parker.

Tester's work on the school board did not necessarily equate with a desire to build a political career. In terms of ambition for *politics,* I detect none. There was no family expectation or honor to redeem. There is no fascination with the political game and its tactics. As far as I know and can determine, it is the first time anyone in his family had gotten involved in politics. Only later does Tester exhibit the characteristics of someone who is progressively ambitious in pursuit of higher office.

## JON TESTER GOES TO HELENA

What took Tester to the next step came from without, as if he had raw political talent just waiting to be discovered. And it was discovered by someone looking for a new kind of Democrat who could compete electorally in rural Montana. That person was Ray Peck, a Democratic legislator from Havre who served in the statehouse from 1982 until 1998 and was his party's minority leader in 1995.[23] Peck passed away a few years ago, and in Peck's obituary, Tester was quoted as saying that Peck first encouraged him to run for the state Senate in 1998.[24] In fact, when I asked Tester who were the most important folks he would talk to when he needed a gut check, for many years Ray Peck headed the list.[25]

Senator Tester's Homestead outside of Big Sandy, Montana in August 2011.

Photo Credit: The author.

Bob Brown says it was Peck that first groomed Tester. Democrats, Brown said, increasingly were having difficulty winning state legislative seats "along the northern border with Canada" which had been "the private property of the Democratic Party" for years.[26] Tester ran for an open seat that stretched across five counties in northern Montana along Alberta's border. Tester's opponent during the 1998 election was Roger Debruycker. Debruycker had served in the House and had earned the nickname "Red Light Roger" because he was notoriously negative. "It didn't make hardly any difference, even if it was the slightest defect in the bill, Roger'd vote against it."[27] Jon—the more personable of the two candidates—beat Debruycker handily. Tester served for four legislative sessions before running for the U.S. Senate in 2006.

Tester began his legislative career later in life, but once he was there, he hustled. After his first session, he was in Senate leadership. In 2003, he became minority leader and then Senate president when the Democrats took the majority in 2005. Part of the reason for Tester's quick rise up the rungs of leadership was the term limits imposed by Montana voters in 1992. Senators who had served for decades suddenly had to leave after eight years; by 2000, all the veterans who had served for decades were gone. Tester stepped into a vacuum artificially created by new institutional rules.

But that sells Tester's abilities short. Leadership made sense for Tester because of his talent for bringing people together. I spoke with Republicans and Democrats who served with Tester in the legislature, and several themes emerged. Tester is affable, funny, and warm. John Cobb, a Republican senator who sat in front of Jon in the chamber, still considers Tester's smile his most endearing trait. "He comes off as a nice person," he told me on a hot summer evening from his ranch in Augusta. "He's not hiding who he is. He's not putting on an act. He's not a professional politician . . . he comes across as he is."[28]

Former Senator, now Representative, Carolyn Squires, who suggested that she could be difficult to manage and sometimes made Tester's job as Senate president harder than it might have been, paid him a great compliment. "If you had a chance to go camping, you'd want to go camping with him," she expressed while we chatted about her time in the legislature serving with Jon. "You'd like to throw down a fishing line and sit on a beach with [Jon] and have a conversation with him. You don't have to put on any pretense or airs," she concluded.[29] In a state that takes both camping and fishing seriously, that's high praise indeed.

He had few, if any, enemies. Most people liked him and considered him friendly. "I never heard bad things about Tester. They didn't cheap shot him," recounted Cobb, which is impressive considering how vitriolic politics has become even in a place like Montana. (Maybe it's because he's funny and pulls pranks. Jon Ellingson's son interned for Jon Tester in Washington, DC. His job? To document photographically the pranks the United States senator played on his staff![30]) Even though Tester did not have much political savvy before appearing in Helena, he was a quick study, and his easy way with people made him an attractive candidate to bring together a fractious party caucus. He didn't step on folks on his way up the ladder of party leadership. Rather, he was pulled up by people helping him along the way. These people say Tester's special qualities allowed the party to push its agenda through a closely divided legislature.

Perhaps the most important trait was that Jon Tester knew the limits of his knowledge. He wanted answers to problems, and he was willing to listen patiently to people as he searched. Bob Brown, a partisan opponent, first met Jon Tester at the Windbag—a popular watering hole for politicians in Helena. He was struck by Jon Tester's presence and perception. "He asked pretty good questions and you could see he was thinking about what my responses were and what his next question would be. And I wasn't the slightest bit surprised when he became whip and the floor leader and then president of the Senate because . . . he was smart and capable."[31] He was patient and respectful as he searched. "Never got frustrated with you," said legislator Carolyn Squires of Tester, a crusty nurse from urban Missoula. "He always had time for you. He had time for the people who came to the door."[32]

Jon Tester had time for people because he could learn from what they had to say. "He has a very welcoming smile and he, when you talk to Jon, he's listening, he looks at the people he's talking with—I think he just very basically and generally cares about people" confirmed Dan Weinberg, whom Jon Tester helped get elected to the Senate in 2004 and provided one of the seats giving the Democrats the majority. "Most politicians would be much better off if they shut up and listened" Weinberg continued. "And heard what people need and expect. . . . He's a listener. And he knows how to learn. That's why he knows a lot more than the next guy because he took the time to listen and just wasn't flapping his lips."[33] "Welcoming," "warm," and "open" are words I heard again and again describing Jon Tester in the Montana Senate.

The senator also has an amazing capacity for work. You might look at Tester and assume a guy his size can't get around and get stuff done. Looks are deceiving. The man knows how to hustle. I've personally witnessed Tester arrive for a radio interview at 6:45 a.m. and spend the rest of the day doing event after event without a break, still going strong after 8 p.m. "He's got enormous energy, and when there's work to be done, he's unstoppable," said Weinberg.[34] Just like the farmer who knows the harvest must come in before the rain even if it takes 20-hour days running the combine with the lights on after dark. And it is not just for himself that he works. Again, it goes back to his relationship to community. "He really feels that responsibility to you and me that he's doing the job," said Squire near the end of our visit.[35]

Tester values a man's word and his handshake as part of what it means to be a Montanan. "I bought that combine out there over the phone," says Tester, pointing to the yellow combine that gave him and Sharla so much trouble that morning. "I didn't sign any papers. I told the guy I wanted it. Period. Over with. . . . It particularly bothers me when I go into an auto dealership and see people have to sign reams, and reams, and reams of paper because there's a lack of trust and a lack of honesty and all that stuff."[36] He kept his word as a businessman and as a neighbor, and he did the same when he ran the Democratic caucus in the State Senate—even when he made promises to Republicans. Tester impressed John Cobb even though they didn't—and still don't—always agree politically. "You never had to worry about him saying one thing and then going and changing it. He would fight for your viewpoint. . . . When he said he was going to do something, he would stick with it."[37] The freshman Democratic Dan Weinberg, who spent his career as a psychologist, boldly asked Jon Tester for a commitment early in the 2005 session to not cut mental health services. Tester made it and kept his word to Weinberg even though Weinberg was "sure that [Jon] had plenty of pressure on him" to find additional cuts to bring the budget into balance. Tester takes his job, his work, and his responsibilities seriously,[38] This trait has been constant in his prepolitical and early political careers and is something he carried with him to Washington during his first term.

## GOING BELLY TO BELLY WITH SENATOR BURNS

In May 2005, Jon Tester announced his candidacy for the United States Senate, running against three-term Republican incumbent Conrad Burns. Although incumbents rarely lose reelection, Tester took a calculated risk in running against Burns—a risk that demonstrated both progressive ambition and strategic calculation. The chattering political class had declared Burns vulnerable. *The Rothenberg Political Report* placed him on its watch list in January, noting that he had won his last election in a "squeaker," and there had been some speculation that he might retire.[39] There were whiffs of trouble in Burns's internal polls if you knew where to look. When asked whether Senator Burns should be reelected, less than half—specifically only 45 percent—agreed that he definitely or probably deserved reelection. And 39 percent agreed with the statement that "Conrad Burns has served for too long already and should retire."[40] Structurally, Burns's campaign struggled raising money, reporting only $740,000 cash on hand at the beginning of 2005—which signaled vulnerability.[41] Republican members of Congress were also going into a midterm election when the president's party often loses seats. Tester had picked an opportune time to make a move to wider and greener political pastures.

### Preliminaries

Throughout 2005, Republican members of Congress faced a scandal of monumental proportions that eventually ensnared House Majority Leader Tom DeLay, Congressman Bob Ney of Ohio, and two White House officials in a wide-ranging federal probe of lavish gifts, travel, and campaign donations given in exchange for legislative favors. At the center of it all was one of Washington's most powerful lobbyists, Jack Abramoff. In addition to kickbacks and questionable campaign contributions, he and his firm had been accused of bilking Native American tribes out of millions of dollars in lobbying fees that were diverted for

Abramoff's personal benefit. Jack Abramoff became the noose around the collective neck of congressional Republicans during the 2006 cycle. Democrats gleefully charged Republicans with creating a culture of corruption on Capitol Hill, demanded lobbying reform, and promised to pursue aggressive oversight hearings to—in the words of House Minority Leader Nancy Pelosi—"drain the swamp" should they win the majority.[42]

Burns himself became ensnarled with Abramoff. The *Post*'s Susan Schmidt wrote a story on March 1, 2005, suggesting a *quid pro quo* between Senator Burns and the Saginaw Chippewa tribe in Michigan.[43] Schmidt noted that Burns, as chairman of the Senate appropriations subcommittee responsible for funding the Department of Interior and the Bureau of Indian Affairs (BIA), slipped a $3 million earmark in an appropriations bill to fund the construction of a new school for the tribe. Concerns had been raised by officials at the BIA about the earmark because the money was designed to help poor tribes replace dilapidated facilities. But this earmark had been specifically targeted to the Saginaw tribe, which was flush with casino revenue and did not qualify for this particular program. The article further documented the fact that Burns's personal political action committee had received 42 percent of its funds from Abramoff, his associates, and tribal clients. In addition, Schmidt reported that Burns and Will Brooke—Senator Burns's chief of staff at the time who later left to work for Jack Abramoff—attended the Super Bowl in 2001 for free on a private jet paid for in part with funds obtained from Abramoff's tribal clients. A March 5th editorial by the *Post* called the Saginaw Chippewa appropriation the "Super Bowl" earmark.[44]

As 2005 unfolded, the news got worse until the bottom simply fell out in late fall. The *Billings Gazette* reported on November 25th that the public integrity and fraud divisions of the Department of Justice were "looking at 'possible influence-peddling' by Abramoff with congressional Republicans—former House Majority Leader Tom DeLay, Rep. Bob Ney of Ohio, Rep. John Doolittle of California, and Burns."[45] Burns was in trouble, and the odds of Tester winning had increased considerably.

## Tester's Campaign Victory

But Tester first had to win the Democratic primary—and he was not the candidate most political observers expected to face off against Burns. John Morrison, the state's auditor who had announced in April 2005, had statewide name recognition and had raised $1.4 million with more than $800,000 cash on hand by the end of March 2006.[46] Tester had raised less than half over the same period, with only $261,000 in the bank for the final push toward the primary.[47] The Burns campaign's internal polls showed Morrison besting Tester by 13 points that spring.[48]

Privately, Republicans wanted Morrison to win the nomination. In preparing their opposition research, they had uncovered evidence that as State Auditor Morrison had asked for outside counsel to investigate a Kalispell businessman on possible charges of securities fraud. Morrison needed said outside counsel to lead the inquiry rather than him because he had engaged in an affair with the businessman's then-fiancé. "We were salivating," confided a Republican staffer.[49] If there was anything that might trump Abramoff, an investigation motivated by a jealous lover was it. The story did not remain quiet, exploding across the pages of Lee Newspapers throughout Montana in early April.[50]

Tester crushed Morrison in June, capturing the Democratic nomination with more than 60 percent of the vote. Although one Democratic operative cited Tester's superior ground game and grassroots organization as important factors in his victory, the affair clearly mattered in an election season focused squarely on ethics.[51] Tester himself never outright mentioned the affair, but he and his campaign made oblique references. In pointing out differences between him and Morrison to Chuck Johnson, Tester claimed he was "literally the only candidate who can go toe-to-toe or belly-to-belly with Burns on his ethical lapses . . . Morrison cannot."[52] In a primary postmortem, Johnson wrote that "Jennifer Duffy, managing editor of the *Cook Political Report* in Washington, DC, said the news of the Morrison affair . . . was the turning point in the campaign."[53] Tester may have won simply because voters in the Democratic primary had no negative association with him.

Tester, the farmer from Big Sandy with no hint of ethics problems and who looked like the regular guy he was, suddenly found himself the Democratic nominee in early June. Still, he was relatively unknown and had bare coffers. The Burns fundraisers were sure they could stop Tester cold with their huge war chest. Underestimating Tester proved a mistake. "[We're] going to bury this fucker in fundraising" said an individual familiar with the Burns fundraising organization. "He's never clipped more than $200,000 or $250,000 in a quarter . . . and in three weeks, he came within $6,000 of [our June quarterly] number. . . . Which all of a sudden said to [us], 'Holy shit, that means the national [Democratic] apparatus is in. . . . This is a real race.'"[54] Tester got the money he needed, and the race became instantly competitive.

The Tester folks doubled down on their advertising, which introduced Tester to the electorate as the farmer who always gets a ten-dollar, flat-top haircut from the same barber in Great Falls, Montana, he's been going to for years. One of the best spots in the series is "Creating a Buzz," an ad that ran in the primary. It shows Montanans admiring Tester's haircut and opting to get buzzed, too. It also displays Tester working his farm and makes mention of how he will go to Washington "to put an end Senator Burns's type of corruption."[55] The message is clear: Tester is not your typical Senate candidate in a year when voters wanted change.

Public polls in August and September showed an average Tester lead of more than five points. Despite another setback in August when Burns made some ill-advised comments about firefighters at the Billings airport, the Burns campaign closed the gap throughout the fall by attacking Tester on taxes and spending. Tester's lead narrowed considerably in the final weeks despite Montana's über-popular Democratic Governor, Brian Schweitzer, campaigning around the state with Tester—even appearing in a series of television ads.[56] The final public poll, done by the Republican firm Rasmussen and released just before Election Day, gave Tester a two-point lead, well within the margin of error.[57]

Election night came, and Tester opened up an early lead that shrunk throughout the evening and into the next day. At 10:33 a.m. the day after the election, the Associated Press (AP) called the election for the dirt farmer. An extra 4,000 or so votes were mistakenly missed in Silver Bow County's initial tally, and once those—along with the few votes from Meagher County—were added, Tester's margin more than doubled to 3,000+ votes. The margin was wide enough that there would be no automatic recount under Montana's election laws. Shortly after hearing from the AP, the Tester campaign held a press conference and proclaimed victory.[58] Senator Burns conceded Thursday in a call to Tester, and then he went hunting.[59]

The official tally shows Tester beating Burns by 3,562 votes.[60] Tester spent $5.6 million on the race, while Burns dropped more than $9.3 million.[61] The Democratic Party helped Tester make up the difference with more than $2.7 million in coordinated and independent expenditures mostly on television and radio against Burns.[62] The Republicans largely abandoned Burns, spending only $700,000 on coordinated and independent expenditures. Outside groups were active, but according to one analysis, accounted for only 10 percent of the nearly $10 million spent on radio and television during the race.[63] This would change dramatically six years later in the post-*Citizens United* world.

Jon Tester was now Montana's junior U.S. senator. He won because Burns had lost touch with Montana. He won because he ran a good campaign. And he won, too, because Montanans saw a reflection of themselves in him. Conrad Burns, who also ran on his relationship to the land, lost to someone who arguably had a greater claim to the land through his generational ties as a farmer who seemed to better reflect the Montana values of honesty and hard work. The election in 2006 came down to each man's connection to place. And Tester's bid was stronger.

## CONCLUSION

Fenno argues that careers provide important contextual clues about how members of Congress behave and the decisions they make both at home and in Washington. At this point, what had Tester learned from his prepolitical career in Montana and from his campaign against Burns? The lessons boil down to three. First, Tester's strength as a politician and as a person was his connection to the land, the way it grounded him in the lives of average Montanans. To stay connected to Montana, he would never stay away from home for long, and he would continue to work his family's land outside of Big Sandy. Second, Tester would not allow himself or his staff to become mired in the murky ethical world of Washington, DC. Tester pledged to hold his office ethics standards above and beyond the letter of the law, including an independent annual review of his office's policies by a judge and the construction of a virtual wall between him and former staffers who left to become lobbyists. Above all else, Tester knew that loose ethical standards among Burns's staff had doomed his reelection campaign and torpedoed his relationship with Montanans. Tester's own credibility with Montanans rested on his campaign's claim that he would never fall prey to K Street's sinister ways. If Montanans ever believed he was no longer "one of them," his time in office would—and should—be short.

Finally, Tester would take the mentality of a farmer—distinctive from that of a rancher—with him to Washington. Ranchers and farmers are both captive of the weather, but the role government plays and how it is played in the lives of each is quite distinctive. This had particular implications for how Tester and Rehberg viewed government and the primary constituencies they saw themselves representing. For Tester, government could lend an important helping hand in protecting community and was a force for good. And as we will discover at the end of the next chapter, Tester's experiences as a state legislator differed substantially from those from his eventual campaign opponent, Denny Rehberg. How both learned to legislate in Helena provided a clear template for their subsequent Washington work, should anyone have cared to notice. Tester sought legislative solutions to policy problems both in Helena and later in Washington in much the same way he looked for and fixed problems on the family farm. It is this effort that becomes critical to understanding not only how Tester represented Montana in the Senate but also in explaining Washington work to his constituents on trips home and throughout his 2012 reelection campaign. And he had to make the most of his opportunities to connect with voters.

From the day Montana farmer Jon Tester got elected to the United States Senate, staying there presented him with a daunting task. Although incumbent senators are difficult to defeat, a number of factors made Tester's electoral situation tenuous. In 2006, he had barely beaten a scandal-plagued incumbent in an electoral environment challenging for Republicans. In 2012, Tester would be the incumbent saddled with hundreds of roll call votes to defend. More important, Tester—as a freshman winning with less than fifty percent of the vote—had to expand his electoral base quickly. Voters had rejected Conrad Burns, but it was uncertain they had embraced Jon Tester and his Democratic Party. In order to widen and strengthen his support among voters, Tester needed to forge relationships with a variety of voting constituencies—some of which had not supported him in 2006. Six years is a short time to build deep impressions. That's exactly why freshmen senators are more vulnerable to electoral challenge than their more experienced colleagues. Tester had no time to savor victory; a lot of tough work would have to be done before voters would render their judgment again.

## NOTES

1. Elizabeth A. Shanahan, Mark K. McBeth, and Paul L. Hathaway, "Narrative Policy Framework: The Influence of Media Policy Narratives on Public Opinion," *Politics & Policy* 39, no. 3 (2011), 374.

2. Ibid.

3. Richard F. Fenno, Jr, *Senators on the Campaign Trail: The Politics of Representation,* (Norman: University of Oklahoma Press, 1996), 19.

4. Joseph A. Schlesinger, *Political Parties and the Winning of Office,* (Ann Arbor: University of Michigan Press, 1991).

5. Fenno, *Senators on the Campaign Trail,* 20.

6. Tim Murphy, "Cowboy Up: Montana's Weird and Wild Senate Race," *Mother Jones,* September/October 2012, http://www.motherjones.com/politics/2012/09/jon-tester-montana-denny-rehberg; Jennifer McKee, "Lawmakers say they pack on between five and 15 pounds during session," *Helena Independent Record,* March 15, 2003.

7. The other farmer in the Senate is Iowa Republican Charles Grassley. He is not actively engaged in farming and hasn't been for some time.

8. United States Department of Commerce, Bureau of the Census, "MONTANA: Population of Counties by Decennial Census: 1900 to 1990," http://www.census.gov/population/cencounts/mt190090.txt.; United States Census, "Quick Facts: Chouteau County, Montana," http://quickfacts.census.gov/qfd/states/30/30015.html.

9. Senator Jon Tester, interview with author, May 17, 2013.

10. Ibid.

11. Ibid.

12. Ibid.

13. Cal Fussman, "What I've Learned: Senator Jon Tester (D, MT)," *Esquire Magazine.* Politics Blog, October 28, 2010, http://www.esquire.com/blogs/politics/jon-tester-interview-1110

14. Ibid.

15. Senator Jon Tester, interview with author, August 16, 2011.

16. Jon Ellingson, interview with author, August 10, 2012.

17. Doris Kearns Goodwin, *No Ordinary Time* (New York, NY: Simon and Shuster, 1994), 16.

18. Perry Backus, "Tester Tells Hamilton Boy with Missing Fingers He 'Can be anything," *Missoulian,* December 8, 2012.

19. Tester, interview, May 17, 2013.

20. Ibid.

21. Courtney Lowery, "The Good Guy Running for the U.S. Senate," New West, August 29, 2005, http://newwest.net/main/article/the_good_guy_running_for_us_senate/.

22. Tester, interview, May 17, 2013.

23. Brown, interview.

24. Charles S. Johnson, "Former Havre Legislator, Education Advocate Peck Dies," *Missoulian,* May 27, 2011.

25. Tester, interview, August 16, 2011.

26. Brown, interview.

27. Ibid.

28. State Senator John Cobb, interview with author, August 8, 2012.

29. State Senator Carolyn Squires, interview with author, August 16, 2012.

30. Ellingson, interview.

31. Brown, interview.

32. Squires, interview.

33. State Senator Dan Weinberg, interview with author, August 9, 2012.

34. Ibid.

35. Squires, interview.

36. Tester, interview, August 16, 2011.

37. Cobb, interview.

38. Weinberg, interview.

39. "2006 Senate Ratings," *Rothenberg Political Report,* January 14, 2005. Provided to the author by Nathan Gonzales via e-mail correspondence dated February 25, 2013.

40. Bob Moore to Burns Political Team, "Montana Voters and the 2006 Senate Race", March 7, 2005. In personal files of author, obtained from e-mail correspondence with Bob Moore dated January 2, 2013. Used with Senator Burns' permission.

41. Burns staff member, interview with author, January 24, 2013.

42. David Espo, "Pelosi Says She Would Drain GOP 'Swamp'," *Washington Post,* October 6, 2006.

43. Susan Schmidt, "Tribal Grant is Being Questioned," *Washington Post,* March 1, 2005.

44. Editorial, "The Super Bowl Earmark," *Washington Post,* March 5, 2005.

45. "Abramoff Probe Includes Burns," *Billings Gazette,* November 25, 2005. It should be noted that the Department of Justice later dropped its probe and Burns was exonerated.

46. All campaign finance statistics obtained from quarterly and year-end reports filed by the campaigns at the Federal Election Commission. These are accessible via the candidate and committee viewer available at http://www.fec.gov.

47. Ibid.

48. Bob Moore, "Montana Voters and Senator Conrad Burns," March 2006, PowerPoint presentation, in author's possession with Senator Conrad Burns's permission.

49. Burns campaign staffer, interview.

50. Mike Dennison and Charles S. Johnson, "Morrison: Personal Conflicts Didn't Alter Investigation," *Billings Gazette,* April 5, 2006.

51. Montana Democratic Operative, interview with author, January 29, 2013.

52. Charles Johnson, "Horse Sense: Tester, Morrison Try to Highlight Differences Before Vote," *Billings Gazette,* May 27, 2006.

53. Charles S. Johnson, "Tester's Decisive Victory Stupefies Pundits," *Billings Gazette,* June 7, 2006.

54. Burns campaign staffer, interview.

55. See the ad on YouTube, https://www.youtube.com/watch?v=DJAn0jqGcTI.

56. Tester campaign staffer, interview.

57. Ibid.

58. Charles Johnson and Mike Dennison, "Now Is the Time: Tester Wins Tight US Senate Race," *Billings Gazette,* November 9, 2010.

59. Charles S. Johnson, "Concession From Burns Clears Way for Tester," *Billings Gazette,* November 10, 2006.

60. Official election results obtained from Montana's Secretary of State's website, http://sos.mt.gov/elections/Results/.

61. Obtained from campaign finance statistics on the 2006 Montana Senate race reported by the Center for Responsive Politics, http://www.opensecrets.org/races/summary.php?cycle=2006&id=MTS1.

62. United States Government, Federal Election Commission, "Party Financial Activity Summarized for the 2006 Election Cycle," news release, http://www.fec.gov/press/press2007/partyfinal2006/20070307party.shtml.

63. Craig Wilson, "The 2006 Montana U.S. Senate Race," in *War Games: Issues and Resources in the Battle for Control of Congress,* eds. David B. Magleby and Kelly D. Patterson, (Provo, UT: Center for the Study of Elections and Democracy, 2007).

# Denny Rehberg: A Man in a Hurry

**W**orking against Tester's reelection bid was Montana's conservative electorate. Montana may consider itself to be fiercely independent, but in presidential and some federal elections, Republican candidates do well. When Jon Tester barely beat Conrad Burns in 2006, the state's lone congressman, Republican Denny Rehberg, coasted to reelection with 59 percent of the vote. Two years earlier, George W. Bush had cleaned up with nearly 60 percent of the vote. In 2008, even with an economy in freefall and voters blaming Republicans, John McCain still managed to beat Barack Obama by two percentage points. Charlie Cook's Partisan Voting Index (PVI) is one way to gauge the partisanship of voters. Cook averages the presidential vote over the past two presidential elections for each congressional district and compares that mean to the national average. Montana, one of seven states where the congressional district is the entire state, has a PVI of Republican +7.[1] All things being equal, Montanans prefer Republican candidates, and as a Democrat, Tester had to run uphill against a stiff conservative wind. A quality challenger would present Tester with problems if one emerged.

It didn't take long for Senator Tester to draw such a quality challenger: Congressman Denny Rehberg. In this chapter, I detail Rehberg's distinctive pre- and early political career, showing how it differed in important way from Tester's. In particular, Rehberg's experiences with a crippling estate tax as a young man and his family's involvement in politics gave him a much earlier push into public service than Tester. Just as Tester was starting his political career, Rehberg had already served in Montana's House, as Lt. Governor, and was on the cusp of successfully running for the House of Representatives. He also viewed government and its role very differently from Tester, as reflected by his family's experiences. Both candidates' political education became the foundation for how they governed in Washington, the primary constituencies they served, and the campaign narratives they constructed during the 2012 campaign.

## THE BILLINGS RANCHER

Elected to the House of Representatives in 2000 and serving continuously since, Rehberg had serious political chops representing a grave threat to Tester. Rehberg enjoyed near-universal name recognition. He had run statewide several times before and had a well-oiled political operation. He did not need to introduce himself to voters; they already viewed him favorably. As a member of the powerful House Appropriations Committee, he became chair of the Labor, Health and Human Services, and Education subcommittee in the 112th Congress when the Republicans gained the majority. The chairmanship had many advantages, but the most critical concerned the ability to tap into substantial financial resources from the many interests and industries wanting the ear of one of Washington's top appropriators. Additionally, as one of the wealthiest members of Congress, Rehberg could also self-fund his campaign. In early February, Rehberg made his challenge official.

Despite their ideological differences, the candidates shared more than either would readily admit. Both had backgrounds in agriculture, linked to Montana's resilient resource extractive economy. Tester was a self-described dirt farmer. Rehberg grew up in a ranching family and himself raised cattle and cashmere goats at various points as an adult. Both had deep family roots in the state: Rehberg was a fifth-generation Montanan, while Tester was a third. Both families homesteaded. Both candidates had experience running close and hard-fought campaigns. Both are baby boomers, born fourteen months apart.

Despite these superficial similarities, Tester and Rehberg were quite different as individuals and as candidates. Their differences, in fact, are critical to understanding the sequence of campaign events that began on February 5, 2011, and concluded in the wee hours of November 7, 2012. It goes without saying that partisan differences were a keystone in the campaign. But just as important to the final outcome were the distinctive personalities and experiences of the two nominees.

Denny Rehberg dresses causally, like the constituents he represents. Rarely is there a tie but always a sport coat, sometimes khakis, more often black jeans or slacks. He, like many Montanans, wears cowboy boots—black leather ones that are well-polished. Rehberg's black, slightly wavy hair is peppered with some gray, as is the neat moustache he keeps carefully trimmed. Rehberg is not physically imposing—he's probably between 5'9 and 5'11 but definitely in solid shape for a man in his mid-fifties. In high school, Rehberg competed on the Billings West state championship gymnastics team. You can still see the body of a competitive gymnast filling out his coat: a classic mesomorph frame with wide shoulders that tapers to a narrow waist. When Congress is in session, Rehberg starts every morning at the House gym where he lifts weights. He also played drums in his high school band. He's still a drummer, full of nervous energy. During a radio interview he gave in Billings on one of our visits, his feet never stopped moving as he kept time to some internal tune while answering questions from a live audience. He even speaks too fast, a trait he readily admits and which is unusual among typically laid back Westerners. Montana's congressman is a man in motion who's in a hurry, which explains his rapid ascent up Montana's political ladder.

Wherever Rehberg travels, he begins his introductory remarks by establishing his Montana credentials. "I'm Denny Rehberg, fifth-generation Montanan, and a rancher from Billings" he might say before launching into his stump speech or opening a listening session. The references to ranching and to family are a conscious bid by Rehberg to signal his authenticity and grounding in place that is so important to Montanans. As discussed in Chapter 2, Rehberg engages in the process of descriptive representation by showcasing the "one of us" representational style described by Richard Fenno. The activity is genuine. Rehberg is deeply proud of his roots in the state and of his family. When I asked him what Montana meant to him, he immediately connected to family. "It's easy for me to get very emotional about Montana because . . . the Rehbergs moved here in the 1860s and the homestead is in Silver City, north of Helena," remembered Rehberg as we drove on a warm August day between Bozeman and Butte. "My great, great grandparents are buried in the Marysville cemetery. . . . I'm fifth generation here. I've got a stake in seeing that my sixth generation relatives have the same opportunity that I had as a fifth generation."[2] Montana's history is the Rehberg family's history, and it is fair to conclude this bestows upon Rehberg a certain confidence that when he speaks, he is speaking for Montana.

Denny Rehberg can readily recite family lore. He seems to know each branch and offshoot of the Rehberg family line well. His roots are scattered wide and far across Montana. But the Rehbergs eventually found their way to Yellowstone County where A.J. Rehberg, the congressman's great grandfather, founded "the Midland Guernsey Dairy Farms on Billings' west side in 1920."[3] According to Ray Ring, senior editor at *High Country News*, A.J. Rehberg set the foundation for his family's future prosperity: "He [A.J.] built an empire of ranchland—more than 7,000 acres with a log ranch house—and ran beef cattle. He died in 1963, when Denny was eight, and his descendants took over."[4] Rehberg remembers his great grandparents fondly and still recalls walking the ranch with his great granddad as a boy. Rehberg grew up with several generations of his family; their stories became part of his early political education.

Rehberg's grandfather and great-grandmother opened the Milky Way Dairy Store in 1952 on Poly Drive in Billings.[5] The store billed itself as "Billings' only drive-in dairy store." Along with staples such as milk, cheese, eggs, and cream, the Milky Way offered customers cones, malts, and shakes at a drive-up window.[6] Eventually, the store added a restaurant in the early 1960s, serving breakfast, lunch, and dinner and was open all night on Friday and Saturday nights.[7] Rehberg recalled his mother working the morning shift and his dad heading off for the night shift, spending hours cooking steaks for customers.[8] In 1963, home delivery of dairy products was also added as a service to Billings residents.[9] The Rehbergs made their living from the land, but they were as much small business-men and entrepreneurs as they were agriculturalists. This important distinction has implications for Rehberg's later representational style and the constituency he viewed as his strongest supporters.

The Milky Way remained open until 1970, when Jack Rehberg changed careers, becoming a successful banker.[10] But that wasn't why the Rehbergs closed the Milky Way. They would say it was government overreach and intrusion. The Montana Milk Control Board set—and still sets—the price of milk sold through-out the state in accordance with federal and state policies developed in the 1930s.[11] Jack Rehberg sold milk by the gallon on a cash basis for five cents less than the price established by the board.[12] Jack Rehberg's action was more than just about making more money: It was a statement about getting government out of private business decisions. Journalist Ray Ring notes that the Milk Control Board sued Jack Rehberg, and the case went all the way to Montana Supreme Court, which eventually ruled against Rehberg.[13]

During a 1996 debate with incumbent U.S. Senator Max Baucus, Rehberg opened by recounting that event. "Many people ask me when I became interested in public administration," he began. "I'm a fifth generation Montanan, but my interest only goes back three generations. My great-grandfather helped create the Milk Control Board, my grandfather served on the Milk Control Board, and my dad sued 'em."[14] In Congressman Rehberg's telling, his dad sued for justice, fight-ing against a capricious bureaucracy. Whatever the facts, Rehberg's version gives us a window into his formative political experiences and how those experiences still shape him. Rehberg grew up skeptical of government and sensitive to the ways regulations intrude on private enterprise. This skepticism remains strong to this day.

Jack Rehberg himself ran for the state house in 1962 and used his fight with the Dairy Board as part of his campaign pitch. [15] He served two terms, and then moved to the state senate in 1966. He later ran for the House of Representatives twice, losing the Republican nomination in the 1969 special election to fill a vacant seat and then falling to incumbent Democratic Congressman John Melcher in the 1970 general election. After the loss, Jack left politics for good.[16]Melcher later became one of the state's two U.S. senators, where he would cross swords again with the Rehbergs.

Jack Rehberg's foray in politics underscores an important point about Denny's prepolitical career: In one sense, a "prepolitical career" never existed because Denny's career was steeped in politics from a young age. He came from a political family and learned to ply the trade early. When I interviewed several former leg-islators who had served with Denny's dad, their first memories of Denny were of him interning in the state legislature in high school. One cannot help speculate about, given his eventual and early involvement in politics, the effects on Rehberg's political development of seeing his dad lose two back-to-back congressional races.

Former Republican Montana Secretary of State Bob Brown thinks the effect is not inconsequential: "[Denny's] a political creature to the depth of his core. And I think it started as a kid and was importantly influenced by that big event in their family's life when Jack Rehberg lost the Republican nomination for Congress [and the race against Melcher]."[17] Rehberg, who can cite election statistics and knows which precincts he's lost when and by how much, surely studied his father's campaigns and drew some conclusions. Jack Rehberg lost the Republican nomination in 1969 to the more conservative candidate. As we will discover, his dad's outflanking from the right affected Denny's tactics in his 2012 race.

While he was away at college at Washington State University, another key formative political moment occurred. And it became the *raison d'etre* for his service in public office. In 1974, Rehberg's grandmother Dorothy passed away—to be followed two years later by his great-grandmother Mary Ada. Much of the ranch land assembled by Rehberg's great-grandfather passed to Denny, Denny's sister Shanna, and their parents.[18] But they had to sell a large chunk of it to pay the federal estate tax. In most public appearances, the story of the federal estate tax—how it affected the family's business and Denny's early adulthood—is told by the congressman. It came up when he visited with my students in 2010. And within ten minutes of our visit in August of 2011, he again recounted the tale as we chatted about family. The story is so central to understanding Rehberg that it is worth reproducing in full:

> One of the things I do get emotional about is the estate tax. When my great-grandmother passed away, we had to sell a third of our ranch. The homes, the corrals, the barns, all the livestock just to pay the estate tax. . . . Why did they have to destroy a small business? And so Jan and I struggled for the first twenty years it took us to pay off the loan and every time I went in to buy cattle, I had to borrow all the money. I had to borrow the money to build all new corrals, to drill new wells. Couldn't afford a house. I lived in town and drove back and forth three or four times a day. Eventually, a house was given to us that we moved up and stuck on a cement slab up on the ranch. Just didn't have the money. Everything we did, we borrowed money because of the estate tax. . . . You don't have the disposal income [in agriculture] to pay an estate tax, so you get caught up in this land rich and cash poor. And that's the situation that's happening with small businesses around America.[19]

Rehberg was (and is still) incensed at what the government did to his family's legacy. The wounds cut deeply; he gets visibly agitated as he tells the story. Rehberg says that he began his professional career and his new family with the burden of a $140,000 personal loan necessary to simply pay a federal estate tax bill in excess of $200,000—a loan he was forced into because of what he perceived to be an unjust federal policy.[20] Again, a remote government and its regulations punished his family's entrepreneurship and ingenuity. And it underscores how the role of government is seen as an intrusion rather than a much needed helping hand, as it was for Tester and his family.

After graduating college, Rehberg sold real estate before landing a job with Montana's Eastern Congressman Ron Marlenee.[21] Rehberg's wife, Jan, had graduated from college and wanted to go to law school after she and Denny got married in 1978. Rehberg wondered if Jan could attend law school someplace where he could get a job. So Denny, smiling as he reminisced, said he picked up the phone and "called up Marlenee and [he] said 'I'd love to have you come on board. Can you be on an airplane tomorrow?' I said, 'Well, I guess so.' That was May 9th of 1979. And off I went. [Marlenee] said 'I don't need you in Washington right this minute; would you mind being my state director in Montana?' So I managed his state operation."[22] Eventually, Rehberg headed to DC, worked for Marlenee there, and Jan attended law school at George Washington University. They later moved back to Billings when Jan joined the state's largest law firm of Crowley, Haughey, Hanson, Toole, and Dietrich.

## FORGET ME NOT: DENNY THE INSURGENT

Between working for Marlenee, and later, freshman Senator Conrad Burns, Rehberg himself became a candidate for office. In January of 1984, Rehberg announced his candidacy for the Republican nomination in House District 88. Interestingly, Rehberg opted to challenge eight-term Republican incumbent Harrison Fagg, an architect and Speaker Bob Mark's majority leader during the 1981 legislative session and the minority leader in the 1983 session.[23] The campaign that unfolded was vicious, intense, and tested Rehberg's political savvy.

Why did Rehberg choose to challenge a well-established incumbent when Rehberg must've known how hard incumbents are to beat, especially in primaries. Former Montana House Speaker Bob Marks thought Fagg's support for a scenic wilderness bill irritated Rehberg and violated Rehberg's firm commitment to private property rights.[24] Rehberg claims he ran because Fagg was too liberal and had drifted too far to the left. In particular, Fagg was an apostate on taxes and this upset Rehberg. Rehberg told me the story during our first trip together as we drove to Butte from Bozeman, passing through Homestake Pass on

Interstate 90. Fagg said he "didn't believe in tax increases. So he goes up and raised the fee on livestock scales. I said, Harrison, to increase a fee is the same as increasing a tax . . . you're actually taxing me and making it harder for me to make a living to support my family." [25] Rehberg linked Fagg's action immediately to the negative consequences for his family and business, reinforcing the impression that Rehberg's early family experiences continues to exert a strong pull on his political worldview.

Old political hands said Rehberg's campaign was unlike anything they had ever seen. Rehberg stormed the district, going door to door months before the June primary. According to media accounts, Rehberg claimed—in addition to Fagg's support for tax increases—that Fagg wasn't an effective legislator, that Fagg didn't pass his bills and had stopped listening to constituents. [26] Royal Johnson, later a state legislator himself and a Rehberg family friend for forty years (but a Fagg supporter during the race), noted that Fagg couldn't respond to Rehberg's aggressive campaign because he was working abroad on a contract for his firm. [27] Rehberg sent mailers late in the campaign accusing Fagg of shirking his duty, missing nearly 25 percent of the recorded votes in the last session. [28] Rehberg demonstrated a propensity to go for the jugular, and it wasn't the last time he would dish out hard hits to a campaign opponent.

The signature moment everyone remembers happened the night before the primary election. Rehberg and his dedicated corps of volunteers knocked on every door in the district, leaving behind a flower for the lady of the house. [29] The story has reached mythical status, with the flower different in each telling. It was a rose, according to Bob Brown. [30] No, it was an orchid, said former Governor Stan Stephens. [31] It was a carnation, at least according to the *Billings Gazette* story reported at the time. [32] Chuck Johnson says it was forget-me-nots. On Election Day, it wasn't even close: Rehberg beat Fagg with 50 percent of the vote in a four-way race. [33] Given the Republican tilt of the district, beating Fagg was tantamount to winning the seat. Rehberg went on to serve three terms in the state house. The race demonstrates Rehberg's political sophistication. He campaigned relentlessly, understood grassroots mobilization, and knew how to raise money. According to Jim Gransbery of the local Billings paper, Rehberg dropped $9,500 on the effort—outspending Fagg by nearly 2 to 1. [34] Rehberg, the competitive gymnast, didn't like to lose and had left nothing to chance.

Rehberg's surprise victory did not go unnoticed by Republican power brokers. They were impressed, as Rehberg, the man in a hurry, arrived at the state legislature at the tender age of 29. As a freshman, Rehberg received a coveted post on the Appropriations Committee. This was unusual—perhaps even unprecedented in the legislature preterm limits. Dennis Iverson, who served on Appropriations with Rehberg for two terms, underscored the uniqueness of Rehberg's appointment.

"Well, obviously, to be appointed to a committee, leadership has to have some confidence in your abilities," he recounted. "Back then, you just didn't appoint somebody to one of those unless they had some talent."[35] Rehberg must have had talent because everyone wanted appropriations as one of the most powerful and prestigious committees. "It's where most of the power is. It's where you get the most done," said Iverson.[36]

Rehberg's work on Appropriations shows us how he governed and viewed representation. First, although the committee is powerful, much of the work is tedious. As Iverson tells it, serving on Appropriations requires fortitude. "You have to be tough," he says in his clipped tone. "It's one of those committees where there's never any opponents. You get beat down. Everybody coming in needs money, and almost everybody coming in deserves it. And you don't always have enough to go around. So you have to make tough choices."[37] After his first session, Rehberg's leadership elevated him to the chairmanship of the subcommittee on general government, where he became responsible for the budgets of the highway department, the executive and legislative branches, as well as the Montana Department of Administration. By all accounts, Rehberg did his homework and was tough. And, as an appropriator, he worked with spreadsheets to hold down the cost of government—not unlike his experience as a rancher and small businessman trying to boost his bottom line.

Denny Rehberg continued to learn the business of politics and expand his political network when the legislature was out of session. The Montana legislature, like many in the West, is part-time. Most members have other jobs. Rehberg paid the bills by ranching and by electioneering. In 1986, he ran Congressman Marlenee's reelection campaign. More important for the development of his career, however, was the 1988 U.S. Senate campaign. Conrad Burns, an auctioneer and Yellowstone County Commissioner, challenged incumbent Senator John Melcher—the same John Melcher who beat Rehberg's father in the 1970 campaign for the House.

Melcher served in the House of Representatives for eight years before running successfully to replace Democratic Majority Leader Mike Mansfield in the United States Senate upon his retirement. Melcher's reelection margin in 1982 dipped below 55 percent, suggesting that he was vulnerable. Melcher, however, had considerable political strengths. He hailed from Forsyth, a small town in the eastern, conservative part of the state where he was a veterinarian. Given his background in rural Montana, he was intimately familiar with Montana's resource extractive economy and had established a fairly moderate voting record. Melcher also served on the Agriculture and Interior committees, two committees important to the state's economic interests. Melcher was beatable, but his loss was not a foregone conclusion.

Burns's campaign was stalled in the summer of 1988. In August, Rehberg agreed to step in as campaign manager.[38] Rehberg righted the ship, and Burns won after an aggressive campaign defining Melcher as out of touch with Montana values. In a postelection story in the *Washington Post,* Senator-elect Burns said, "taxes and a Montana wilderness bill sponsored by Melcher and vetoed by Reagan were the keys to his victory."[39]

Recall that onerous restrictions on land usage motivated in part Rehberg's early involvement in politics. Perhaps Rehberg saw this as the perfect issue to use against Melcher. We cannot know for certain if Rehberg's machinations brought the wilderness issue to the fore, but it is clear that Rehberg deserves credit for engineering Burns's eventual victory. And it is a window into Rehberg's later career in the House of Representatives. Cutting taxes and fighting preservationists, too, became positions central to Rehberg's representational style. After the dust settled, Rehberg worked on Burns's Senate staff as state director and managed the eight field offices scattered around Montana. He continued to serve in the state legislature, resigning only after the conclusion of the 1989 legislative session.

Rehberg's early political career is marked by ambition and a rapid ascent of the state's ladder of political opportunity. Dennis Iverson believes that Rehberg always intended to run for the United States Senate, and that each step was carefully calculated to that end.[40] That next step came open in 1991 when Montana's Lieutenant Governor, Allen Kolstad—after losing the 1990 Senate race to Sen. Max Baucus—resigned unexpectedly.[41] Rehberg threw his hat into the mix for the vacancy, and Governor Stan Stephens selected him because of his legislative experience.[42] The job gave Rehberg the opportunity to build his name recognition statewide and to develop his skills as an executive. It also demonstrated his political growth from the insurgent conservative challenging the establishment to a team player.

Rehberg, as the newly appointed Lieutenant Governor, was positioned to run for Governor if he wished. Attorney General Marc Racicot, a popular politician who himself had established solid statewide name recognition, also hoped to run. Rehberg understood his weaknesses relative to Racicot. He had only been serving in the Number 2 slot for eight months and had no experience as a candidate in a statewide campaign even though he had successfully managed two races himself. Rehberg's experience as a campaign manager taught him the virtue of playing a deep game of political chess. "I am not so egotistical that I believe that I have to be the one" is how Rehberg put it to the Associated Press (AP) reporter asking about his willingness to step aside for Racicot.[43] Rehberg would bide his time, but he needed the Lieutenant Governorship to build a statewide network to run for higher office. By threatening to run for Governor himself, Rehberg put Racicot's own ambitions at risk. Given Rehberg's previous

Congressman Denny Rehberg receiving an award from the United States Chamber of Commerce in Bozeman in early September 2012.

Photo Credit: The author.

willingness to challenge the establishment, the threat was credible.

In the end, an arranged marriage was agreed to "in a little log cabin on the West side of Helena" that February according to former Republican Montana Secretary of State Bob Brown. Rehberg and Racicot aired their differences, and Rehberg stepped aside for Racicot, who gave him the second spot on the ticket.[44] That fall, they won a tight race. Rehberg got four more years as Lieutenant Governor, serving in one of the most popular gubernatorial administrations in recent memory. In my estimation, Rehberg never wanted to run for Governor—he wanted to keep his job, build a resume, and aim for something else down the road that fit his larger ambitions.

## DENNY AND MAX

In 1995, Rehberg did exactly as Dennis Iverson and others anticipated. He announced for the Senate, challenging the state's senior Senator, Democrat Max Baucus. His 1996 Senate campaign against Max Baucus was a watershed moment for Rehberg. The forty-one-year-old Billings politician *cum* rancher appeared unstoppable. Baucus was in serious trouble politically, and politically savvy Rehberg had chosen his moment carefully. First, the national political environment favored the Republicans. The Clinton administration was wildly unpopular nationally and especially so in Montana. Although Clinton had won Montana in 1992, the electoral college victory was more a testament to the political strength of Ross Perot's independent candidacy than Clinton's. The 1994 midterms swept Republicans into control of Congress for the first time in forty years, and Clinton's reelection was imperiled.

When Republicans captured the Senate, Baucus lost his chairmanship of the Environment and Public Works Committee and much of the clout his seniority provided. He was on the defensive, having voted for Clinton's assault weapon ban and the administration's 1993 Omnibus Tax Reconciliation Act, which contained the largest federal tax increase in history during peacetime. National observers called Baucus the most vulnerable senator going into the 1996 cycle.[45] Rehberg, the aggressive campaigner who had visited all 56 counties yearly as Lieutenant Governor (a *Roll Call* article in 1996 called him the "Lee Atwater of Montana"[46]), had built an impressive political organization. The seat looked to be his for the taking.

In the end, the most vulnerable Senate Democrat beat Rehberg by five points while Governor Racicot won reelection handily. Rehberg did give Baucus the toughest fight of his long Senate career. No other Republican had managed to come so close to vanquishing one of the Senate's great political survivors. How did Rehberg manage to lose when the political stars seemed so well-aligned?

In some respects, the surprise is that Rehberg did so well. A postelection summary by the *Associated Press* noted that polls in early fall showed Baucus with a 14 point lead, a lead that only closed in the final days of the campaign.[47] Financially, Rehberg spent only $1.4 million to Baucus' $4.3 million.[48] In fact, the National Republican Senatorial Committee paid for much of the advertising in the race, using $300,000 in independent expenditures to blast Baucus as a tax-and-spend liberal.[49] Rehberg closed the gap by criticizing Baucus for accepting a series of pay raises while serving in Congress—pay raises Rehberg promised to forego.[50]

Money is clearly one reason why Rehberg did not win, although seventeen years later, Rehberg does not emphasize that fact. He blames Becky Shaw, who ran as the nominee of Ross Perot's Reform Party. Shaw pulled more than 19,000 votes—more than the margin separating Baucus from Rehberg. Rehberg believes that Shaw's candidacy was engineered by Democrats as a spoiler from the get-go, as Shaw had worked for Baucus on his Senate staff and had run in the Democratic Senate primary in 1994.[51] Politicians draw political lessons from elections, and Rehberg's interpretation of his 1996 loss haunted him during his race against Jon Tester in 2012.

Other factors provide equally plausible explanations for his defeat. Rehberg won 41 counties but lost all the major media markets.[52] This supports the money explanation as the reason for Rehberg's loss: Rehberg simply could not afford to compete with Baucus on television. Dig deeper and we find that Baucus crushed Rehberg in his home county of Yellowstone, 51 percent to 44 percent.[53] Despite having served in the legislature for three terms and having strong family connections, Rehberg could not prevail at home. This points to a problem with Rehberg's base and perhaps the lingering fallout of the old feud between establishment and conservative Republicans in Billings.

The now-defunct Voter News Service conducted exit polls for the Montana Senate race in 1996, and the original data are available for download and analysis

## TABLE 4.1
*How Montanans Voted in the 1996 Montana Senate Race*

| | Vote for Senator | | |
| --- | --- | --- | --- |
| Party ID | Baucus | Rehberg | Other |
| Democrat | 83% | 11% | 6% |
| Republican | 14% | 84% | 1% |
| Independent | 51% | 41% | 9% |
| Something Else | 47% | 32% | 21% |
| Total | 49% | 45% | 6% |

## TABLE 4.2
*Vote by Party and Ideology in the 1996 Montana Senate Race*

| | Self-Described Republicans | | | | Self-Described Democrats | | |
| --- | --- | --- | --- | --- | --- | --- | --- |
| | Vote for Senator | | | | Vote for Senator | | |
| Ideology | Baucus | Rehberg | Other | Ideology | Baucus | Rehberg | Other |
| Liberal | 36% | 64% | 0% | Liberal | 92% | 5% | 3% |
| Moderate | 22% | 75% | 3% | Moderate | 84% | 8% | 9% |
| Conservative | 9% | 90% | 1% | Conservative | 62% | 35% | 3% |
| Total | 14% | 84% | 1% | Total | 83% | 11% | 6% |

## TABLE 4.3
*Vote by Ideology in the 1996 House Race (Republicans Only)*

| | Self-Described Republicans | |
| --- | --- | --- |
| | Vote for Representative | |
| Ideology | Yellowtail (Dem) | Hill (Rep) |
| Liberal | 29% | 71% |
| Moderate | 14% | 86% |
| Conservative | 6% | 94% |
| Total | 9% | 91% |

*Source*: Voter News Service, "Voter News Service General Election Exit Polls, 1996," ICPSR06989-v2, (Ann Arbor, MI: Interuniversity Consortium for Political and Social Research [distributor], 2011–07–06), doi:10.3886/ICPSR06989.v2. The VNS exit poll was conducted as voters left polling sites. A sample of 1,184 Montana voters participated.

at the Interuniversity Consortium for Political and Social Research (ICPSR).[54] I reviewed the data and found some telling clues about Rehberg's support among Republicans and the effect of Shaw's independent bid. Approximately 16 percent of Democrats surveyed did not vote for Baucus, and about the same percentage of Republicans defected from Rehberg (see Table 4.1). Where those votes went is interesting. Ten percent of Democrats voted for Rehberg, while the remaining six percent supported Reform Party candidate Shaw. Among Republicans abandoning Rehberg, nearly all voted for Baucus. Rehberg lost his 1996 Senate campaign because of Republican defections to Baucus and not Shaw.

Who were these Republicans? Both Rehberg and Baucus did well with the ideological bases of their parties: 92 percent of liberal Democrats voted for Baucus and 90 percent of conservative Republicans supported Rehberg (see Table 4.2). It is among Republican liberals and moderates that Rehberg lost critical support; 36 percent of liberal and 22 percent of moderate Republicans voted for the Democrat Max Baucus. Although Baucus lost about the same percentage of conservative Democrats—35 percent—only eight percent of moderate Democrats voted for Rehberg. Rehberg also lost independent voters by ten percentage points, but had Republicans stayed home, he might have pulled out a win.

## MONTANA'S LONE CONGRESSMAN

Rehberg's political career was far from over. He caught a timely break when Congressman Rick Hill, after serving only two terms, resigned for health reasons, leaving Montana's at-large House seat open in the late summer of 1999. Rehberg jumped into the race without any opposition for the Republican nomination. His general election opponent was State Superintendent of Public Instruction Nancy Keenan, who—as a three-time statewide candidate—had strong name recognition and a well-developed campaign organization. In fact, Rehberg—according to veteran political observer Charlie Cook—began the race as the underdog. Cook rated the race a toss-up, citing Keenan's high favorability rating, her strong fundraising, and a spring 2000 poll showing her with an eight-point lead over Rehberg.[55]

The campaign was rough and centered on "abortion rights, inheritance taxes, and a prescription drug benefit."[56] Outside groups spent substantial sums on negative advertisements, and Rehberg "ran ads with strong endorsements from Governor Racicot and often depicting his family."[57] One advertisement stood out: An ad titled "Elsie." In it, Rehberg talks about family, the importance of protecting the next generation, and of working across party lines. The ex-Lieutenant Governor walks among his cattle and his goats, his children sitting on a fencepost. But the main star is his then two-year-old daughter, Elsie.

Rehberg tells the viewer that Elsie was a "precious gift," and he walks with her hand in hand, carries her with a diaper bag on his shoulder, and sits with her in a field of flowers surrounded by baby goats. It is a wrenchingly warm advertisement, and Rehberg radiates genuine affection.[58]

Craig Wilson, a MSU-Billings political scientist, says the focus on family smoothed out Rehberg's rough edges, who had a "reputation as aggressive and assertive, as seen in . . . his unsuccessful U.S. Senate race against Sen. Max Baucus."[59] The Almanac of American Politics suggests cynically that the advertisements drew attention to the fact that Keenan was unmarried and didn't have children.[60] Perhaps, but it is telling that the campaign felt compelled to show the softer, human side of Rehberg—a side that apparently never emerged in the 1996 campaign. Denny won with 51 percent of the vote.

That first House race proved to be Rehberg's closest. He never got less than 59 percent of the vote during any of his ensuing House campaigns. His fundraising prowess kept quality challengers from emerging, and Democrats had difficulty finding strong candidates. And Rehberg never faced a substantial primary challenge during his twelve years in office. Rehberg could have held onto the seat for as long as he wanted as he continued to amass seniority and the power that came along with it in the House. But, back in the recesses of his mind, that loss to Baucus still loomed. Perhaps if the right circumstances came along, he would give the Senate another shot.

## TWO EARLY POLITICAL CAREERS, TWO DIFFERENT PATHS

The personal experiences of both Denny Rehberg and Jon Tester are fundamental to their representational styles. In that 1996 debate with Senator Max Baucus, Rehberg said, "I am a reflection of my family's values." Those family values included individual entrepreneurship in the shadow of a government eager to snatch up the rewards of that entrepreneurship. Rehberg had learned from his father and from his grandmother's death that government takes your land and dishes out financial hardship. "What do you want your federal government to do for you or not do to you?" asked Rehberg when we talked about economic regulation.[61] The final clause is important: Rehberg wants government to leave him and Montana alone. Government hurts a society of rugged individuals.

Tester's experiences were very different and, as one might expect, he arranges Montana values in his personal and political solar system differently. Tester's ancestors did not have a wonderful time in Montana when they first moved to the state. In fact, their experience is much closer to the norm than the Rehberg's. Tester's family, like most of the homesteaders in the early 20th century, lost everything and left. But they came back without resentment. In fact, they were grateful to their community and the government for helping them to survive. Tester's dad relied on the New Deal to give him work when he was starving. It was the government that brought electricity to the homestead and provided the roads necessary to get crops to market. And it was community that came together to build the Big Sandy schools and make them work. Jon Tester's worldview was that government did work and without it, community suffered. At its best, government helped people build upon their rugged individualism to better themselves and make the whole prosper more than it could alone.

What can we conclude from the pre- and early political careers about Rehberg and Tester to help us better understand their respective representational styles? Both considered themselves attached to Montana and the land by virtue of their deep family roots in the state. Both were connected to the state's most important economic engine, agriculture. But how they connected to agriculture created distinctively different linkages to primary constituencies within Montana. Ranching and farming are distinctive agricultural enterprises and highlight different aspects of the state's political culture and history.

Rehberg described farming as "a monoculture" distinct from ranching, which he described as "holistic resource management" that balanced a variety of competing needs driven both by the producer's interests and the land's inherent characteristics.[62] And, the best person to navigate those needs and the land's potential bounty is the rancher, not the federal government. Tester at first downplayed the differences between farming and ranching: "agriculture was agriculture."[63] He admitted, though, that ranchers and farmers relate differently to government. "When I was growing up, ranchers prided themselves on not taking any subsidies. I don't know that's [true] as much anymore even though the ranchers don't take any subsidies [per se], and the people in production agriculture do" said Tester from his machine shop in Big Sandy.[64] Ranching and farming are different and yield competing worldviews concerning government— especially the federal government. And each candidate developed a perspective on government based on the type of agriculture they practiced. This then affected who Tester and Rehberg saw as their core supporters within Montana and the representational styles they later adopted in Congress.

When I asked Rehberg who his primary constituency was he said small businessmen because "he was one."[65] The annual awards Rehberg received from the Chamber of Commerce serve as testament to the closeness of the relationship. Tester drew a bigger circle. His core supporters were the "young and the old" because "they deserve the attention."[66] As we talked about the young and the elderly, Tester noted that "government touches a lot of our lives. And it's not bad. It's pretty good."[67] Implicit in his comments is the fact that government had an important role in helping especially vulnerable constituents. The early political careers of Rehberg and Tester not only shaped how they viewed the role of government, it affected the constituencies within Montana who became their natural supporters. Rehberg, having personally felt the heavy hand of government, looked out particularly for those businessmen and resource extractionists who felt government too often got in the way of entrepreneurship. Tester, alternatively, was drawn to those constituents who saw government as providing an essential helping hand and necessary for the protection of community. As we will see, one group in particular—veterans—received a lot of Tester's attention.

Prepolitical careers highlight the development of both Tester and Rehberg's political values and gives a clear picture of the constituencies that later become important to their distinctive congressional careers. To provide one final glimpse into their development as lawmakers, I dug through the legislative records Tester and Rehberg compiled in the Montana State legislature. I gathered the bills Tester and Rehberg wrote as primary sponsors. Why? Because drafting legislation as the chief sponsor requires considerably more effort than simply agreeing to cosponsor someone else's bill. Bill sponsorship is a much more meaningful measure of where a member's policy priorities lie because it represents an intensity of effort and intention.[68]

## TABLE 4.4
*Bill Sponsorship Patterns of Jon Tester and Denny Rehberg in the Montana Legislature*

| | Tester's State Legislative Track Record | | | | Rehberg's State Legislative Track Record | | |
| --- | --- | --- | --- | --- | --- | --- | --- |
| | Bills Introduced | Bills Becoming Law | Passage Rate | | Bills Introduced | Bills Becoming Law | Passage Rate |
| 1999 Session | 9 | 6 | 67% | 1985 Session | 7 | 5 | 71% |
| 2001 Session | 17 | 10 | 59% | 1987 Session | 3 | 1 | 33% |
| 2003 Session | 12 | 5 | 42% | 1991 Session | 3 | 1 | 33% |
| 2005 Session | 11 | 7 | 64% | | | | |
| Totals | 49 | 28 | 57% | | 13 | 7 | 54% |

*Source*: Data collected from author from the records of the Montana State Legislature. For Tester, see the Montana State Legislature's online bills database, http://leg.mt.gov/css/bills/Default.asp. For Rehberg, see the *Montana State Legislature's Index to the House and Senate Journal*, (Helena: State of Montana, 1983, 1985, and 1987).

Rehberg and Tester present strikingly different legislative patterns during their service in the Montana State Legislature. Rehberg has always told me that, as an appropriator, you legislate less. Dennis Iverson confirmed this when I asked: Appropriators pore over budget numbers and don't spend much time drafting bills.[69] During his three sessions in the House, Rehberg sponsored thirteen bills—seven of those during his freshman year. Tester, on the other hand, carried forty-nine bills across four legislative sessions. Both enjoyed similar success in winning support for their efforts: 54 percent of Rehberg's bills became law, while 57 percent of Tester's bills did. Of course, as a member of party leadership, Tester would carry far more bills than Rehberg, who was not in leadership. Nevertheless, both had chosen carefully in terms of where to spend their legislative efforts. One might argue that Tester's decision to become a party leader reflected an interest in solving big problems. Rehberg, on the other hand, preferred to make policy decisions by choosing how and where government spent its money.

The type of legislation each sponsored also is revealing. I coded each bill into one of nineteen different, discrete subject categories based upon the abstract of the bill and, if available, the text of the bill itself (see Table 4.5).[70] Nearly half of Rehberg's bills concerned government operations, the bailiwick of his appropriations subcommittee. A third of the remainder dealt with either property rights or real estate development. For example, in the 51st legislative session—Rehberg's last—he sponsored a bill revising the criteria to review subdivision proposals. Another, during his first session, dealt with freeholder rights concerning annexation into municipalities for the provision of services. Rehberg, when he drafted legislation, stuck closely to what he knew. He was a specialist, focusing on the inner workings of government—important to his subcommittee—and issues of property, about which he drew from his personal experiences as a realtor and as a rancher. Rehberg, like many members of Congress in an earlier area, was content to specialize, to learn from more senior members, and to work his way up the seniority chain as an appropriator.

Tester's legislative work patterns were completely different. He sponsored a bill in every policy category save three during his eight years in the state Senate. He exhibited some particular interest in agriculture, health, and budgetary policy, but overall, Tester is a classic legislative generalist. This is not surprising given that Tester seems to be a fixer, and when he identified a problem, he'd try to repair it. Some of the most important bills he carried during his time in the legislature included Big Sky Rx, the State of Montana's prescription drug program for the elderly, tax credits for wind energy, a study to address funding inequalities in state education, and a fund for economic development.

**TABLE 4.5**
*The Policy Generalization of Jon Tester versus the Specialization of Denny Rehberg*

| Subject Areas | Tester's Bills | Percentage | Rehberg's Bills | Percentage |
|---|---|---|---|---|
| Macroeconomics | 6 | 12% | 0 | 0% |
| Civil Rights and Civil Liberties | 2 | 4% | 0 | 0% |
| Health | 5 | 10% | 0 | 0% |
| Agriculture | 10 | 20% | 0 | 0% |
| Labor, Employment, Immigration | 1 | 2% | 0 | 0% |
| Education | 2 | 4% | 1 | 8% |
| Environment | 3 | 6% | 0 | 0% |
| Energy | 2 | 4% | 0 | 0% |
| Transportation | 2 | 4% | 0 | 0% |
| Law, Crime, Family | 2 | 4% | 1 | 8% |
| Social Welfare | 3 | 6% | 0 | 0% |
| Community Develop. and Housing Issues | 1 | 2% | 4 | 31% |
| Banking, Finance, and Domestic Commerce | 3 | 6% | 1 | 8% |
| Defense | 0 | 0% | 0 | 0% |
| Space, Science, Tech, Communications | 1 | 2% | 0 | 0% |
| Foreign Trade | 0 | 0% | 0 | 0% |
| International Affairs/Foreign Aid | 0 | 0% | 0 | 0% |
| Government Operations | 4 | 8% | 6 | 46% |
| Public Land and Water Management | 2 | 4% | 0 | 0% |
| Total | 49 | | 13 | |

*Source*: See Table 4.4.

Even though Tester is classified as a generalist, many of his signature accomplishments stem from his experiences as a farmer in rural Big Sandy. Tester's interest in health care came from having elderly parents and from experiencing his daughter Christine's precarious health as a baby. Many of the best locations for wind turbines exist on agricultural land, and his experience on the school board in a community losing kids and dollars every year had to help in addressing education funding inequalities in Montana. Tester's programs again show how he saw government as a positive force in the lives of Montanans. Government could work, and his legislative efforts sought to fix some big problems facing average Montanans.

## CONCLUSION

Jon Tester and Denny Rehberg were both products of Montana, but they reflected different elements of the state's conflicted political psyche. Their approach to governing diverged, too. Tester, the farmer, saw government as an important difference maker, especially in the lives of citizens living on the margins. His primary constituents were those who needed government the most, and he worked as a legislative generalist to help make government work better particularly for those relying on government programs as a social safety net. Rehberg, alternatively, was a government skeptic who feared government growing too big and too distant. He identified—as a rancher—with small businessmen trying to balance the books while navigating increasingly onerous federal regulations. As an appropriator, Rehberg wanted government to work well and efficiently but within very narrow and clearly defined boundaries. Both Tester and Rehberg's prepolitical careers provided the foundation for their distinctive representational styles both in Montana, and later, in Washington.

Despite their clear differences and approaches to governing, Tester and Rehberg were elected, together and on the same ballot, to represent Montana in Washington. When they got to Capitol Hill, how did their formative experiences—both familial and political—shape their representational styles? And directly for our purposes, when Montanans had to choose between their approaches and styles, which one would win? The first question is the subject of the next chapter. The final question is the subject of the final five chapters of this book.

---

## NOTES

1. See "Senate Scatterplot," *Cook Political Report,* http://cookpolitical.com/senate/charts/scatterplot.

2. Congressman Denny Rehberg, interview with author, August 22, 2011.

3. Ray Ring, "Who is Denny Rehberg, Really?" *High Country News,* September 3, 2012. Online edition, http://www.hcn.org/issues/44.15/who-is-denny-rehberg-really.

4. Ibid.

5. Today it is the site of MSU-Billings.

6.  The store advertised its grand opening in an advertisement in the *Billings Gazette,* April 5, 1952 on page 12.

7.  For example, see the "Sunday is Family Day" advertisement for the Milky Way in the *Billings Gazette,* August 18, 1962.

8.  Rehberg told the story of the Milky Way as we walked the floor of the Montana Energy 2012 Trade Show and Conference at the Billings MetraPark Expo on April 4, 2012.

9.  See the advertisement for the Milky Way in the *Billings Gazette* on August 25, 1963, page 22.

10.  See "Thank You" advertisement posted in the *Billings Gazette* on June 22, 1970, page 3. Also Brown, interview.

11.  Donald Blayney and Alden C. Manchester, "Milk Pricing in the United States," *Agricultural Information Bulletin (AIB-761),* February 2001, http://www.ers.usda.gov/media/306460/aib761c_1_.pdf.

12.  "Price Slashes Asked on Big Milk Cartons," *Billings Gazette,* June 28, 1961.

13.  Ring, "Who is Denny Rehberg, Really?"; Also *Milk Control Board v. Rehberg* 1962, Montana Supreme Court, http://www.hcn.org/external_files/rehberg/rehberg_1962_court_ruling.pdf.

14.  "Montana Senatorial Debate," October 28, 1996, *C-SPAN,* http://www.c-spanvideo.org/program/76280–1.

15.  "Elect Jack D. Rehberg," *Billings Gazette,* June 3, 1962, p. 3.

16.  Brown, interview.

17.  Ibid.

18.  Ring, "Who is Denny Rehberg, Really?"

19.  Rehberg, interview.

20.  Ring, "Who is Denny Rehberg, Really?"; Rehberg, interview.

21.  Until 1990, Montana had two congressmen representing the state. One represented roughly the mountainous western third and the other the remaining two thirds covering most of the high plains in the East.

22.  Rehberg, interview.

23.  Jim Gransbery, "Two Challengers Seek to Unseat Incumbent Fagg in HD 88," *Billings Gazette,* June 2, 1984.

24.  Bob Marks, interview with author, December 10, 2012.

25.  Rehberg, interview.

26.  Gransbery, "Two Challengers Seek."

27.  Royal Johnson, interview with author, December 13, 2012.

28.  Fagg later filed a complaint with state elections commission about that mailer; Gransbery, "Two Challenger Seek"; Jim Gransbery, "Fagg Blames Defeat on GOP Purge," *Billings Gazette,* June 10, 1984.

29.  I first heard the tale when Rehberg spoke to my congressional campaigns class in spring of 2010.

30.  Brown, interview.

31.  Governor Stan Stephens, interview with author, December 10, 2012.

32.  Gransbery, "Fagg Blames Defeat."

33. "Election Results," *Billings Gazette,* June 7, 1984.

34. Gransbery, "Fagg Blames Defeat." Rehberg's primary campaign cost more than $21,000 in 2013 dollars.

35. D. Iverson, interview.

36. Ibid.

37. Ibid.

38. Rehberg, interview.

39. Bill McAllister, "Montana: Negative Ads, Visits by Bush Helped Produce Victory for Burns," *The Washington Post,* November 10, 1988.

40. D. Iverson, interview.

41. Brown, interview; Stephens, interview.

42. Stephens, interview.

43. Associated Press, "Rehberg, Racicot Consider Strong Ticket," *Billings Gazette,* February 4, 1992.

44. Brown, interview.

45. Associated Press, "Baucus Prevails Again for 4th Term," *Billings Gazette,* November 6, 1996.

46. Benjamin Sheffner, "On the Road," *Roll Call,* July 10, 1996.

47. Associated Press, "Senate Summary," *Billings Gazette,* November 6, 1996.

48. Michael Barone and Grant Ujifusa, *The Almanac of American Politics 1998.* (Washington, DC: National Journal, 1999), p. 857.

49. Ibid., 853.

50. Charles S. Johnson, "Rehberg Beaten in Home County," *Billings Gazette,* November 7, 1996; Montana Senatorial Debate, October 28, 1996.

51. Rehberg and I discussed that campaign on several occasions. Craig Wilson, a political scientist at Montana State University Billings who observed the race, also mentioned the Shaw factor in an election postmortem. See Johnson, "Rehberg Beaten."

52. D. Iverson, interview.

53. Johnson, "Rehberg Beaten."

54. Voter News Service, "Voter News Service General Election Exit Polls, 1996." ICPSR06989-v2. Ann Arbor, MI: Inter-university Consortium for Political and Social Research [distributor], 2011-07-06. doi:10.3886/ICPSR06989.v2, data downloaded on June 20, 2013.

55. Charlie Cook, "A Look at Key Races in the House and Senate," *National Journal,* May 6, 2000.

56. Michael Barone, Richard E. Cohen, and Grant Ujifusa, *The Almanac of American Politics, 2010.* (Washington, DC: National Journal Group, 2009), p. 904.

57. Ibid.

58. Watch the ad on *YouTube,* https://www.youtube.com/watch?v=SuSnHudfUkA.

59. Associated Press, "Rehberg Takes 44 Counties," *Billings Gazette,* November 8, 2000.

60. Barone, Cohen, and Ujifusa, 2009, p. 904.

61. Rehberg, interview, August 22, 2011.

62. Ibid.

63. Tester, interview, August 16, 2011.

64. Ibid.

65. Rehberg, interview.

66. Tester, interview.

67. Ibid.

68. I used two sources to gather the bills. For Tester, I used the Montana State Legislature's online bills database, http://leg.mt.gov/css/bills/Default.asp. For Rehberg, I had to resort to the Montana State Legislature's Index to the House and Senate Journals for the three terms Rehberg served in the Montana State Legislature, *Index to the House and Senate Journals,* (Helena: State of Montana, 1983, 1985, and 1987).

69. D. Iverson, interview.

70. The topics coding system is borrowed from the Policy Agendas Project. Their coding scheme can be viewed here: http://www.policyagendas.org/page/topic-codebook.

# CHAPTER 5

# Representational Style: How Congressman Rehberg and Senator Tester Govern

How do representatives cultivate trust? They engage in the process of representation, a series of complex negotiations with constituents. In Chapter 2, I discussed one important aspect of building trust: Richard Fenno's presentation of self. Presentation of self is a particular representational style members of Congress display to build constituent trust. In the American West (and Montana especially), presentation of self often centers on linkages to the land and a common set of shared historical experiences. And this is true of representation elsewhere: constituents want to know if their elected officials truly understand them and their shared stories—if they are "one of us." To understand how a member of Congress represents, you must begin with place and the geographic constituency the member serves because that shapes constituent expectations.

Presentation of self is only one aspect of what Fenno calls "home style." There are others, including the member's perception of a personal constituency—as distinct from a geographic constituency—the allocation of resources, and the explanation of Washington work.[1]

In this chapter, I pay particular attention to constituencies within a member's district or state and ways in which members of Congress explain their Washington work to the folks back home. By understanding these elements separately as well as their intersection, we gain a better understanding of how representatives negotiate trust with their constituents.

The remainder of this chapter takes a close look at the legislative records and activities of both Senator Tester and Congressman Rehberg in Washington. They are compared to each other and Montana's senior U.S. Senator, Max Baucus. I first look at the bills sponsored by Montana's congressional delegation, classifying them by issue to comprehend their legislative priorities. I then examine their work to obtain federal grants and projects for the state. Finally, to better understand explanations of Washington activity which Senator Tester and Congressman Rehberg undertook to build their distinctive reputations among Montanans, I explore their press releases and their interactions with constituents in town hall meetings. Throughout, I paint a picture of the representational styles present in the Montana congressional delegation—styles that are the cornerstone of the arguments and counterclaims both candidates made in the 2012 Senate race. Campaigns, at their core, are about presenting narratives to the voters that win the candidate the most votes. To understand those stories and unfolding events, it is important to begin with the raw materials: the home styles and Washington work of Jon Tester and Denny Rehberg.

## HOME STYLES IN THE BIG SKY

Perception of constituency begins with the observation that members of Congress purposefully carve the district or state into a series of constituencies, managing their representational relationship differently with each piece. Fenno outlines three types of constituencies that members have in the districts they represent: the reelection, primary, and intimate constituencies.[2] The reelection constituency is the broadest, representing those individuals who voted for the member in the last election. To be considered part of a member's reelection constituency, a person simply has to vote for them in the general election. Constituents populating the primary constituency have deeper connections to the member. They do more than vote for the member; they contribute money, volunteer, and keep close tabs on the doings of the member in Washington. Often, they have a policy or partisan connection to the member that explains their greater intensity of support.

Both the election and primary constituencies can be thought of in terms of geography and groups. All members, for example, begin with a base of support often centering in their home town or county. Conversely, there are places in a state or district that are remote physically, economically, or politically from that home base where the member has little presence. Correspondingly, there are groups—diverse demographic or interest groups—varying in their intensity of support for a member. The intimates—the final constituency—are the member's inner circle of friends and advisors. They guide the member's career and often are called upon by the member when making difficult representational decisions. Frequently, intimates have a long relationship with the member going back to their earliest political and even prepolitical careers. In the last chapter, I noted that the prepolitical careers of Tester and Rehberg established different core supporters, or primary constituencies, for each of them. Tester saw himself as a protector of those most reliant upon government programs—the young and the old. Rehberg, the self-described rancher, saw small businessmen and entrepreneurs as his primary constituents that he paid the most attention to politically and in his representational efforts.

Allocation of resources represents the decisions a member makes concerning the disposition of his time and staff. Two key components are the member's travel back to the district or state and the location of his staff. Does the member spend much of his time in Washington, or is he flying home every weekend? Does the member have multiple offices spread throughout the constituency, or is his staff concentrated in Washington? Both decisions are representational choices communicating particular priorities. Travelling back home frequently suggests that the member feels a need either to deepen or expand trust with his or her constituents. It also suggests a desire to emphasize constituent problem solving. Conversely, a member who does not travel home often and locates most of his staff in Washington signals an interest in legislating and working on national issues. It also may suggest that the member feels secure with his constituent groups. Members early in their careers or less electorally safe often travel home more often and have more staff devoted to constituency service.[3] Members who have more seniority and have built up durable, trusting relationships with constituents divert a larger portion of their resources to legislating and policy matters.[4] Finally, the allocation of resources is also driven by constituency demand and expectations. Some constituencies want their members to be personally accessible to them while others are content to read about their members in the paper or watch them on the local news. More rural and less densely populated constituencies put a premium on access to their members, while this is less the norm in urban communities and more populous states.[5] The allocation of resources also drives presentations of self, with constituent service types spending lots of time at home and policy types spending more time in Washington working the Sunday talk show circuit or advancing to positions of party leadership. That said, all members of Congress act as policy experts, constituent servants, and "one of us" to some degree—but each member crafts a particular apportionment as his presentational style.

Members decide who and how to represent by slicing their constituencies into groups, carefully allocating their time and staff members, and presenting themselves stylistically to their constituents when travelling home. The final piece pulling this all together is what Fenno describes as explaining Washington work. "They *explain* what they have done while they have been away from home," writes Fenno.[6] It is not enough to show a connection, be an expert, or solve the problems of constituents. Members must justify their actions and put them into a context constituents understand. "Show me the money" is pro football wide receiver Rod Tidwell's response when hot shot sports agent Jerry McGuire asks him what he can do for him in the movie *Jerry McGuire*. Representatives must show constituents the money, the rationale for keeping them in office, to validate their trust in them. Sometimes this means explaining a difficult vote. Other times it is educating constituents about how Washington operates so they can appreciate what the member does for them. When performed well, the process is iterative and self-sustaining: If the member has laid the groundwork through his allocation of resources and presentation of self, explanations of Washington work are more likely to be accepted. The more these explanations are accepted, the more trust is built, and the more the member's presentation of self is reinforced. Of course, the opposite is true, too. If a member's explanation of his or her Washington work does not match his or her presentation of self, trust erodes and the member's image can be in jeopardy—which hurts his or her chances of reelection.

What members do also is shaped by the representational space they cohabitate. Members of Congress do not walk the representational stage alone.[7] This is particularly true of senators, who share their geographic constituency with another senator and a governor. And, in the case of small states like Montana, senators also compete with the lone congressman for attention. This creates additional considerations. If one senator has built a reputation as a policy expert in agriculture, say, this constrains the other senator or congressman from doing the same. Wendy Schiller explains this dynamic, writing that it is particularly important in the case of junior senators serving with much more senior colleagues: "Encroachment into the senior senator's territory becomes expensive," she explains. "The senior senator will also have built successful relationship with key local actors, such as reporters, issue activists, campaign contributors, and interest groups. If the junior senator does decide to specialize in areas similar to a more senior colleague, based on preexisting interests or experience, the junior person faces higher costs of reputation building because of the senior colleague's established visibility in the Senate in those areas."[8] Members must develop individual brands and relationships with constituents, so pre-existing reputations in a geographic constituency affect the choices a senator or congressman makes when crafting his or her own reputation. In other words, in a given state, there are multiple primary and reelection constituencies that can be knitted together by a member and maintained by his or her Washington work and by the allocation of resources. And some combinations are more fruitful, generating more representational bang for the buck, when they have not already been co-opted by another representative. Presentations of self, allocation of resources, and decisions concerning which constituents to represent are choices not made in a vacuum.

Finally, representational choices depend upon the capacity in which a member represents a constituency. Expectations for congressmen, senators, governors, and presidents differ. Even Montanans don't expect their president to come their county fairs or ice cream socials.[9] The conventional wisdom is that House members are perceived as the closest to their constituents and are more in touch or "one of us." They represent smaller constituencies and run for reelection every two years, both of which necessitate that they develop more intimate connections with a larger segment of their constituency than they might in comparison to senators. Furthermore, House members are generally seen as more likely to adopt a presentation of personal style and of resource allocations that prioritize constituent service and frequent travel home.[10] Senators, on the other hand, are expected to be a bit more detached from their constituents. They are seen as national figures; they are less likely to involve themselves in parochial concerns or constituent service work. Senators represent states, but at the same time, they represent the nation.[11] Part of the reason these expectations differ is by design. There are fewer senators than House members, and senators have additional responsibilities in making national policy—the ratification of treaties and the provision of advice and consent on judicial and executive branch appointments. In combination, senators and representatives have distinctly different jobs and roles even if they are both members of a common legislature. And these different roles are anticipated and expected by constituents.

Except in Montana; in those states with three or fewer representatives, constituents report similar levels of contact with their senators and representatives on a whole host of measures, according to Frances Lee and Bruce Oppenheimer.[12] Constituents meet with, attend meetings, speak to congressional staff members, receive franked mail, and seek help with problems from their senators and congressmen at comparable rates because they are seen as equally accessible in these less-populated states. Montanans, unlike Californians or New Yorkers, do not think of senators as terribly distinctive from their congressman. Why not contact your senator with an issue or concern? The senator is equally accessible and, better yet, has more power and resources with which to address your problem. On the one hand, this makes it more difficult for senators in smaller states to be policy experts or do work on the national stage. On the other hand, it makes it increasingly difficult for House members to distinguish themselves from senators and show their constituents the money. With fewer resources and the same constituency, the House member is relegated often to second tier status because the senators seemingly provide a better return on the constituent's investment of resources.

And while the existence of different constituencies within a state or district suggests that successfully crafting a representational relationship built on trust can take different forms even in the same place, there are limits to what that relationship can look like—particularly in smaller and less densely populated states with high expectations of access to the entire congressional delegation. In my research with fellow political scientist Craig Goodman, we find that constituent service work is particularly beneficial for junior senators in garnishing positive attention from constituents in states with widely dispersed citizens.[13] If we apply this same analysis to Montana, we might expect that while Senators Baucus and Tester and Congressman Rehberg will establish unique reputations among their constituents, all three will attempt to ground themselves as constituent servants. Second, given the fact that smaller states are prone to less diversity in terms of issues and groups, we should expect to see greater overlap in the reelection and primary constituencies of Montana's congressional delegation—particularly among the two Democratic senators.[14] Finally, we should expect to see that the work patterns Senator Tester and Congressman Rehberg established in the Montana legislature re-emerge in their Washington work and their explanation of that work to their constituencies. Tester should continue to author a good bit of legislation and to pass it successfully across a range of issues. Rehberg should author few bills focusing mostly on private property and the circumscription of government while specializing in appropriations work behind the scenes. To see if this is the case, we now turn to bill sponsorship and congressional earmarks.

## WASHINGTON WORK

Members of Congress engage in a host of representational activities, some on Capitol Hill and others back home. Roll call votes receive extensive attention from political scientists as a metric of representational style. Although roll call votes in the aggregate can tell us a bit about the governing philosophies of members of Congress, they present three distinct problems. First, members need to vote for or against literally thousands of bills and procedural motions throughout their time in office. Many votes are routine and uncontroversial. Even if it is possible to separate procedural votes from substantive votes, roll call votes still do not signal intensity of support. Also, aggregate measures of roll call votes tell us nothing about a member's legislative priorities.

A better indicator of a member's priorities is bill sponsorship. Sponsorship tells us in what issues a member is most interested. It also signals preference intensity.[15] It takes more effort by a member and his or her staff to draft legislation than it does to cast a vote. The legislation a member puts his or her name on tells the casual observer about his or her priorities. It gives us a window into the member's governing philosophy, and tells us which constituencies a member choses to represent legislatively.

I compiled the bills sponsored by Congressman Rehberg, and Senators Tester and Baucus from the 107th Congress through the 111th Congress.[16] I include Baucus as a baseline comparison. Generally speaking, Montana's senators draft more bills. Senator Baucus wrote the most legislation, sponsoring no fewer than 34 bills and as many as 64 bills per Congress during the period. Senator Tester during his first two years in office introduced 17 bills as primary sponsor, following up with 31 additional bills and resolutions in the 111th Congress. Congressman Rehberg penned as few as 11 bills in the 108th Congress but then introduced 35 bills—by far the most bills he's sponsored—in the 111th Congress.

On average, House members passed less than one bill in the 109th through the 111th Congresses that became law, according to data compiled by the Congressional Bills Project. In the Senate, it isn't much better: Senators passed fewer than two bills on average that were signed by the president over the same period.[17] Of the 42 bills and resolutions sponsored by Tester during his first four years in office, two passed. Rehberg passed seven of the 82 bills and resolutions he introduced between 2001 and 2010.[18] In neither case do Rehberg nor Tester stand out as successful legislators, but their efforts are less reflective of their individual abilities than they are of governing in an era of polarization and divided government. Senior members of both chambers tend to be more successful because they often have committee chairmanships that provide them with the opportunity and responsibility to advance legislation central to their party's legislative agendas.[19] Montana Senator Max Baucus's experience illustrates the point. As one of the most senior members of the chamber and chairman of Senate Finance, Baucus had 14 bills become law in the 111th Congress alone. This represents a passage rate of 24 percent (well above the chamber average of about three percent).[20] Finally, the ideas introduced in bills often can migrate into other legislative vehicles and become law that way. More on this later.

Why are Senator Tester and Baucus more active legislatively than Congressman Rehberg? The differences reflect both institutional and personal factors. Institutionally, senators have more staff resources than congressmen to devote to drafting legislation. House members are restricted to no more than 20 staff members on their payrolls—and Rehberg often adheres to the maximum. According to the House Clerk's *Statement of Disbursements* for 2009, Rehberg had exactly 20 staffers working for him, one who was part time and another who was shared with other members.[21] By comparison, Senator Baucus had 42 individuals working for him at home and in Washington on his personal staff as of the spring of 2008. Tester employed 37.[22] Senators do not face the same restrictions as House members on the number of the staff they can hire save for the money they have available in their Senator's Official Personnel and Office Expense Account.[23] This disparity of resources is particularly important to understand in states like Montana where the congressman represents the same geographic constituency but is stretched thinner in terms of official resources. It makes it harder for congressmen to do Washington Work and to create Washington successes to tout back home—especially when compared to what senators can do.

Senate rules also provide more points of access to the legislative process than do House rules. In the House, bills are introduced and referred to the jurisdictionally appropriate committee. In the Senate, this, too, often is the case; however, senators may opt to introduce legislation directly on the Senate floor. In addition, senators can use floor amendments much more readily to influence the content of individual bills—allowing them to transport ideas expressed in bills stuck in committee into other bills being debated on the floor. In the House, this is much more difficult owing to tighter rules on germaneness—meaning amendments must adhere strictly to the subject of the bill or they are ruled of order—and the increasing use of so-called closed rules which restrict considerably the amendments allowed during debate on the House floor.[24] It is much easier as a senator—with fewer members and less restrictive rules—to insert oneself into the legislative process than it is for a member of the House.

Still, more than institutional differences explain the legislative patterns of Congressman Rehberg and Senator Tester. Both men approach legislating in much the same way as they did when serving in the state legislature. There Tester was by far more active in sponsoring bills and steering them through the process than was Rehberg. And this pattern recurs on the national stage. In both the 110th and 111th Congresses, Senator Tester introduced almost as many amendments as he did bills: 38 amendments compared to 48 bills. And he achieved far greater success in amending legislation than in sponsoring it. To compare apples to apples, I pulled out the freshman class of the 110th Congress—the first in which Tester served—and studied their work in this and the 111th Congress. I looked collectively at the bills and amendments the freshmen senators sponsored in their first four years of service. Tester ranks second to last with a bill passage rate of four percent. However, he is the second most successful sponsor of amendments among his peers with a 29 percent success rate.[25] Tester, much as he had in the state legislature, used whatever vehicle was available to him in order to achieve positive legislative outcomes.

As an appropriator in the state legislature, Congressman Rehberg was a legislative specialist concentrating on his committee work. He stuck closely to legislative areas in which he had personal knowledge and interest. When I asked him why he didn't sponsor much legislation while in the House of Representatives, he said that House Appropriators legislate less than their colleagues.[26] This pattern was certainly true in the state legislature.

Rehberg used budgets, not legislating, as the manner with which to make decisions and policy as an appropriator. Data further confirm that House appropriators are less active legislators. On average, members of House Appropriations sponsor fewer bills than their colleagues serving on other committees. According to the data I compiled for the 109th, 110th, and 111th Congresses from the Congressional Bills Project, members on appropriations sponsored about five fewer bills on average than other House members.[27] This is also the pattern observed by Richard Fenno when watching congressmen and senators doing their committee work in Washington in the late 1960s and 1970s. Members choosing to serve on House Appropriations had power and prestige as their chief goal, not policy *per se*. What Fenno wrote is equally important now as it was four decades ago: "Their main goal as committee members does not concern policy.... These congressmen are attracted, in other words, more by the putative 'importance' of their subject matter than by its content."[28] Again, the early political careers of both Tester and Rehberg explain how each approached their Washington work distinctly. Tester was still the generalist and Rehberg the specialist. Tester used all the levers of the legislative process available to create statutory change, while Rehberg preferred sticking to spreadsheets and budgets to produce the limited government he wanted.

As much as bill sponsorship tells us about how members allocate their time, it communicates even more about their issue priorities and the various constituencies they choose to represent within their district or state. It also tells us about the distinctive reputations they wish to showcase.

I took the bills sponsored by Congressman Rehberg and Senators Tester and Baucus in the 110th and 111th Congresses and coded them according to the 19-point issue categorization scheme used by the Congressional Bills and Policy Agendas Projects, two massive database projects classifying the legislative output of Congress.[29] The results appear in Table 5.1 with each cell representing the percentage of total bills sponsored by the member falling in the category.

Senators are policy generalists and House members are policy specialists. It seems to be the case among the Montana congressional delegation as well. Nearly half of Congressman Rehberg's bills fall into the category of Public Lands and Water Management or Congressional Operations, with each category representing 36 and 11 percent respectively. No other category breaks the ten percent threshold. Remembering Congressman Rehberg's priorities as a state legislator, recall that he worked mostly on government operations and community development issues, especially private property development. Much of Rehberg's focus on public land and water management in the House also addresses private property rights. Rehberg's early political career predicts well his Washington work.

Senators Tester and Baucus cast their legislative efforts more broadly afield. Part of this is a function of the fact that they—like all senators—serve on far more committees than the average House member. This pattern happens to be attenuated among the Montana congressional delegation because Rehberg serves only on House Appropriations. As a prestige committee, members of the House get to serve only on Appropriations if they are lucky enough to get appointed.[30] We would expect to see a much broader legislative portfolio among Baucus and Tester when compared to Rehberg due to these particular institutional circumstances.

## TABLE 5.1
*Bill Sponsorship by Issues, 110th and 111th Congresses*

|  | Baucus | Tester | Rehberg |
|---|---|---|---|
| Macroeconomics | 12% | 2% | 1% |
| Civil Rights and Civil Liberties | 0% | 0% | 4% |
| Health | 11% | 13% | 3% |
| Agriculture | 5% | 11% | 8% |
| Labor, Employment, Immigration | 4% | 2% | 3% |
| Education | 1% | 2% | 3% |
| Environment | 2% | 4% | 4% |
| Energy | 3% | 13% | 5% |
| Transportation | 7% | 0% | 3% |
| Law, Crime, Family | 4% | 4% | 3% |
| Social Welfare | 4% | 0% | 0% |
| Community Development and Housing Issues | 0% | 2% | 0% |
| Banking, Finance, and Domestic Commerce | 3% | 9% | 5% |
| Defense | 5% | 9% | 8% |
| Space, Science, Tech, Communications | 2% | 0% | 1% |
| Foreign Trade | 19% | 0% | 1% |
| International Affairs/Foreign Aid | 3% | 0% | 0% |
| Government Operations | 4% | 4% | 11% |
| Public Land and Water Management | 9% | 22% | 36% |

*Source*: Data on bill sponsorship collected from the Library of Congress's THOMAS database located at http://thomas.loc.gov/home/thomas.php and then coded by the author using the subject protocols developed by the Policy Agendas Project available at http://www.policyagendas.org/.

Jon Tester, much like his days in the state legislature, appears to be a legislative generalist in the Senate. In the state legislature, he concentrated mostly on taxes, healthcare, and agriculture—representing 42 percent of the bills he sponsored in terms of issue content. In the Senate, given Senator Baucus's role on finance, Tester shies away from tax policy in deference to his more senior colleague who has established a clear reputational advantage on the issue. Tester focuses his efforts on public land and water management (22 percent of his legislation), health (13 percent), energy (13 percent), and agriculture (11 percent). Fewer than half of Tester's bills were referred to committees on which he served, while the number for Baucus was 65 percent during the same period. This seems to be a conscious shift in style because in his first two years in office, more than 70 percent of Tester's legislation was referred to his committees. It then dropped to a third in the next congressional session.[31] Again, the data show in stark relief what we have already observed from their careers in the state legislature: Rehberg has a proclivity to specialize legislatively while Tester generalizes.

Three additional observations confirm that the legislative work of Congressman Rehberg and Senator Tester reflect their experiences in their early political careers. First, consider the role of appropriators in the legislative process. Appropriators make policy by choosing what programs to fund and—at least until the elimination of earmarks in the 112th Congress—to designate funds for particular projects back in their states and districts. Derided as "pork barrel spending" by critics, this process of earmarking funds is why House Appropriations was such a powerful and sought-after committee for so long. Members could unveil a whole host of projects with which to credit claim among constituents. To understand the work of an appropriator, it is important to look at earmarks.

A series of recent reforms made the earmarking process more transparent in both the House and Senate, and we have earmark data for three years that are easily accessible: 2008, 2009, and 2010. After 2010, when the Republicans took over the House, earmarks were banned first in the House and later in the Senate.[32] The Center for Responsive Politics compiled the total number of earmarks every member requested in 2008, 2009, and 2010 as well as the dollar total of these solo earmarks.[33] Table 5.2 details the earmarking behavior of Montana's congressional delegation during this period.

Congressman Rehberg used earmarks aggressively to demonstrate power and influence as a *geographic agent*. A geographic agent brings particularistic benefits to a congressional district or state. During the three-year period, Rehberg was responsible for 40 earmarks totaling more than $19 million. This is the average amount produced by a congressman for his district. However, the amount looks more impressive when compared to what Montana's Senate delegation brought home. Rehberg far outpaced Tester—who served on Senate Appropriations starting in 2009. Tester was responsible for only $11 million in solo earmark requests, far less than the average small state senator (defined as a state with only three members in its congressional delegation).[34] Senator Baucus brought in more than $30 million in earmarks by himself, exceeding Rehberg even if the amount is less than the average senator from a small state successfully requests. What is striking is how well Rehberg does as a House member with far less clout than any individual senator, especially when compared to a senator of Baucus's seniority. Rehberg clearly preferred using earmarks as a policy tool as opposed to bills, again demonstrating the importance of his early career to his learning as a congressman.

**TABLE 5.2**
*Congressman Rehberg as a Geographic Agent and Legislative Specialist*

| Year | Member | Number of Solo Earmarks | Dollar Total of Solo Earmarks |
|------|--------|-------------------------|-------------------------------|
| 2008 | Baucus | 16 | $8,375,430 |
| | Tester | 8 | $1,890,070 |
| | Rehberg | 11 | $6,037,000 |
| | Average Small State Senator | 21.0 | $37,525,852 |
| | Average Congressman | 9.2 | $6,802,575 |
| 2009 | Baucus | 12 | $10,896,750 |
| | Tester | 4 | $1,863,000 |
| | Rehberg | 9 | $3,242,000 |
| | Average Small State Senator | *16.0 | $24,594,153 |
| | Average Congressman | 8.9 | $6,903,972 |
| 2010 | Baucus | 8 | $11,054,500 |
| | Tester | 11 | $7,342,750 |
| | Rehberg | 20 | $9,645,600 |
| | Average Small State Senator | 11.9 | $10,971,995 |
| | Average Congressman | 7.9 | $5,700,448 |
| Totals | Average Baucus | 12 | $10,108,893 |
| | Average Tester | 7.7 | $3,698,607 |
| | Average Rehberg | 13.3 | $6,308,200 |
| | Average Small State Senator | 16.3 | $24,364,000 |
| | Average Congressman | 8.7 | $6,468,998 |

*Source*: Data on earmarks collected by author from the Center of Responsive Politics, http://opensecrets.org.

Tester seemed less interested in earmarking. This might be a residual of his campaign against Senator Burns where he railed against special interests and the use of earmarks to reward contributors. It wasn't that he was opposed to earmarks; in fact, he disagreed with the earmark ban because he believed it gave the executive branch more power in the appropriations process. In 2008, he told the *Billings Gazette* that "now more than ever, large, rural states like Montana need funding for basic infrastructure" and he "prioritize[d] projects that improve roads, water systems, health care facilities and research projects that are critical to Montana's future."[35] But earmarking was not central to his governing style, perhaps because it was earmarking that got his predecessor Conrad Burns into so much trouble—trouble which the Tester campaign capitalized on to allege that Burns had become out of touch with Montanans and too connected to special interests in Washington.

It might appear that Tester's legislative efforts lack clarity. No—Tester involved himself in problems that he felt needed solutions. He was assigned to the Veterans Affairs Committee when he first got to Washington, and it is this assignment that begins to define him as a legislator who is a *generalist* working as a *group agent*. Group agents identify a particular constituency that needs assistance and makes it their mission to produce policy aiding that constituency. Tester identified veterans early as an important constituency. Montana has the second-highest number of veterans as a percentage of population, exceeded only by Alaska.[36] Tester made veterans the target of his generalist legislative efforts. Again, remember how Tester defined his core supporters as the young and the old, those most needing an effective government providing a social safety net. Veterans are another group facing similar needs that must be advanced and protected.

Why veterans in particular? We can trace Tester's interests in veterans to two distinct events. First, even prior to his appointment to the Senate Veterans Affairs Committee, Tester felt that veterans slipped through the cracks.[37] If one uses bill sponsorship as a metric measuring concern for veterans' issues, this is true. Searching THOMAS for bills sponsored by the Montana delegation using the words *veteran* or *veterans* yields exactly seven bills between the 107th and 109th Congresses.[38] Senator Burns sponsored four and Baucus sponsored three. Congressman Rehberg did not sponsor a single bill mentioning veterans during this period, according to this metric. Clearly, here was a constituency group that was not receiving any intense legislative attention from the delegation. This provided Tester with an opportunity.[39]

Second, on Tester's first trip back to Montana following his swearing in, he held a town hall meeting in the Bitterroot Valley.[40] During that meeting, many veterans mentioned several problems they were having with the Veteran's Administration (VA), including the low mileage reimbursement rates they received when travelling for medical care. Mileage reimbursement became one of Tester's first major legislative wins. The victory was an amendment increasing the reimbursement rate to the military construction appropriations bill passed in September 2007.[41] In this instance, Tester used the more open and fluid amendment process in the Senate to make his legislative mark.

Tester's interest in veterans' issues only grew. In his first Congress, Tester sponsored two bills—or 12 percent of his legislative efforts—mentioning veterans. This grew to five or 18 percent of the bills he sponsored in the 111th Congress. Finally, in the 112th Congress—when he was running for reelection—fully 31 percent of

Tester's sponsored bills concerned veterans across a range of issue areas including housing, healthcare, and education. Although Rehberg and Baucus also sponsored veterans' legislation, their efforts did not represent as sizeable a portion of their bill sponsorships. Tester concentrated his policy efforts on providing benefits for an underserved group. One might also surmise that this legislative push represented an effort by Tester to expand his reelection constituency, although neither Tester nor his staff members have ever characterized his work in this way to me.

Bill sponsorship also broadcasts how members think about government and their roles as legislators—especially if you look closely. Two bills are emblematic of how Rehberg and Tester approach legislating and government differently. Both were introduced in the 111th Congress and, while neither passed, were reintroduced in the succeeding Congress. The first bill, sponsored by Rehberg, would prohibit the expansion or establishment of national monuments in Montana.[42] A later version became known as the Montana Land Sovereignty Act.[43] The second is Tester's Forest Jobs and Recreation Act.[44]

In 2010, Congressman Rehberg submitted legislation curtailing the 1906 Antiquities Act in response to a leaked internal memo from the Department of Interior.[45] The memo suggested that large swaths of land in the West were candidates for national monument status should the president wish to designate them.[46] According to the Antiquities Act, the president may, at his discretion, issue an executive order protecting "objects of historic and scientific interest."[47] Rehberg's bill would permanently exempt Montana from the act, much in the same way that Wyoming was exempted in 1950 as a concession to the establishment of Grand Teton National Park.[48]

Less than three weeks after the memo leaked, Rehberg dropped a bill in the House clerk's hopper. Rehberg warned that the Department of Interior would "federalize potentially millions of acres of private lands in Montana" and that the actions of the agency were nothing short of a "naked abuse of power."[49] The Department of Interior memo touched a raw nerve with Rehberg and his primary constituency, entrepreneurs in the extraction industry. Rehberg saw the Obama administration threatening private land holdings. His response was instinctive: Stop the land grab and abusive federal power. It was a reaction that shouldn't surprise anyone who had followed Rehberg's political career or understood his family's negative experiences at the hands of federal bureaucrats. Rehberg wanted to be seen as the protector of the small guy, as a supporter of Pinchot conservation, and as a vigilant defender of private property.

On the opposite side of the spectrum, in 2009, Senator Tester introduced his Forest Jobs and Recreation Act. The bill was Tester's bid to bring a variety of Montana stakeholders together to resolve three public land issues: first, the perceived need by environmentalists to designate more land in Montana as wilderness; second, the desire to create jobs in a timber industry beset by increasing foreign competition and the loss of thousands of jobs over the past two decades; and third, the necessary clearing of trees killed by pine beetles, which presents a serious fire hazard in an ever-warming and drying West. The problem is that all three purposes did not necessarily sit well together. Which for problem-solving Tester, I suspect, was exactly the point.

Those supporting Tester's bill "said it came from a broad coalition of loggers, hunters, anglers, outfitters, snowmobilers, motorized user proponents and conservation groups, who spent years in meetings, hammering out a compromise everyone could live with."[50] Recently, Tester rallied support for his bill. "It is important to note that many of the stakeholders that have helped to write this bill used to only meet in the courtroom. Now they meet to find common sense solutions that create jobs and protect Montana's outdoor heritage," he testified in front of a Senate committee.[51] Critics of the bill, including Rehberg, indicated that it had been written in secret and didn't actually create a single job. "All that you're really guaranteeing in there is more wilderness" and not a single job Rehberg told me as we travelled together.[52]

What is important is the reflection of Tester's legislative instincts in the bill. On his Senate website, Tester provides extensive information about the bill in its current form. In a letter, how Tester pitches the bill to Montanans is revealing. He writes that "by working together, we will create jobs. We will create new opportunities for recreation. We will protect Montana's clean water. We will protect our communities from wildfire. And we will keep Montana's fishing, hunting and hiking habitat around for our kids and grandkids." Tester's bill is an attempt to do the impossible: find common ground between the traditional, Pinchot-style conservationists and Muir preservationists. Perhaps that is why the bill is controversial and why it's not overwhelmingly popular with any one group. But it is exactly because Tester attempts to square a circle that it is notable. Tester believes his job is to make government function well while addressing a seemingly irresolvable difference. Perhaps the bill will not pass, but it demonstrates Tester's gut instinct as a farmer: There's a job that needs doin'. Let's pull together as a community and get 'er done.

In summarizing the Washington work of Congressman Rehberg and Senator Tester, we see Rehberg as a legislative specialist in the House who secured earmarks for Montana. Tester, alternatively, is a legislative generalist who looks for problems to solve. A particular constituent group, veterans, receives his attention across policy areas. In both instances, the legislative tastes of Rehberg and Tester reflect their previous experience working in the Montana legislature. And their formative prepolitical experiences continue to motivate the types of legislation they draft. Legislating is important and signals the issue priorities of legislators.

But just as important is how constituents perceive what members of Congress do in Washington, and how constituents learn about what members do comes from the explanations the members themselves provide to constituents when they come back home.

## EXPLAINING WASHINGTON WORK TO CONSTITUENTS

What members do in Washington represents only one side of the representation coin. The obverse is how members communicate their work on Capitol Hill to their constituents. There are a variety of ways to observe this process of explanation. I concentrate on two: press releases and town hall-style meetings with constituents. Both venues provide different glimpses of the home styles of Senator Tester and Congressman Rehberg, serving to deepen our emerging impressions of them as legislators. They also provide us an early and telling look at their strengths and weaknesses as Senate candidates.

Although they must consider the prevailing news environment when sending press releases to the media, members of Congress use news releases in an attempt to set the media's agenda while burnishing their own reputational images. Press releases are distinct from newspaper articles. Journalists and editors decide what is newsworthy and then strive to provide largely evenhanded and balanced coverage. Press releases often appear in these articles but rarely verbatim—especially in larger newspapers. News stories never tell a story exactly as a member of Congress would like it to be told, but news releases sent by the member's communications office are unmediated versions of events as they would tell them. Short of observing members of Congress visiting constituents, news releases are the best way to witness how they want their legislative activities communicated to folks back home.

I obtained 1,675 news releases sent by Senators Max Baucus and Jon Tester and Congressman Denny Rehberg from 2007 through 2010. A team of students and volunteers coded the releases to reflect the substantive policy areas discussed in the news release, the type of activity the member engaged in, and the constituent needs primarily addressed by the member's Washington work.[53] Tester was the most prolific in sending releases, accounting for 726 during the period (43 percent of the total). Baucus had fewer press releases (500), and Rehberg the fewest (449). Unsurprisingly, both Senators sent out more press releases than Montana's lone congressman. This reflects the greater staffing resources of senators. Most congressmen have only a press secretary, while senators often have a press secretary, a deputy press secretary, a communications director, and a deputy communications director. It is also perhaps not surprising that Tester sent more press releases given the stage of his career. Unlike Baucus and Rehberg, who were fairly well-established in their careers and well-known public servants statewide, Tester was in his first term in office. He had yet to establish a particular reputation among Montanans. Having a more robust press operation was one way to spread the word quickly to the folks back home.

In Table 5.3, I report the percentage of news releases falling into each issue categorization scheme as highlighted throughout the book. Releases not centering on a particular issue are excluded so we can more clearly detect patterns. Jon Tester's reporting of his Washington work through press releases matches fairly closely the bills he chooses to sponsor. His propensity to scatter his legislative efforts comes through as before, and he chooses to communicate that to his constituents. Tester issued press releases in every issue category save one (space,

## TABLE 5.3
*News Releases by Issues, 110th and 111th Congresses*

|  | Baucus | Tester | Rehberg | Total |
|---|---|---|---|---|
| Macroeconomics | 8% | 6% | 11% | 8% |
| Civil Rights and Civil Liberties | 1% | 3% | 3% | 2% |
| Health | 14% | 7% | 8% | 9% |
| Agriculture | 9% | 5% | 5% | 6% |
| Labor, Employment, Immigration | 2% | 3% | 3% | 3% |
| Education | 7% | 5% | 6% | 6% |
| Environment | 12% | 11% | 15% | 12% |
| Energy | 4% | 10% | 11% | 8% |
| Transportation | 9% | 4% | 8% | 6% |
| Law, Crime, Family | 5% | 2% | 2% | 3% |
| Social Welfare | 3% | 8% | 4% | 5% |
| Community Development and Housing Issues | 3% | 1% | 1% | 2% |
| Banking, Finance, and Domestic Commerce | 8% | 10% | 7% | 9% |
| Defense | 5% | 12% | 5% | 8% |
| Space, Science, Tech, Communications | 0% | 0% | 0% | 1% |
| Foreign Trade | 0% | 2% | 2% | 1% |
| International Affairs/Foreign Aid | 0% | 6% | 3% | 3% |
| Government Operations | 0% | 1% | 0% | 0% |
| Public Land and Water Management | 9% | 6% | 7% | 7% |

*Source*: News releases obtained by author from the offices of Senators Baucus, Tester, and Congressman Rehberg. Coding of issues based on the Policy Agendas Project Topic codes available at: http://www.policyagendas.org/.

science, tech, and communications). The top five issue areas in order are environment, energy, health, banking, and defense. The main difference is his work on public lands, which represents the largest single area of legislative concentration (22 percent of bills sponsored) but is only emphasized six percent of the time in his releases. The main point is that Tester is a legislative generalist and portrays himself as such; this is consistent with what we have thus far observed in his bill sponsorships and prepolitical career.

Tester's communications efforts stand in contrast to Congressman Rehberg's and Senator Baucus's—both of whom do not communicate the same mix of issues in their releases relative to their legislative efforts. Senator Baucus, who spends considerable effort legislating on trade and macroeconomic issues, hardly talks about these issues in his public communications. Macroeconomics consists of eight percent of issue mentions (6th out of 19 possible issue areas), and international trade, the single largest issue category of bills sponsored (19 percent), is completely absent from news releases. Senator Baucus, like Senator Tester, is most likely to discuss health, the environment, and agriculture in his releases—plus transportation. It should be noted that Senator Baucus, in addition to his perch on finance, served on the public works and environment, agriculture, and transportation committees in the Senate.

Congressman Rehberg, who prefers the work of a legislative specialist as a House appropriator, strikes a different pose in his press releases. Public lands and congressional operations, consisting of nearly 50 percent of his legislative efforts, do not appear in his releases with any great regularity (seven and zero percent). The top five issues in Rehberg's releases are the environment, energy, macroeconomics, health, and transportation. Only energy appears in the top five of Rehberg's legislative efforts. Rehberg's communication of his Washington work is very different from his legislative priorities as expressed in bill sponsorship, his earmarking behavior, and his prepolitical career.

What to make of these patterns? In all three instances, Montana's congressional delegation prefers that Montanans see them as legislative generalists doing the work of Montana across issues important to them. Senator Baucus and Congressman Rehberg appear to legislate more as specialists than Senator Tester; both Baucus and Rehberg focus on work related to their committees and of personal interest to them. When communicating with Montanans, however, all three stress their work in areas central to the functioning of Montana's economy and the perceived needs of its citizens.

This observation is especially interesting given the need of each individual member to craft distinctive reputations among constituents. Congressman Rehberg, as the lone Republican in the Montana delegation, is under less pressure to carve out a distinctive issue reputation because, as a Republican, his positions—by virtue of his ideology—are different from the Democratic senators. Senators Baucus and Tester, while exhibiting distinctive tastes legislatively, are more alike than one might expect in their issue portrayal to constituents. If there is a distinction, it is the apparent willingness of Tester to communicate more willingly his work on the banking committee than Senator Baucus does with his work on finance. One might conjecture that Senator Baucus's choice to eschew talk of larger economic issues such as budgets and trade is a function of those issues being removed from the lives of the average citizen and the necessity of carrying the water of the administration and toeing the party line more closely as a committee chair during a period of unified government. This might put him at odds with his Montana constituents more than he might like, so it gets downplayed.

Aside from issues and their work on bills, members of Congress also use press releases to claim credit for particularistic benefits they bring back to their constituents. Earmarks, already mentioned, are one way that members can demonstrate their work as geographic agents. Members also can work to attract benefits aiding the state or to protect from cuts benefits already obtained. If a reference to obtaining or protecting benefits aiding the state is mentioned in the press release, it is coded to reflect the member behaving as a geographic agent attempting to draw attention to their work. The specific forms of behaving as geographic agents coded here are favoring a proposal to obtain geographic benefits, working to acquire benefits, announcing success in obtaining benefits, claiming credit for benefits, explaining why desirable benefits are not available, and educating constituents about geographic benefits.

Table 5.4 shows the incidence of behaving as a geographic agent by Montana's congressional delegation for the entire period of 2007 through 2010, broken down between these six categories. The figure separates 2010 for comparison to 2007 through 2009. This allows us to evaluate the effect of the Tea Party and a shift in the national political conversation away from particularistic spending.

Generally speaking, the three members representing Montana in Washington, DC are more likely to portray themselves as legislators than as local agents bringing benefits home. About 60 percent of the time their releases make no mention of acting as local agents seeking to claim geographic benefits. By comparison, two-thirds of releases discuss work on behalf of legislation.[54] The aggregate picture of communicating the obtaining or protection of local benefits obscures some important patterns, however. About 30 percent of the time, Tester either claims credit for bringing geographic benefits to the district, discusses working to acquire such benefits, or announces success in bringing spending to Montana. Tester is the least active in this regard during the entire period, with 35 percent of Rehberg's releases portraying him as an active geographic agent and 49 percent

**TABLE 5.4**
*Montana's Congressional Delegation as Geographic Agents in News Releases, 2007 to 2010*

| | 2007–2010 | | | Before 2010 | | | 2010 | | |
|---|---|---|---|---|---|---|---|---|---|
| | Baucus | Tester | Rehberg | Baucus | Tester | Rehberg | Baucus | Tester | Rehberg |
| No portrayal as a local agent | 51% | 67% | 63% | 49% | 64% | 59% | 66% | 72% | 78% |
| Favoring proposal to acquire geographic benefits | 0% | 2% | 2% | 0% | 3% | 3% | 0% | 0% | 0% |
| Working to acquire geographic benefits | 15% | 17% | 18% | 15% | 18% | 17% | 17% | 15% | 19% |
| Announcing success in acquiring geographic benefits | 10% | 7% | 6% | 9% | 4% | 7% | 15% | 12% | 2% |
| Claiming credit for geographic benefits | 24% | 6% | 11% | 25% | 9% | 14% | 2% | 1% | 1% |
| Explaining why benefits aren't coming | 0% | 0% | 0% | 0% | 0% | 0% | 0% | 0% | 0% |
| Educating constituents about geographic benefits | 0% | 1% | 0% | 0% | 2% | 1% | 0% | 0% | 0% |

*Source:* News releases coded by author using scheme developed by R. Douglas Arnold in his book, *Congress, the Press, and Political Accountability.* The coding protocols are available at: http://www.princeton.edu/~arnold/research/data_archive.htm.

of Baucus's releases making such claims. Political science scholarship suggests that House members are much more likely to engage in producing and claiming credit for particularistic benefits for consumption back home. In Montana, at the very least, this seems to not be the case because of Baucus's considerable efforts to communicate this aspect of his Washington work, which overshadows the rest of the delegation.

An interesting wrinkle is added when looking at the patterns longitudinally. The Tea Party movement undermined the value of credit claiming activities, especially for Republicans who were likely to be challenged from the right in primaries. The center and right-most panel in Table 5.4 compare the period before the Tea Party rise in 2010, the height of the movement's strength. Note that all three members are less likely to portray themselves as local agents, but the differences are most notable for Rehberg and Baucus. Rehberg is portrayed as a local agent in some capacity 41 percent of the time through 2009 in his releases. This drops by 19 percentage points to only 22 percent of the time in 2010. The drop is almost as precipitous for Baucus: 17 percentage points. Tester, by comparison, is only 8 percentage points less likely to claim credit in some capacity for bringing geographic benefits to Montana. Clearly, Baucus and Rehberg wanted the public to pay less attention to their roles as local agents. This is especially true for Rehberg, worried the most about a Tea Party challenge and being abandoned by hardline conservatives.

One final point can be gleaned from news releases. I claim that Tester's generalist approach as a legislator is directed at one particular constituency group: veterans. Of the hundreds of issue codes available to coders of press releases and news articles, three address veterans' issues: appropriations for veterans' programs, veterans' health care, and veterans' benefits broadly. In all other cases, coders were instructed to code press releases in the issue area regardless of the particular group served. A bill concerning education but directed to veterans would be coded as education and not veterans' affairs, for example. The main point is the issue variable is a conservative measure of policy involvement concerning veterans. Nevertheless, the pattern in releases concerning attention to veterans' affairs matches that uncovered legislatively. Neither Rehberg nor Baucus are coded as working extensively in veterans' affairs: Only five and four percent respectively of releases sent by their offices mention veterans' issues. Fully 12 percent of news releases issued by Tester, however, deal directly with veterans' issues. Overall, the match between the actual Washington work and the explanation of that work overlap considerably for Jon Tester. Rehberg and Baucus, alternatively, present their Washington work to their constituents differently from the work they actually do.

It is as important to understand how members of Congress communicate their representational activities as it is to examine those activities within the context of Washington, DC. Sometimes those views are congruent. This is the case with Jon Tester. His legislative work is general in its approach, looks to bring diverse stakeholders together, and is aimed toward making the lives of veterans better. That work is conveyed in his press releases and his legislative priorities.

Rehberg's explanation of his Washington work, however, varied somewhat from his governing activities. There are two factors at play here. First, as a congressman who is in the rare (but not unique) position of sharing a geographic constituency with the state's two senators, Rehberg needs to address a broader range of issues than most congressmen. This makes it harder to develop an issue monopoly, but perhaps this is less problematic when communicating Washington work because as the lone Republican his positions can be distinctive. Indeed, Rehberg can and does represent primary constituencies distinctive from Tester and Baucus who, as Democrats, likely exhibit considerable overlap in the primary constituencies they serve. Second, Rehberg's work as an appropriator, which has long been a part of his political career, is now a political liability among his primary constituency—those same small businessmen and ranchers who often found themselves at the center of the Tea Party's emergence nationally and in Montana. Rehberg continued to work to secure geographic benefits for Montana through the earmark process in 2010. Indeed, it was his best year to date with the most money obtained from the most earmarks requested during the three years for which we have data. But Rehberg chose not to publicize those activities as widely as he once did. This, as we will see, becomes a considerable problem for him in the campaign when attempting to explain his legislative successes to constituents back home—a liability that Jon Tester did not have. Tester's legislative activities and explanation of Washington Work exhibited consistency, while Rehberg's and Baucus's did not.

## HOME STYLES AND TOWN HALLS

The final part of explaining Washington work is how members portray themselves when visiting with constituents. During the early stages of the campaign between Senator Tester and Congressman Rehberg, I observed both participate in town hall meetings. About a month after he announced his bid for the Senate, Congressman Rehberg held a town hall in Livingston, about twenty-five minutes east of Bozeman in Park County. Four months later, Senator Tester held a listening session for veterans in Billings. Both Senator Tester and Congressman Rehberg pride themselves on coming back to Montana frequently to interact with constituents.[55]

Senator Tester held his hour-long listening session near a newly constructed Veterans Affairs Clinic on the west side of Billings, the building of which he claimed credit. The hotel conference room selected for the event was nearly full with perhaps 100 or so veterans. Tester began his remarks noting his appointment to the Senate Veterans Affairs Committee, the listening sessions he held immediately upon his first trip back to Montana after his swearing in, and how those sessions led to a series of improvements in veterans' benefits including the increased mileage reimbursement that served as his first major legislative victory.

Three things were notable about Tester's interaction with veterans on that warm July day. First, he was at ease, answering questions comfortably while demonstrating his expertise on veterans' issues. His tone was quiet and even, almost understated. He opened directly for questions and even told folks that they could "go wherever they want to go." It is clear that Tester believed he is among friends. It seems that feeling was mutual.

Second, most of the veterans expressed concern about veterans' benefits being cut in the current climate of fiscal austerity. In fact, Tester's first question came from an elderly woman expressing worry about the debt ceiling negotiations and the possibility that, should the government shut down, veterans would not receive their disability payments. Tester put to rest her concerns in a way that demonstrated both his expertise on veterans' issues and the trusting relationship he has established with this primary constituency:

> I don't think you have to worry about your disability payments. That's not something people in Congress have an appetite to go after. It's not ... well, it just isn't going to be right. .... As we look at opportunities to save money, opportunities to reduce programs, it is my opinion that is not the place to look. And I'll tell you why. We're in two conflicts right now, one in Iraq and one in Afghanistan. .... Those troops [coming home] have issues. And the signature injury that's coming out of [that conflict] revolves around mental health, PTSD, TBI. And in Montana, we are woefully short of people dealing with mental health issues. .... To cut the budget now would make no sense at all because demand is growing, not receding. .... You're darn right you should get your payment on August 1.

Tester's answer allayed fears, demonstrated his understanding of veterans' needs, and—perhaps most importantly—underscored his role as a group protector. Throughout the hour-long session, Tester expressed the hallmarks of a classic group agent by mentioning repeatedly how he's fought for veterans.

He also demonstrated a command of the problems facing veterans and, when he didn't know the answers, he had the appropriate staff members on hand who could respond. The issue of orthopedic surgery was raised early, specifically the backlog for such surgeries, the scarcity of orthopedic surgeons working in Montana, and issues of payment when soldiers sought emergency treatment. A staff member from the main VA clinic in the state tackled the questions, but Tester—sensing this was a bigger problem—asked members of the audience who had orthopedic questions to raise their hand. He then steered the conversation to that issue so that the VA staffer could respond. It was a small but significant example of Tester demonstrating his understanding of the needs of this primary constituency.

Finally, Tester spent much of the time acting as a constituent servant. Time and again, Tester was presented with stories of benefits denied, medals never received, and the inconveniences veterans faced when seeking medical treatment. He would direct folks to his staff to make sure casework files were opened and the problem resolved. Bruce Knutson, Tester's chief veterans' affairs liaison in the state, was pointed out frequently by Tester as the individual responsible for veterans casework. And Tester would do so directly, quickly, and efficiently: "Bruce Knuston? Raise your hand. You get his card before you leave, and we'll follow up" was a typical response. I understand you, the response says, and I'm going to help you. What is important about these interactions is the fact that, in many states, this is the type of work that House members would devote themselves to and not a United States Senator. It is clear that Tester, however, does not agree. When I asked his staff after the campaign whether Tester saw himself primarily as a constituent servant, policy maker, or as "one of us," the answer came back universally: constituent servant. Tester may look like "one of us," but the heart of his representational style lies in solving constituent problems. Other senators might concern themselves with statecraft and bigger national issues. Not Jon Tester. Again, it was about making government work better for his people.

Veterans knew that Tester was the voice for their concerns in Washington, and they frequently expressed their gratitude for Tester's attention to them. I spoke with a few in Billings, as well as some in Bozeman the previous day, and the praise was universal. A 40-year army veteran told me that Tester was "the best veterans have ever had" in Washington, citing his position on veterans' affairs, the new Billings clinic, and his work on mileage reimbursement as examples of how Tester "fights" for them. When I said that Rehberg lived in Billings and worked on veterans' issues, he said that Rehberg "shows up" to veterans events but when he goes "back East he forgets about us." Even the 58-year-old Republican woman from Billings who said she had been raised in Republican politics and noted that her family was close to the Rehbergs admitted that the choice between the two of them would be "difficult" because

"Tester is a wonderful man" who has done "great things, especially for veterans." A Vietnam veteran who attended the Bozeman veterans' event the previous day focused on the many bills Tester had introduced for veterans and echoed the oft-noted view that Tester's support among veterans was nearly universal. Tester's strength among veterans flows from his Washington work but really began with, and is sustained by, the listening sessions he's held throughout his time in office. He had built trust by making himself available to a group that felt underappreciated. The Billings veterans' event provided ample evidence of that. It was a good example of Tester connecting with a primary constituency that relied upon government benefits and how his explanation of Washington work matched his legislative activities and priorities.

Rehberg's town hall fulfilled a promise he made to constituents upon his reelection: to hold listening sessions in each of Montana's 56 counties each congress. This is something he began annually as a lieutenant governor and an activity that he believed central to his representational style. "I need to see it. Touch it. Smell it. Feel it. I just . . . there's nothing like the personal experience of being in the communities and seeing and talking and hearing," responded Rehberg when I asked him why he came home so often.[56] When he became a congressman, Rehberg found going to all 56 counties every year to be impossible given the schedule in Washington, so he made it to all 56 counties every congressional term. The Park County session in March was one of the last listening sessions held by the congressman during the 112th Congress.

The session was held in the basement of the Park County administration building, which was a more intimate venue than Tester's session with veterans. It was well-attended, particularly for a Saturday morning in late winter. About 60 folks packed the room to interact with Congressman Rehberg, many standing in the aisles. Rehberg began the meeting by shaking hands, noting that the listening session was a continuation of his commitment to staying in touch with Montanans, and indicating his new responsibilities as Chairman of the Labor, Health and Human Services, and Education Subcommittee of Appropriations. Like Tester, Rehberg appeared comfortable, even funny at times, saying before turning to questions that "I don't need to introduce myself. I'm your congressman. We only have one." He noted that half of his staff was in Montana and encouraged folks to contact them with issues and concerns. He took questions for 90 minutes.

It was immediately apparent that Rehberg faced substantial challenges in portraying his Washington work with this group. Congressman Rehberg had been a champion of earmarks for much of his career, and one of the first questions from the audience concerned wasteful federal spending. Rehberg, the appropriator, stressed support for zero-based budgeting and eliminating earmarks. In discussing appropriations, he demonstrated his chops as a policy expert when confronted by constituents upset with the newly passed healthcare law. Rehberg gave a textbook political science answer in discussing what he could do on appropriations concerning the law: "We can't legislate in an appropriations bill. We can only give money or take it away." Rehberg could have an effect, and the biggest effect he could have would be to defund the law and take money away from enforcement.

Rehberg's talk about his Washington work was a far cry from Tester's in that, despite his position on appropriations, he spent almost no time—if any—talking as a protector of either geographic or group benefits. He rarely had the opportunity to credit claim and ran into a barrage from the individuals upset with the cuts he and the Republican majority were making. The one opportunity he had to distinguish himself from Republicans on this issue he used to point out that he agreed with the Tea Party. When asked about whether he, as a supporter of defense, would be willing to look at waste in defense programs, he responded: "Sure. I have continually said that's one of the areas where I separate myself from the Republicans. You can't tell me there can't be savings that can't be found. . . . I voted for amendments to reduce defense and homeland security waste just last week." Rehberg had to lock down a primary base that was clearly unhappy with Washington's fiscal profligacy, and this made him steer away from all the earmark work he had done, successfully, for Montana.

It was clear from the start that the audience was divided in their loyalties toward the congressman, unlike the Kumbaya treatment given Tester in Billings. About half of the audience represented the core of Denny's primary constituency: conservative Republicans who took a hard line on spending, many from a small business background. The other half of the audience voiced their concerns about impending cuts to community health care centers and Medicaid. At one point during the meeting, the anger between these two groups erupted in raised voices and bickering. Rehberg was composed throughout, but expressed frustration—particularly over the charge that Republicans and his committee would be cutting funding for community hospitals. An exchange between the congressman and two upset individuals working at community healthcare centers went on for several minutes.

Laurie, a healthcare provider in Livingston, claimed Rehberg had cut services for poor Montanans in need of healthcare. "Under your charge, they [community health centers] will not be able to see patients . . . and they already can't keep up with demand. With your change, the Kalispell clinic will have to close. Your cut will block 26,000 Montanans from access to healthcare." And, she further noted, this would increase healthcare costs because the folks served by community health care centers would go to emergency rooms. She asked the congressman if he would be willing to drop his healthcare, a choice many Montanans did not have because they couldn't afford insurance.

The congressman pushed back hard: "It is untrue. In the year 2008 there was $2 billion spent on community health centers. Now, let's talk about the stimulus. What was it intended to do? To turn the economy around. It was a one shot opportunity." In a refrain I had heard before, he said that a stimulus should address economic crises, but this stimulus increased social spending. The dollars spent on these programs were neither honest nor stimulative. He maintained that "88 cents on the dollar . . . went to social spending." Now that the economy has turned around, he claimed that the one shot, $1 billion stimulus was no longer necessary, and that the budget could return to the $2 billion that had been appropriated in 2008. Rehberg returned repeatedly to this point when accused of cutting spending for community clinics in his budget. "There is no cut. We didn't reduce the budget. We didn't allow them to keep the extra billon." Rehberg was calm and careful as he explains, but it was clear he didn't think the charge was fair.

Rehberg spent about half of the time defending himself against charges of emasculating the Affordable Care Act and the rest bolstering his fiscal credentials with conservative Tea Party type supporters. While it was apparent that he had scored some points with those conservatives, it was not a comfortable meeting for Rehberg. Tester clearly had the affection of veterans; this group's view of Rehberg was mixed. When given the opportunity to discuss policy detail, he enjoyed it. You could tell. But when pushed to defend his efforts to defund Obamacare, he found himself returning to generic Republican talking points about how the law would not reduce healthcare costs, did not include provisions dealing with defensive medicine, and how the whole process lacked transparency. One audience member said accusingly of Rehberg that "a lot of what I'm hearing you say today sounds like cable news." Rehberg responded cuttingly that "some of them might be true, you know." The biggest challenge Rehberg faced related to the difference in his personal appropriations experiences. In the state legislature, Rehberg tried to impose fiscal austerity on the actual operations of government—the expenditures made by the executive and legislative branches. Now, he was attempting to implement austerity on programs benefiting various subconstituencies—something which he and Republicans felt was essential to balancing the budget but which generated backlash among supporters and users of those particular programs. It was an uncomfortable and an unenviable position and highlighted some of the challenges Rehberg faced in the general election against Senator Tester.

## CONCLUSION

Congressman Rehberg and Senator Tester share one representational trait: How they communicate their Washington work centers heavily on a home style of travelling around the state, listening to and interacting with constituents. It is something they both believe is a necessary precondition to building a lasting and durable relationship with Montanans. And this is likely a reflection of place; that is, Montanans demand a representational style sensitive to the uniqueness of place. This means coming home often to be physically and mentally rejoined to the land and the people who share that special connection to it. Staying in Washington and away from the land imperils, in the minds of Montanans and its representatives, the intimate understanding of place necessary to represent it.

Beyond that, Rehberg and Tester chose different representational paths in Washington. Those differences reflect patterns established in their pre- and early political careers. Rehberg had been in politics a long time and understood the ins and outs of policy well. When interacting with constituents, Congressman Rehberg comes off as a policy expert willing to dive headlong into the details of policy making, proclivities that served him well in his legislative work as a specialist and appropriator. Tester, on the other hand, never comes off as wonkish. Knowledgeable, yes; but while Rehberg never turns to an aide to address a concern or question, Tester will and does. He has always been a policy generalist—looking for opportunities to solve problems rather than getting immersed in details. He also demonstrates a willingness to help with constituent problems and oriented much of his Senate office around constituent service. Rehberg does this as well, but with fewer staff resources, found it difficult to get the attention that either Tester or even Baucus did as a constituent servant. Finally, and most importantly, Tester seemed to have a stronger relationship with his primary constituency than Rehberg had with his. Rehberg's work as an appropriator painted a target on him from both the conservative businessmen and ranchers that had become the core of the Tea Party's support. It also made him unpopular among those who relied upon the programs cut by his subcommittee. Tester, on the other hand, navigated well his meeting with veterans, who clearly respected him and appreciated the work he did for them to make the gears of government grind more smoothly in the provision of important benefits they earned by serving their country.

The difference in legislative styles between Rehberg and Tester is notable given that they represented the same geographic space but in different offices and constituencies. The ultimate test of their styles hinged on who would be seen as the most authentic, consistent, and honorable by Montanans in the upcoming race. In fact, I argue that the race itself ultimately boiled down to these three characteristics and which candidate best exhibited them convincingly for Montanans. It is to that campaign that we now turn for the remainder of the book.

---

# NOTES

1. Fenno, *Home Style*.
2. Ibid., pp. 1–29.
3. John Hibbing, "Congressional Careerism: For Better or For Worse?" in Lawrence C. Dodd and Bruce I. Oppenheimer, eds., *Congress Reconsidered*, 5th ed. (Washington, DC: CQ Press, 1993). This is not necessarily the case in rural and less densely populated states.
4. Ibid.
5. Parker and Goodman, "Making a Good Impression"; Parker and Goodman, "Our State's Never Had Better Friends."
6. Fenno, *Home Style*, 136. Emphasis in the original.
7. Parker and Goodman, "Our State's Never Had Better Friends," 381.
8. Schiller, *Partners and Rivals*, 24.
9. Although Iowans do.
10. Richard F. Fenno., Jr., *The United States Senate: A Bicameral Perspective*. (Washington, DC: American Enterprise Institute, 1982).
11. Barbara Sinclair's work suggests senators who appear on the national scene reap positive constituent benefits. See Barbara Sinclair, "Washington Behavior and Home-State Reputation: The Impact of National Prominence on Senators' Images," *Legislative Studies Quarterly* 15, no. 4 (1990), 475–494; Richard F. Fenno, Jr., *When Incumbency Fail,*. (Washington, DC: CQ Press, 1992).
12. Frances E. Lee and Bruce I. Oppenheimer, *Sizing Up the Senate: The Unequal Consequences of Equal Representation,* (Chicago, IL: University of Chicago Press), 63–73, especially tables 3.3 and 3.4.
13. Parker and Goodman, "Our State's Never Had Better Friends."
14. Lee and Oppenheimer implicitly argue this, connecting a state's population size to interest heterogeneity. Smaller states are more homogenous and overlapping interests conflict less often. See pages 68–69 in particular.
15. Intensity can be signaled in other ways, too. See Richard L. Hall, *Participation in Congress* (New Haven, CT: Yale University Press, 1998).
16. See http://thomas.loc.gov.
17. See Congressional Bills Project, http://congressionalbills.org/, analysis conducted by and available from author.
18. Bills and joint resolutions have the force of law if passed by both Houses and signed by the president. Concurrent or simple resolutions do not require the signature of the president and are used to either express the sense of the chamber on an issue or makes changes to the internal rules of the chamber. Walter J. Oleszek, *Congressional Procedures and the Policy Process,* 6th ed., (Washington, DC: CQ Press, 2004).
19. See Hibbing, "Congressional Careerism: For Better or For Worse?."

20. Congressional Bills Project.

21. United States Congress, House of Representatives, *Statement of Disbursements of the House, July 1-September 30, 2009,* http://disbursements.house.gov/2009q3/2009q3-single volume.pdf; This is also what Congressman Rehberg told me during our first trip together. Rehberg, interview with author, August 19, 2011.

22. Calculated by author from congressional staff directories published by CQ Press.

23. Ida A. Brudnick, "Congressional Salaries and Allowances," *Congressional Research Service,* January 7, 2014.

24. Barbara Sinclair, *Unorthodox Lawmaking: New Legislative Processes in the U.S. Congress.* 3rd Edition, (Washington, DC: CQ Press, 2011); Barbara Sinclair, *Party Wars: Polarization and the Politics of National Policy Making,* (Norman: University of Oklahoma Press, 2006).

25. Analysis available from author.

26. And when they do have an impact on a law, it usually gets wrapped up in the chairman's mark. We discussed this as I arrived for our trip together on August 22, 2011, in the anteroom of KMMS radio in Bozeman.

27. Available from author.

28. Richard F. Fenno, Jr, *Congressmen in Committees,* (Boston, MA: Little, Brown, and Company, 1973), 4.

29. See the online appendix for further discussion.

30. Rehberg petitioned to be on House appropriations.

31. None of Congressman Rehberg's bills were sent to appropriations, but this is not surprising. Appropriations is not an authorizing committee, so it does not create programs. To create new programs or to change existing programs requires a bill to be sent to the appropriate authorizing committee. Legislation coming out of appropriations consists almost exclusively of the 13 annual bills authorizing federal government spending or continuing resolutions continuing existing spending levels. The primary sponsors of these bills are the chairs of the various subcommittees.

32. Earmarking has not ended. It has just gone underground. See Ron Nixon, "Lawmakers Finance Pet Projects without Earmarks," *The New York Times,* December 27, 2010.

33. "111th Congress Earmarks," *The Center for Responsive Politics,* http://www.opensecrets .org/bigpicture/earmarks.php. Earmarks that are jointly requested are also available, but given that we are interested in the individual member behavior, it makes most sense to restrict the analysis to solo earmarks.

34. It makes sense to compare congressmen who, aside from those who represent whole states, serve roughly the same number of constituents. Senators represent geographic constituencies that vary greatly in terms of population, so a Senate average is not terribly meaningful. It is more useful to compare states of similar population size when looking at the earmark dollars.

35. Noelle Straub, "Baucus, Tester oppose ban on earmarks," *Billings Gazette,* March 13, 2008.

36. Niraj Chokshi, "MAPS: What Each State's Veteran population looks like," GovBeat blog, *The Washington Post,* November 11, 2013, http://www.washingtonpost.com/blogs/ govbeat/wp/2013/11/11/maps-what-each-states-veteran-population-looks-like/.

37. Aaron Murphy, interview with author, November 19, 2012. "Nobody was there to help them. And [Tester] think[s] all of a sudden, 'I'm listening, I'm here to help you and I'm going to start by doing this.' And all this work was sort of like sitting out there and nobody's picking it up. And he realized it early and said, 'I got to take this.' Not because it's popular and not because it's good for [Tester] politically but because it has to be done."

38. Technically, I searched using the term "veteran*" with * a wildcard character.

39. There are other ways to represent veterans besides legislation, and it is very likely—indeed probable—that Rehberg, Baucus, and Burns expended considerable effort doing casework for veterans to help them obtain existing benefits.

40. "Tester Blasts VA: 'Veterans Are Hurting,'" Helena Independent Record. Feb 2, 2007; Aaron Murphy, interview with author, November 19, 2012.

41. Press Release, "Senate Passes Tester Amendment Funding Vets' Mileage Reimbursement," September 6, 2007, http://www.tester.senate.gov/?p=press_release&id=2251. This was mentioned repeatedly as a pivotal moment in Senator Tester's development as a legislator and group agent by Tester's staff.

42. Introduced in 2010 H.R. 4754. See THOMAS, http://thomas.loc.gov .

43. Introduced in 2011 as H.R. 845. Ibid.

44. Introduced in 2009 as S. 1470. Ibid.

45. Kirk Johnson, "In the West, 'Monument' is a Fighting Word," The New York Times, February 19, 2010. The article discusses Western outrage over President Clinton's designation of the Grand Staircase-Escalante National Monument in 1996, which is emblematic of conservative suspicion of the Antiquities Act.

46. Mike Dennison, "Salazar: No Plans in Montana," Billings Gazette, March 9, 2010.

47. American Antiquities Act of 1906, 16 USC 431–433, http://www.cr.nps.gov/local-law/anti1906.htm.

48. Robert W. Righter, Crucible for Conservation: The Struggle for Grand Teton National Park. (Moose, WY: Grand Teton History Association, 1982), 140.

49. Dennison, "Salazar: No Plans in Montana."

50. Eve Byron, "Tester Unveils Forest Bill," Helena Independent Record, July 18, 2009.

51. Matt Gouras, "Panel Takes up Embattled Tester, Baucus Forest Bills," The Bozeman Chronicle, July 31, 2013.

52. Rehberg, interview, August 22, 2011.

53. For the coding instrument used for news releases, please see the online Appendix. Other than issue areas, I adopt a modified version of Doug Arnold's elaborate mechanism used in his book, Congress, the Press, and Political Accountability. His coding mechanism is also available on his website: http://www.princeton.edu/~arnold/research/data_archive.htm; R. Douglas Arnold, Congress, the Press, and Political Accountability, (New York, NY: Russell Sage Foundation, 2004).

54. Coders were asked if the news release mentions the introduction of a bill, committee work on a legislative proposal, taking a position on legislation, work marking up a bill, cosponsoring or endorsing legislation, or building a coalition to pass a bill. Adding these creates a legislative work index which is the basis for this number.

55. Travel records obtained from the Secretary of the Senate and the House Clerk confirmed that each travelled between 156 and 270 days in Montana each year. Tester travelled the most—270 days in 2010. Rehberg travelled more than 200 days in 2007 but in 2010 came home for only 156 days. Much of the time at home was spent visiting with and listening to constituents.

56. Rehberg, interview, August 22, 2011.

# CHAPTER 6

# Campaigning in *a Citizens United* World: The Early Days of the Race

eam Rehberg and Team Tester both recognized early on two important facts about the upcoming race. First, substantial sums of money were necessary to implement their respective campaign plans. When I visited with Rehberg in late summer of 2011, he estimated that eight million dollars would be necessary to confront the ten million Tester would likely spend.[1] After the election, Tester's campaign manager Preston Elliot confirmed that ten million dollars was the Tester campaign's goal.[2] Second, outside groups—courtesy of the recent Supreme Court decision in *Citizens United* that allows corporations and labor unions to spend directly on electioneering—would dump substantial resources into Montana. This would make it difficult, especially when the race heated up through the summer and fall of 2012, for the campaigns to communicate their own messages. Both Tester and Rehberg acknowledged fundraising would consume much of their time. Whether both candidates fully appreciated that their campaign would be the most expensive in Montana history and that more than half the money spent would come from outside groups is unknown. The race was targeted early as one of the top two or three in the cycle that would determine party control of the Senate, but no one could have predicted the more than $50 million spent collectively.

In this chapter, I discuss how campaigns make decisions about messaging and targeting, focusing on the particular choices made by the Tester and Rehberg campaigns that shaped their ensuing campaign narratives. These choices carefully reflected how each candidate viewed his relationship with various constituent groups in Montana as well as his political experiences over two decades. Next, I discuss the strategic tasks facing each campaign in the context of the electoral constituencies each campaign had constructed in previous election cycles. To illustrate how each campaign viewed the political landscape, I focus on two important issues: federal spending and the Affordable Care Act (ACA). In both cases, we glean important insights into how each campaign would proceed in the months ahead as they laid their respective cases before Montanans.

Finally, I show how the Supreme Court's landmark decision in *Citizens United* transformed the ability of candidates to control their own campaign narratives. When the Supreme Court struck down corporate and labor union bans on independent election expenditures, it opened the floodgate for outside organizations to engage in electioneering much earlier and more intensely than ever before. Although launching an election ad advocating support for or defeat of a candidate early in a cycle is not new, the scope of participation by interest groups and the vast sums of money commanded was. Previously, interest groups could pay for express advocacy advertisements but were hampered by strict limits on contributions and reporting requirements. Now, labor unions, corporations, and individuals choosing to form new organizations devoted to political action could raise and spend unlimited sums to support direct and express electioneering.[3] The early spending by outside groups on television and radio affected the dynamics of the campaign, creating opportunities and frustrations for both Rehberg and Tester as they struggled to frame the election on terms favorable to them. I conclude with a failed effort by the Tester campaign in February 2012 to address outside spending by pledging to renounce all outside money and impose a spending cap. This pledge spoke volumes about the two campaigns and their strategies, and it is a fitting place to pause as it came just before the general election campaign kicked off earnestly in the spring of 2012, when Tester and Rehberg took to the airwaves with their own ads.

## PRIMING AND FRAMING

Campaigns decide first which voters they must target. Once that decision is made, campaigns then develop the messages necessary to persuade and remind those targeted voters. Political scientists talk about persuasion through ads and paid media by using the terms *priming* and *framing*. Priming is "the activation of issues that voters use to evaluate candidates" while framing is putting issues into a particular context that can activate certain cognitive shortcuts in the minds of voters.[4] For example, some research demonstrates campaigns successfully prime voters to make decisions based upon the issues they communicate in earned media, and that exposure to media affects how citizens evaluate presidential performance.[5]

Framing is related to priming but distinct. Framing provides the lens through which a campaign or the media prefers information to be viewed. A campaign might prime a particular issue in a campaign, say spending, but use certain phrases or images to lead voters to certain conclusions when that issue is referenced. As Shanto Iyengar's research demonstrates, how poverty is discussed by the media elicits particular responses from voters.[6] Poverty can be discussed in terms of personal responsibility, which might make voters less sympathetic to social programs designed to alleviate poverty. Alternatively, a discussion of poverty can emphasize social factors underlying the phenomenon, which might elicit more support for government efforts to address the problem.

Campaigns must decide which issues to prime and how to frame them favorably for their candidate and unfavorably for their opponent. They use message grids to help with this. Message grids are simple two-by-two tables outlining reasons why the candidate should be supported by voters, why voters shouldn't support the opponent, and the messages the campaign expects the other side to make for and against their preferred candidate. Good campaigns build a campaign message based upon candidate track records, informed by polling.

Excellent campaigns strive to stay on message, pivoting back to the core themes at every opportunity. Both the Rehberg and Tester campaigns decided which issues to prime and how they would be framed at the start of the race. At the macrolevel, the issues and frames the campaigns chose never changed. The narratives, however, unfolded in a carefully scripted fashion designed to provide maximum impact on particular constituencies at critical moments. That is to say the campaigns primed particular issues and framed the choice for voters at a metalevel, but which pieces of information they primed and how that information was framed to support that metanarrative evolved as the campaign progressed throughout 2011 and 2012.

## FARMER JON OR BARACK TESTER; RANCHER DENNY OR IRRESPONSIBLE DENNIS?

Congressman Rehberg officially jumped into the Montana Senate race on February 5, 2011, at a party fundraiser in Helena. Republicans, eager to close ranks behind their best shot to win back the Senate seat lost to Jon Tester in 2006, stuffed the ballroom at the Red Lion Inn to the rafters. Minnesota Congresswoman Michele Bachmann, a Tea Party favorite, was the keynote speaker, but the main event was Congressman Rehberg's much-anticipated announcement. Shortly after Rehberg took to the podium to Kid Rock's "I Was Born Free," he thanked Bachmann for coming. Her presence had been at the request of the party, but Rehberg helped orchestrate the appearance. His efforts testify to the work Rehberg still felt he had to do in order to swing the conservative base of the party behind him.

Rehberg began his speech with the familiar. He noted his connections to Montana as a fifth-generation rancher and retold the stories about his father's fight with the Montana Milk Control Board and the loss of one-third of their ranch to the estate tax. Everyone knew the tale, but it reminded the crowd that Rehberg had personally felt the sting of big government's regulatory overreach. He understood, viscerally, Tea Party skepticism and animosity toward Washington and the federal government.

What followed next, however, was unlike any campaign announcement I had witnessed. The congressman apologized for much of his service in the House of Representatives over the past decade. Rehberg noted that the he and the Republican Party had lost their way. "I've had to do a lot of repentance myself over the years," said Rehberg quietly. "I stand before you as a reformed earmarker. I recognize how the Real ID was a really bad idea. I welcome constructive criticism from my fellow conservatives." Criticism, Rehberg said, he had heard loud and clear.[7] Rehberg, who began his career as an unapologetic conservative, had become more pragmatic over time. Long-time political associate Dennis Iverson noted that the journey had begun during his stint as a lieutenant governor and continued during his service in the House of Representatives.[8] That night, Rehberg cast all that aside—the pork, the earmarks, and compromises. Rehberg needed to make sure that the Tea Party was firmly ensconced in his corner during the long campaign ahead.[9]

Rehberg's efforts to lock down the party base made sense. It was early in the campaign and he would—as he admitted that night—need every last bit of effort from everyone there to help him with what was going to be a hard-fought, expensive battle against incumbent Senator Jon Tester. It is noteworthy that Rehberg and his campaign felt insecure about the more libertarian-minded Tea Party-types throughout the entire campaign. When I asked Rehberg six months later about his biggest concern during the race, he mentioned Libertarians, again referencing the 1996 campaign that he had narrowly lost to Baucus.[10] In that campaign, he had been outspent three to one and the Reform Party candidate had taken five percent of the vote—the difference between him and Baucus. And that, according to Rehberg, is the main reason he lost then. In this campaign, Rehberg believed that as it got nastier, voters upset with the tone would cast about for a third alternative.[11] Rehberg was determined not to let those voters abandon him again.

Why was Rehberg concerned about his right flank?[12] Neither Rehberg nor his campaign staff felt that Rehberg had to grow his constituency. When asked what Rehberg's strength was as a candidate, campaign manager Erik Iverson noted that he had run statewide five times, often winning with sixty percent of the vote or more; he had visited all fifty-six counties each congressional session; and he was more philosophically in tune with the state than Tester.[13] Rehberg merely had to protect what he had already won and mend fences with Libertarians in the Republican Party. Jake Eaton, who had worked for Rehberg over the past ten years in a variety of capacities and was the campaign's chief of staff, stressed their efforts to lock down that constituency from the very beginning. "We made a pretty heavy investment in terms of libertarian outreach, trying to get the people whom we thought were the actual libertarians. . . . We had a guy that did that full time. . . . We made a huge effort to try to steal back as many of those people as were possible."[14] Rehberg himself told me in August of 2011 that he was down among independents by fifteen points but was still up by two points overall in a matchup with Tester—a testament to the number of Republicans in the state and the advantage it provided him.[15]

Throughout the campaign, I heard from Democrats and Republicans alike that Republican voters refused to commit to a candidate early, coming home to the Republican nominee only at the last minute. In 2006, Tester—who had been ahead much of the campaign—almost lost because enough Republicans who had been upset at Burns began to forgive him in the campaign's closing days. This might explain Rehberg's persistent confidence throughout the campaign. Even a small Tester lead could be remedied if Republicans simply came home in November. If Rehberg could succeed where Burns failed, Rehberg would be Montana's next U.S. senator.

If the Rehberg folks had any hopes of expanding their reelection constituency, it would require tying Senator Jon Tester to Barack Obama. In March 2011, just three weeks after Rehberg's announcement, Lee Enterprises (the company owning most of the large daily newspapers in Montana) released a poll conducted on its behalf by Mason Dixon. President Obama, who came within two points of carrying the state in 2008, had a job approval rating of only 40 percent in Montana.[16] From the opening bell that night in Helena, Rehberg made it plain to anyone listening that Jon Tester was more than a simple farmer from Big Sandy. He belonged to a great Democratic conspiracy orchestrated by Majority Leader Harry Reid and President Obama that foisted freedom-killing, costly policies on Montanans which would only bankrupt the nation. "When Harry Reid wanted a trillion dollar stimulus bill, Jon Tester voted yes" lambasted Rehberg. "When Harry Reid wanted to pass Obamacare on Christmas Eve, Jon Tester voted yes. Half a trillion dollars in higher taxes? Jon Tester voted yes. Half a trillion dollars in cuts to Medicare? And Jon Tester voted yes." In what became the key tagline of the Rehberg campaign, Rehberg noted that "Jon Tester has become a reliable yes man for Barack Obama and Harry Reid, and he's voted with the Obama administration 97 percent of the time."[17]

The point? Rehberg stood with Montanans on the issues. Not Tester. If Rehberg could get them to see that point clearly, the choice would be simple. By focusing on how Tester was a tool of the Obama administration while simultaneously working to nail down Libertarians by distancing himself from his work on appropriations, Rehberg hoped to retain the electoral coalition that had reelected him to the House in 2010. Quite simply, Rehberg believed that his primary constituency—Republicans—was big enough to carry him to victory in the general election. In fact, Tester's chief of staff Tom Lopach admitted as much: "When the majority of Montanans wake up and look in the mirror," he told me during a very busy day on Capitol Hill, "if they see a political party, they see Republican."[18]

The path forward for Tester was as twisted as Rehberg's seemed straightforward. Jon Tester won in 2006 with less than a majority. He had won only 15 counties out of the total 56, splitting the eight largest counties with Burns. Although Tester clearly held down Republican vote totals in rural Montana, Tester won because he rolled up large margins in the state's most reliable Democratic counties (Missoula, Silver Bow, and Deer Lodge) while holding Burns to only a 1,000 vote plurality in Yellowstone (home to the state's largest city, Billings). Unless Tester broadened his appeal beyond the narrow Democratic base, he would be a one-term senator. At the same time, however, Tester had to do even better in traditionally Democratic strongholds to counter the possible loss of those same Republicans and conservatives who supported Tester in 2006. This presented him with a tricky electoral path: Build his base *and* expand beyond it.

To beat the Republican numerical advantage, Tester had to assemble a diverse coalition. Lopach called the strategy "base plus plus": "The way I've always thought about it, the staff has thought about it, is 'base plus plus.' . . . You take the Democrats and you add in those communities he's worked his tail off for."[19] Nail down the Democratic base, which included labor, environmentalists, and young voters. Then add "women, senior citizens, veterans, and small businessmen and women who had benefited from Jon's efforts in the Senate."[20] To do that, the Tester campaign needed to convince voters to make a more complicated calculation at the polls.

How Team Tester chose to define this race was clear from the start, back at the Mansfield-Metcalf dinner in March 2011. The largest and most lucrative fundraiser for Montana Democrats, it was held in Helena almost exactly a month after Rehberg's announcement. During this rousing speech to the party faithful, Tester pointedly did not talk about President Obama. Instead, he reminded Democrats and Montanans more generally of his record as an independent-minded public servant who made a living moving dirt. He spoke of that record in terms of the constituency groups he had helped as senator and whose support he would need to win in 2012.

Tester began with veterans and his accomplishments for them. He stressed how he "brought Main Street Montana values to Congress" to change the way Wall Street does business—a nod to the small businesses in Montana that may have been disadvantaged by previous federal regulations.[21] He discussed his support for the Lilly Ledbetter law equalizing pay for women. And, more generally, he framed his support for the stimulus as providing investments in infrastructure critical for Montana to compete economically. This was a pointed contrast to how Rehberg discussed spending. In speaking directly about concerns central to veterans, women, and small businesses throughout Montana, Tester demonstrated how his legislative efforts during the past five years represented a Montana beyond his party base. Exactly as Lopach had said: base plus plus.

The speech reintroduced Montanans to Tester while stressing independence from the national party. Andrew Maxfield, Tester's pollster, emphasized that although some of the national narrative about the Democratic Party had stuck to Tester in the months following the disastrous 2010 midterm elections, Montanans did not know much specifically about Jon Tester other than he was a farmer and "down to earth."[22] Tester's speech reminded Montanans of what he had done over the past four years and that much of what he had done was popular among the voting public even if they didn't associate the specifics yet with Tester. I asked Lopach about Tester's biggest challenge going into the race against Rehberg. He responded that it "is how you get a Republican-majority state to appreciate the hard work, sincerity, intellect, commitment, and honest nature of Jon Tester so that they vote for him."[23] This speech was the first effort to meet that challenge, to focus voters on the Tester brand and less on the Democratic brand.

If Montanans didn't know much about what Tester had done for them, they also had trouble associating Rehberg with specific accomplishments. They "knew he was a rancher. They knew his Montana roots. They knew he was a conservative," said Maxfield.[24] The vagueness surrounding Denny the person provided the Tester campaign with an opening. To grow Tester's reelection constituency, they would repeatedly contrast the personalities and accomplishments of Tester to what they characterized as Rehberg's lackluster record and, as the campaign framed it, "irresponsible" decision making.

In front of the raucous Democratic crowd, Tester began the task of defining Rehberg as an unpalatable choice for Montanans. He might be their guy, but he's not nice and he's not conservative. And Rehberg has done almost nothing to help Montana during his decade in Congress—and the record he did compile is one that Rehberg won't even now acknowledge. Tester scoffed at Rehberg's legislative history, dismissing it as "naming a few post offices."[25] And then, Tester painted Rehberg as a rich, ne'er-do-well who uses his position in Congress to enrich himself. Rehberg, according to Tester, was "the 14th wealthiest member in Congress" who gave himself pay raises while he "refuses to give up his taxpayer-funded healthcare."[26] Tester described the choice facing Montanans as between "a multimillionaire who has spent years putting his wallet ahead of his public service" and the only farmer in the Senate. Tester's characterization of Rehberg was not just to excite the partisan crowd. It became the linchpin of his campaign's election strategy. Preston Elliot, Tester's campaign manager: "At the end of the day

Rehberg was a self-serving politician, that hurt voters, and . . . moving people past that partisanship" was the campaign's Number 1 goal.[27] The Tester campaign would go so far as to call Denny Rehberg "Dennis" Rehberg because Dennis polled less favorably than Denny.[28]

Part of the strategy was to highlight Rehberg's personal failings. The other key part of the Tester strategy was to shake loose the Republican base that Rehberg was rallying. Refusing to mention Rehberg's name, Tester said that the congressman had "suddenly found religion when it comes to federal spending. This from a guy who squandered a $130-billion-dollar surplus in his first year in Congress. Who was recently named the Tea Party Caucus' 'Number 1 Porker.'"[29] Tester would circle back to the theme that Rehberg is not who Montanans think he is, I suspect, to keep Rehberg's campaign focused on his Republican base at the expense of outreach to independents. Independents represented the single largest group of voters in the state and are notoriously fickle. They were critical to Tester's effort to expand his reelection constituency. Tester's strategy shrewdly not only kept Rehberg tied up with Libertarians, it also helped remind those Republicans who were not supporters of the Tea Party that Rehberg had recently abandoned pragmatism in favor of the Tea Party's more strident conservatism.

A Republican political consultant who was not involved in the Rehberg-Tester race but had done work in Montana in the past helped put the strategies of the two candidates into a broader perspective. "Senate races are large enough and spend enough money so that the personalities, the personas of the candidates are a larger portion of the pie than just the general tide of the year," he said. "And contrast that with House races for example where those guys try to latch on to a national camp."[30] He succinctly encapsulated the differences in the strategies between Tester and Rehberg. Tester would run a classic Senate campaign emphasizing his distinctive personality and independence from the Democratic Party. Rehberg, alternatively, would run a campaign on national images and themes in an effort to make the election a referendum on President Obama—a campaign very much like his House campaigns.

According to Erik Iverson and Jake Eaton, the Tester campaign had to resort to a personality-based campaign because on the issues, Tester was not where Montanans were. This was the fundamental precept of the Rehberg campaign. For example, consider both the stimulus act and the ACA, both of which Tester supported. Both seemed unpopular. When asked about their thoughts on "Obamacare" by Bob Moore, Rehberg's pollster, 60 percent of Montanans indicated they opposed it.[31] The 2011 Mason Dixon poll, which described the law more neutrally as "recently passed federal healthcare law," showed that 57 percent of Montanans wanted to repeal it.[32] When Moore asked respondents about the stimulus, 50 percent of respondents indicated they were more likely to vote for

Rehberg once they knew he voted no. Similarly, they were much less likely to vote for Tester because he had supported it. Add the fact that Montanans believed that the national economic recovery was headed in the wrong direction and the top concern among voters in 2011 was the economy, and it seemed that an issues campaign would advantage Rehberg.[33]

Yet certain ambiguities in the minds of Montanans about issues created opportunities for the Tester campaign that may not have been readily apparent. It is well-known that polling questions can be extremely sensitive to word choice, and polling about the ACA is no exception.[34] Call it Obamacare, and there is much less support. In a national poll completed nine months after the campaign had concluded, CNBC found that 46 percent of Americans opposed Obamacare but only 37 percent opposed the ACA.[35] A Kaiser Family Health poll conducted in November 2011 demonstrated that portions of the law received widespread support. In particular, 67 percent of poll respondents liked that the new federal healthcare law prevented insurance companies from denying coverage based on pre-existing conditions.[36] Montanans, too, expressed support for "coverage for pre-existing conditions, coverage for young people on their parents' policies, ending abuses by health insurance companies (such as the practice of using minor paperwork mistakes to cancel people's coverage if they were diagnosed with a serious disease like cancer), [and] ending lifetime limits or caps," according to Tester's pollster, Andrew Maxfield.[37]

Even if Montanans were unhappy with Obamacare (or the ACA) and Tester's vote for it, this did not translate into a universal push for repeal. Only 45 percent supported efforts by the Montana State Legislature to block implementation of the ACA in March of 2011, and Moore's poll in early 2012 showed that only 46 percent supported a full repeal of the law.[38] Maxfield elaborated, indicating that the Tester campaign's polling showed that "a fairly significant proportion of the electorate . . . would say repeal some, but not all, of the law even when asked about it broadly as Obamacare."[39] Furthermore, even using the term *Obamacare* was potentially problematic: 47 percent of Montanans said that the term itself was partisan and disrespectful.[40] Although Montanans clearly had concerns about the ACA, the issue presented problems and opportunities for Rehberg and Tester alike. Tester never referenced the ACA during his remarks at Mansfield-Metcalf, but he did mention healthcare, noting that jobs were created by "investing in quality healthcare" and attacked Rehberg's efforts to defund the ACA while he himself "refused to give up his taxpayer-funded health care."[41]

Elections are often referenda on incumbents. The challenger must demonstrate they are an acceptable alternative to an incumbent that has done a bad job. The problem for Rehberg was that the Tester folks were determined to demonstrate that Rehberg was an unacceptable choice. And Montanans were not quite willing to lay all the blame at Tester's feet for their personal problems and the nation's economic woes, which made the election less of a referendum on Jon Tester than the Republican campaign may have preferred. Maxfield said at the very beginning of the race that Montanans "were unhappy with the economy.... They liked Jon Tester and they were unaware of many of his achievements but they weren't gonna lay the blame of the deficit...at Jon Tester's feet."[42] Some of the blame they put squarely on the shoulders of the Bush administration, an administration which had received substantial support from Congressman Rehberg during his time in Congress. It was certainly a situation that Tester's campaign staff eagerly exploited in the months ahead.

To summarize, the Rehberg campaign framed the choice as a referendum on President Barack Obama's policies with Tester as the supposed handmaiden of the administration. The hope was to convince Republicans and conservative-leaning independents to cast their vote for Rehberg as they had in the past but this time for the Senate and not the House. The Tester campaign framed the choice differently. They emphasized the personal brand of candidate Tester juxtaposed against candidate Rehberg, who—as we will discover—was not viewed as positively as a person by constituents. They also worked to remind Republican voters in particular that Rehberg had occasionally supported policies, particularly concerning civil liberties and earmarks, more in tune with the national Republican Party's positions and less in line with the more libertarian-minded Republican philosophy predominant in Montana. Team Rehberg hoped to nationalize the election while Team Tester hoped to localize it.

## *CITIZENS UNITED*: MORE MONEY, LESS CONTROL

Through the spring and summer of 2011, as Tester and Rehberg sought to reintroduce themselves to the electorate and make their respective cases to their reelection constituencies, the candidates found themselves confronted with the harsh reality of campaigning in a new world with new rules. The Supreme Court's decision in *Citizens United* opened the floodgates to other political players—namely, newly organized interest groups that could raise huge sums of cash without disclosing their donors—who could intrude on Montana's landscape with their own issues, messages, and agendas. During all of 2011, not a single campaign advertisement hitting the airwaves was sponsored by either Senate candidate. To understand how *Citizens United* changed campaigning henceforth, it is important to discuss briefly how federal campaigns have been financed in the modern era, the changes to that financial structure implemented by Congress, some key Supreme Court decisions, and how *Citizens United* altered the financial resource structure facing parties, candidates, and interest groups.

The modern era of congressional campaign finance began with the passage in 1974 of the Federal Election Campaign Act (FECA).[43] The law accomplished four important objectives. First, it placed limits on what candidates for federal office could raise from individuals and political action committees (PACs) while forbidding candidates from accepting donations from labor unions or corporations. Second, labor unions and corporations could not pay for advertisements expressly advocating the election or defeat of a candidate. PACs and individuals could pay for such advertisements so long as they did so without coordinating with the candidate advantaged by the ad. These types of advertisements and activities became known as independent expenditures. In the case of individual independent expenditures, a person could spend as much as they wanted on these advertisements. PACs could spend whatever they wished, so long as they pay with money raised, collected, and reported under the auspices of the Federal Election Campaign Act and its contribution limits. Third, restrictions were put in place concerning what political parties could raise and contribute to candidates. Finally, money spent on electioneering activities or contributed to candidates had to be reported to the newly established Federal Elections Commission (FEC). In short, the law established the principle that electioneering activities were subject to restrictions and transparency.

Various provisions of FECA were declared unconstitutional in the Supreme Court's *Buckley v. Valeo* (1976) decision. The most important part of the decision was buried in a footnote establishing the so-called "magic words" test. If a paid political advertisement did not expressly advocate for the election or defeat of a candidate, then the expenditure did not fall under the FECA restrictions. These ads, a form of political speech known as "issue advocacy," received greater First Amendment protections according to the Court. Later, Congress passed amendments to FECA in 1978 allowing political parties to raise and spend money on voter mobilization and party building activities that were not subject to the contribution limits. Parties used this so-called "soft money" loophole to raise millions of dollars from individuals, labor unions, and corporations to purchase facilities, buy voter lists, and engage in voter outreach. Later parties used these unrestricted and unregulated monies to pay for issue advocacy ads in congressional campaigns after it was sanctioned by the Federal Election Commission in 1995.[44] In 1996, the Supreme Court then gave parties the green light to engage in express advocacy advertisements paid for with "hard" dollars—monies raised under the restrictions imposed by FECA—as long as the ads were not coordinated with the candidate.[45]

By the late 1990s, corporate, labor, and large individual donations flowed into the political system through political parties at an unprecedented rate. Because these so-called "soft" dollars were not spent on electioneering outright, they were not subject to the stringent reporting requirements enforced by the FEC. Most troubling, in addition to the volume of dollars spent by groups who could not legally give to candidates, was the fact that much of this money supported issue advocacy ads that, while avoiding the magic words outlined in *Buckley v. Valeo,* looked like electioneering ads designed to advocate for candidates.

Senators Russ Feingold (D-WI) and John McCain (R-AZ) wrote legislation to remove soft money from the political system and eliminate the legal distinction between issue advocacy and direct electioneering advertisements. After several years of effort, they won passage of the Bipartisan Campaign Finance Reform Act (BCRA) in 2002. The bill changed existing campaign law in three significant ways. First, it banned political parties from raising and spending corporate, labor, or individual donations for issue advocacy, party building, or any other activity. Second, corporations and labor unions—that previously could spend money from their treasuries on issue advocacy ads—could do so no longer. All political advertisements sent over the airwaves would have to be financed by their affiliated political action committees, which could only raise money under the tight restrictions of FECA in limited amounts from individual donors. Finally, all broadcast advertisements within sixty days of a primary or ninety days of a general election for federal office had to be paid for with hard dollars. This meant that PACs, parties, and other organizations had to pay for the ads with money raised in $2,000 increments from individuals, now adjusted annually for inflation.

Political entrepreneurs probed for loopholes in the law. In 2007, the Supreme Court essentially reestablished the issue advocacy distinction eliminated by Congress when it ruled in *FEC v. Wisconsin Right to Life* that the ban on issue advocacy advertisements identifying federal candidates for office in the months preceding an election was unconstitutional.[46] And, most famously, the Supreme Court affirmed in *Citizens United* that corporate and labor union organizations could use their treasuries without restriction to fund not only issue advocacy ads but also electioneering ads calling on voters to support or defeat a federal candidate. In some cases, depending on the organization and the type of electioneering activity sponsored, the dollars raised and spent would not have to be disclosed to the Federal Election Commission.[47] The decision received a storm of protest from good government and transparency groups. Some claimed that the decision gave First Amendment rights to corporations and labor unions. Others expressed alarm at the return of unregulated dollars spent on political advertising, money that once flowed through political parties but now could be spent by shadowy organizations and individuals accountable to no one. The campaign finance regulatory regime established in 1974, based on transparency and privileging candidates and their parties in electioneering efforts, lay in shambles.

From the perspective of the Montana Senate candidates, *Citizens United* had important consequences for their campaign. The first concerned the ability of the candidates to control the framing of the campaign during 2011—the year when both Tester and Rehberg needed to raise money, build their organizations, and frame the election on terms favorable to them. Although the candidates received important benefits from the involvement of these outside groups, Tester and Rehberg also suffered the consequences of a campaign finance system giving nearly free and unfettered reign to organizations and individuals who did not live in Montana and had little, if any, interest in the state save for the consequences the Senate campaign had on the Senate's partisan balance.

The first rude awakening came in March of 2011—just a few weeks after Rehberg announced his intention to run against Tester. An environmental organization called the Environmental Defense Fund launched what became the first campaign advertisements of the Senate race. The group placed an ad called "Mercury and Children" on television stations in Billings and Missoula. They also bought radio time on several stations.[48] The ad displayed a sonogram of a fetus, made the viewer aware of the dangers of mercury pollution to unborn children, and intoned that "Congressman Denny Rehberg sides with corporate lobbyists to block limits on mercury pollution. Did he think we wouldn't notice?"

Under the federal tax code, the Environmental Defense Fund is incorporated as a 501c(4), which is a social welfare organization devoted to "further[ing] the common good and general welfare of the people of the community (such as by bringing about civic betterment and social improvements)."[49] These organizations can engage in political activities so long as they are not the primary function of the organization. They are also not required to divulge the source of their contributions. So the first advertisement aired in the Montana Senate campaign was not sponsored by a candidate or party. It was paid for, instead, by an organization headquartered in Washington, DC, spending the very "dark" money on issue advocacy ads now legally sanctioned by *Citizens United*. Given all the attention focused on how corporate money would flood the political system to Republican advantage, it is interesting that a nonprofit, pro-environmental organization launched the first salvo at the expense of the Republican candidate, Denny Rehberg.[50]

In 2008, the last campaign cycle conducted under the pre-*Citizens United* rules, candidates still had a fair amount of control over priming and framing during the early days of the campaign. I identified the most competitive Senate elections during that cycle using three criteria: Did the Senate incumbent win the previous election with less than 55 percent of the vote? Did the Senate incumbent represent a state won by the opposing party's presidential nominee in the last presidential election? Was the nominee running against a quality challenger? This yielded twelve potentially competitive Senate races during the 2008 election cycle. I then examined data from the Wisconsin Advertising Project, which collected information on all broadcast advertisements for federal candidates aired in every media market during the 2007 to 2008 campaign cycle.[51] In each case, it was the candidate who aired the first ad during the campaign. No campaign advertisement aired more than a year before the November election. On average, candidates launched their first ad in these potentially competitive contests 160 days before Election Day. Political parties and interest groups, when they spent money on advertisements, did so during the campaign's final months.

The midterm election in 2010 represented the first cycle contested with the new *Citizens United* rules in place. Again, using the same criteria above, I identified seven competitive Senate campaigns featuring an incumbent that cycle. In three cases, an interest group aired the first advertisement in the race. The average number of days before Election Day of the first television ad airing increased by 39 days to 199. In 2012, again I identified seven competitive Senate races. This time, interest groups sponsored the first ad in five out of the seven competitive Senate races with an incumbent running for reelection. And the average number of days between the airing of the first ad and the general election? Nearly a full year—330 days. One consequence of *Citizens United* is a loss of candidate message control to outside organizations and ads appearing on television much earlier during the election cycle.[52]

In the Tester-Rehberg campaign, the first ad aired on March 2, 2011, 604 days before the general election![53] The amount of money spent by the Environmental Defense Fund was a harbinger of things to come. As spring faded into summer and then fall, more groups and more advertising dollars flowed into the race. By January of 2012, 15 groups had spent more than $1.8 million on advertising in the race. Not a single dollar had been spent by Tester or Rehberg on television or radio. The political parties had also spent virtually nothing. The Montana Republican Party aired one ad during the college football championship games featuring the University of Montana and Montana State University, and the National Republican Senatorial Committee created and posted an online television spot which they promulgated via YouTube. Otherwise, all advertisements were sponsored by interest groups, most headquartered outside Montana. Much of the money spent was donated by individuals who did not have to disclose either the amounts they contributed or their identities to the public.

What were the consequences of all this money spent so early in the Senate campaign? There were both positive and negative effects from the standpoint of the campaigns. One negative consequence was the loss of message control by the candidates and their campaigns during a period when they needed to establish their bona fides and communicate their representational work to constituents to build voter support. Most of the advertisements launched during this period were negative, attacking the legislative records of the two candidates. Senator Tester, in particular, bore the brunt of the early assault. Crossroads GPS, Concerned Women for America, the United States Chamber of Commerce, and the 60 Plus Association all targeted Tester for supporting the stimulus, deficit spending, and his vote for "Obamacare" that took money from Medicare. They also blamed him for the slow economic recovery. All four themes were the ones primed and framed by Rehberg either in his February announcement of his candidacy or on the stump afterwards. In essence, these Republican-allied groups provided heavy artillery fire for Rehberg, while drawing upon his carefully prepared ammunitions dump for their assault. The advertisements helped Rehberg prime his message and frame Tester as a national Democrat in the pocket of Obama.

Sixty percent of the money spent during the period appeared as negative ads attacking Senator Tester. Although Tester bore the brunt of the advertising barrage in the aggregate, he too, received some cover fire from outside organizations. According to data I compiled by visiting Montana's television stations and visually inspecting advertising contracts, pro-Rehberg groups aired substantially more spots and spent more money than pro-Tester groups in July 2011, December 2011, and February 2012.[54] Pro-Tester groups, although spending less than the pro-Rehberg groups, controlled the airwaves for five months: March, May, June, September, and October. The Democratic-allied organizations, while not as well coordinated in terms of how they primed and framed issues as they would become later during the campaign, did follow the breadcrumbs laid by the Tester campaign in their press releases and public statements. Advertisements extolling the need to protect Medicare and Social Security were paid for by AARP, the Coalition to Protect Medicare (a group sponsored by labor union organizations), and Patriot Majority.

More importantly, a Montana-based organization called Montana Hunters and Anglers aired a series of ads in November skewering Rehberg's support for HR 1505—the same bill Tester himself mentioned as a "land grab" and an unprecedented expansion of federal control.[55] It was a bid to shake Rehberg's right flank, as Rehberg had feared all along.[56] These outside groups, by beginning the attack early on both candidates on issue terrain already primed by them, provided critical support to their favored candidates while allowing the candidates to salt away their own money to spend later in the cycle.[57] It also gave the candidates plausible deniability, mitigating against a backlash for the tone of the ads and the early start to the campaign season—neither of which were likely popular among voters.

For all the benefits accrued by the candidates thanks to this spending, a campaign dominated by outside groups brings risks. Groups pursue their own interests and agendas that are not always aligned with the candidates they support. While Rehberg was getting attacked for his votes on mercury regulations, another group entered the fray on the side of Tester that spring airing ads thanking Tester for working with them to remove a cap imposed on debit card swipe fees in the Wall Street Reform and Consumer Protection Act (known popularly as Dodd-Frank).[58] Swipe fees are charged to retailers by banks on every transaction made with a debit card by a customer and are an important source of revenue for banks, especially smaller banks in rural states like Montana.

Both advertisements provided possible attack lines Rehberg could leverage. In the case of mercury regulations, the Rehberg campaign could and did use the opportunity to suggest that Tester was beholden to the environmentally extremist fringe—a charge that did not particularly help Tester in a state split between extractionists and preservationists. The Rehberg campaign, the Republican Party, and Republican-allied groups all framed Tester's support for removing the swipe fee cap as proof Wall Street banks owned him. Tester's work on the swipe fee issue had actually been done at the behest of Montana banks who believed the proposed regulation placed them at a competitive disadvantage relative to bigger, national banks—but those same banks also applauded the move. The Electronic Payments Coalition (EPC) chose to launch the ads when it did likely to inoculate Tester on the issue because they knew his stance would be framed as catering to Wall Street. In any case, the heavy and early investment by outside groups in the campaign belied the efforts of both candidates to focus on their homespun appeals to average Montanans, who were now treated to a slew of ads claiming neither Tester nor Rehberg represented them.

What did the candidates think of all this outside money? Rehberg expressed frustration after the Environmental Defense Fund ad aired, indicating that the advertisement misrepresented his position. He believes that certain clean air and water standards are absolutely necessary, but that many new regulations promulgated by the Environmental Protection Agency yielded few environmental benefits at great cost. He stressed this when we visited the Ash Grove Cement Company in Helena. Meeting with the company's owners and representatives of the boilermakers union in their conference room, Rehberg heard company owners complain that the single largest capital expense in the company's history was in response to new particulate standards developed by the EPA. The cost to the company would be between $300,000 and $500,000 during a time when the company had its profits per unit slashed in half.

Rehberg noted his position that regulations on mercury or on particulate matter needed to be "common sense," acknowledging that "the expense goes up relative to the gains you get" as more exacting standards are imposed. The mercury regulations he voted against, he said, imposed costs on American businesses when "most of the problem with mercury over here is coming from Asia. Most of the American impact is from overseas coming this way from weather patterns." The end result, according to Rehberg, was increased costs on American businesses that would drive business overseas, close American companies, and continued production of mercury that Congress could neither regulate nor control. Rehberg, the rancher and small businessman who saw his family struggle with government-imposed directives, understood exactly what Ash Grove was facing and agreed with Ash Grove's plant manager. It upset him that what he saw as common sense was twisted into "Denny Rehberg wants your kids to get asthma."[59] It would not be the last time Rehberg would express frustration with outside groups' spending money during the campaign.[60]

The mercury pollution ad and the swipe fee issue were early lessons in how outside groups use advertisements to frame an issue for their political gain and how hard it is for candidates to respond effectively when the response is complex. As Tester's Communications Director Aaron Murphy confirmed, the swipe fee issue was hard to explain to the average voter and Tester's position and rationale for it could not be quickly summarized. "Try to explain that in a TV sound bite" he told me, tacitly acknowledging that while he believed Jon took the right position on the issue, it presented opportunities for Rehberg and his allies to make Jon look out of touch and in the pocket of special interests.[61]

Tester, too, was upset, but he and his campaign tried to use the early expenditure of money as motivation. I asked him in Big Sandy about all the special interest money attacking him on the airwaves throughout the summer and the claim that Tester was the Number 1 recipient of lobbyist cash. (A claim, by the way, that Denny Rehberg echoed the following week during my visit with him.) Tester threw his head back, laughed, and looked me straight on: "Any moment in time I could be. Look, Rehberg and his cronies dropped $500,000 on my head the first of June and the middle of July and that sent me a message loud and clear, Jonny, you'd better raise the dough, or they're going to roll you. We'll raise it in a month."[62]

Tester took the outside money as a challenge to raise the money he needed and then some. More to the point, Tester didn't think that anyone would buy the fact that he, the dirt farmer from Big Sandy, was in the pockets of special interests. Tester might have the most lobbyist cash, but the Republican frame would not be deemed credible if Tester could effectively remind Montanans why they elected and trusted him in the first place. Tester knew from his 2006 race against Conrad Burns that his personal reputation had to be completely above reproach if he had any hopes of winning reelection exactly because of attacks like this.

Tester's campaign decided to use the attacks to their political advantage both in the earned media and among their activist base. Fundraising appeal after fundraising appeal sallied forth from the Tester campaign, slamming the outside money smearing Tester. In one e-mail sent in July 2011, during the middle of the $184,000 Crossroads GPS ad buy attacking Tester for his debt and deficit busting votes, Tester wrote that "it's no surprise that the very worst of these attacks are the ones engineered by Karl Rove himself—and funded by Big Oil and Wall Street millionaires. You can tell they're pretty confident—after all, Karl Rove has thrown around all sorts of smears and insinuations in states all across the country. **But this is Montana**, and things are different out here."[63]

Team Tester often circled back to this point in discussing outside groups attacking him. They assaulted the messenger, playing on two key points sure to strike a chord with Montanans. First, the money attacking Jon was not from Montana. It was money from "outsiders." Second, they attacked *Citizens United* as undermining Montana values. "We believe that corporations do not have the right to spend unlimited money buying power and influence.... The copper kings of Butte and Anaconda tried that once. And they got away with it ... until Montana voters set things straight a century ago," rasped Tester to great applause at the Mansfield-Metcalf dinner in March of 2012.[64] *Citizens United* was unseemly because it did not reflect the Montana values of trustworthiness and community. The message boiled down to this critical point: You don't trust outsiders, these are outsiders, so why believe what they say about me? You know me—they don't. Do you trust them or your own instincts?[65] The Rehberg camp did the same, painting outside interests with the brush of Hollywood, Washington elites, and radical environmentalists, but given their support of *Citizens United* in principle, their criticism seemed more muted. It is yet another example of how both Rehberg and Tester understood Montanans and their wariness of outsiders unduly influencing their affairs.

Outside money can bolster a campaign's existing messaging, and powerfully so when it does, because the outside groups carry negative messages. That advantage evaporates, however, when the outside groups become the issue. Candidates try to shred the credibility of outside organizations with the voters. The best case scenario is when these groups do the damage to themselves. The Tester campaign capitalized in the fall of 2011 when two pro-Rehberg organizations made missteps in their advertisements.

In an Internet advertisement released in September, the National Republican Senatorial Committee (NRSC) again made the standard claims about Tester's support for President Obama. To drive the point home, they included a picture of Jon jovially slapping the president on the arm during a visit to Montana. The problem is, in cropping the picture, it appeared that the NRSC had added the three fingers missing from Tester's left hand. The Tester campaign jumped all over the mistake, posting pictures of Jon with his missing fingers. The message—that Tester was an Obama clone—was lost in the fallout.[66]

Shortly after the NRSC debacle, GPS Crossroads released an ad called "Dirt" which claimed that Tester voted for EPA regulations that would classify dust kicked up in agricultural operations as a pollutant.[67] The ad's claim, if true, had the potential to damage Tester's image as a farmer because it would show that he really didn't understand agricultural interests and that, perhaps, the dirt farmer had been captured by the environmental left during his time in Washington.

The Tester camp's response was immediate: The ad, at best, misrepresented the facts. They sent letters to Montana television stations stating that the claim was an outright lie, that the vote cited in the commercial had nothing to do with farm dust but with currency regulations and China. A couple of television stations refused to run the ad, and several independent fact checking groups agreed with the Tester campaign's characterization of the ad.[68]

In both instances, two organizations that spent and would spend substantial sums of money on the air war during the campaign unwittingly played into Tester's frame about *Citizens United* and outside money. It certainly didn't help the Rehberg campaign any because the narrative became about Rehberg and the company he keeps and not about "liberal" Jon Tester. "Congressman Rehberg's allies have already dumped one and a half million dollars into ads attacking me and my record. With no regard to the truth," Tester told the party faithful in March 2012. "One of the TV ads, from President Bush's top strategist, Karl Rove, made the claim that was so false, it was pulled off the air. Another ad had a picture of me with all five fingers on my left hand. The last time I had all fingers on this hand [Tester sticks his left hand up] was also the last time I stuck it in a meat grinder."[69] The insinuation was plain: Rehberg and his pals lie and "they'll stop at nothing" to beat Tester. Who do you believe? Them or the guy with the flattop, the big belly, and the mustard stain on his shirt? If the campaign became about personalities, Tester—for a variety of reasons—would have the edge. That's exactly what the NRSC and GPS Crossroads did not want; yet, their ineptitude made Rehberg's essential job harder.

By the time February ended, it was clear that the Montana Senate race would be expensive and hard-fought. Public polls from the beginning showed a tight race, and despite the early advertising of interest groups that began the previous spring, intensifying over the summer and fall, nothing had changed. The race remained tied statistically. Although both sides stood to benefit from having additional sources of cash from outside groups to prime and frame their issues, relying upon these outside groups to carry these messages came at the cost of uncertainty. Would these groups continue to frame the campaign in ways useful to the candidates? Would they stay involved in Montana or shift their resources to other competitive Senate races? Worse from the perspective of both Tester and Rehberg: Would they inject issues into the campaign that might take on a life of their own while undermining the veracity of candidate claims made in their own paid and free media advertising efforts? All of these remained open questions as the campaign moved into the spring of 2012 when the candidates would begin airing their own advertisements, and voter outreach efforts would intensify.

## THE PLEDGE THAT WASN'T

Soon after the Supreme Court's decision in *Citizens United*, Tester began a concerted effort to mitigate what he perceived to be the negative consequences of the decision. Like most Democrats, he characterized the decision as wrongly granting corporations First Amendment speech rights, and he cosponsored legislation to bring greater disclosure of donations made to 501(c) organizations engaged in issue advocacy advertising.[70] In early February of 2012, consistent with his position on transparency and *Citizens United*, he offered the Rehberg campaign the chance to join in an effort to ban all television and radio ads sponsored by third party organizations.[71] This would effectively eliminate independent expenditures and issue advocacy from Montana's airwaves. Third party groups would be encouraged to abide by the restriction, otherwise their favored candidate would be assessed a financial penalty equal to the amount spent by the offending third party group. The pledge was similar to an agreement inked by Massachusetts Senate candidates Scott Brown and Elizabeth Warren.[72] The Tester campaign gave Rehberg a week to respond.

Congressman Rehberg told me he was not surprised by the Tester proposal, calling it a "typical Democratic campaign tactic." He countered with a more stringent proposal. "The Made in Montana Pledge" allowed only Montana money to be donated to and spent by the candidates. Neither campaign could accept PAC money nor money from registered lobbyists (whether registered in Montana or not). Any money already collected from non-Montana donors or special interest groups would have to be returned, and no coordination with parties or interest groups would be allowed. Finally, if either campaign violated the pledge, the offending party would be assessed a penalty equal to the expenditure to be donated to the charity of their choice.[73]

As both campaigns relied heavily on contributions from out of state donors (according to data compiled by Open Secrets, about 80 percent of the amounts raised by both candidates during the election came from individual contributors and groups outside of Montana), the net effect of the Rehberg pledge would be to reduce severely the amount of money either campaign would have to spend on their operations.[74] Tester rejected Rehberg's more restrictive pledge, suggesting that the pledge was disingenuous and would be ignored by Rehberg anyway because "he's broken every clean campaign pledge he's signed. Montanans won't fall for yet another promise Congressman Rehberg knows he can't keep."[75]

Rehberg knew that the Tester campaign was unlikely to agree to his proposal and saw the whole affair as a means to put the Tester campaign in a bind politically. For Rehberg, the legislative insider who had been running campaigns since his twenties, it was all about the tactics. "We're not stupid," he relayed to me as we sat in his car before going to his next appointment in early April. "We ran the numbers. And by the time he gave all his money back and we gave all our money back, he would have been $1.5 million in the hole and I would have had about $100,000 to the good. . . . And under the current system, the advantage goes to him because he's the incumbent."[76] Rehberg acknowledged that he would have more difficulty raising money, and that the third party money coming into the state would keep him in the game: "So he's gonna beat me in PACs, he's gonna beat me in New York City and around the country and the great equalizer is the third-party spending. The ones that are whacking him are going to be bringing in more money than the ones that are going to be whacking me. So I think, frankly, they blew it on their strategy."[77]

The early outside money coming into the state in the form of television ads probably did help Rehberg, even accounting for the mistakes made by his allies. Most folks watching television likely saw and understood efforts to equate Tester with the Obama administration while never hearing about the ruckus over fingers added in or the vote that wasn't on EPA dust regulations. But two questions remained going forward: Would that benefit continue to accrue to Rehberg as the campaign heated up, and what would be the cost of relying so much on money controlled by other groups whose interests would not always align with Rehberg and his campaign?

## CONCLUSION

Candidates frame and prime issues in ways most favorable to them. In the 2012 Montana Senate race, the Rehberg campaign framed the choice for voters between a Democrat who supported an unpopular presidential administration and a Republican who was more closely aligned with the majority of Montanans on the issues. They primed in particular the issues of spending and healthcare, both of which were foremost in the minds of Montanans and favored Rehberg. The Tester campaign, alternatively, framed the campaign as a choice between two people—one that was in touch with the land and reflected of Montana and one who was rich, irresponsible, and ineffective. But as much as they candidates tried to dominate the messaging in the race, they had to contend with outside organizations that had their own political agendas and interests, which did not always align with the interests of the candidates they purported to assist with their television and radio advertisements.

This spending by outside groups, coming as a result of the Supreme Court's decision in *Citizens United,* clearly had consequences for Montana's Senate campaign. Political scientist Michael Franz found that interest groups advertised at historic rates in congressional races during the 2012 cycle, displacing the traditional role of political parties in the campaign process. Franz suggests that the "existing structure of rigid contribution limits acts as a handcuff. Parties are increasingly less relevant to the deployment of resources in competitive elections and are unable to play the lead in the plotting of strategy between elections—and candidates are coming to understand that outside groups loom large in any competitive contest."[78] The consequence, he says, is the need for candidates to spend more time on fundraising and less time on constituent outreach. Reliance of candidates on outside money leads to a loss of campaign control, and more time raising money from interests and groups with views that may not be well-aligned with the interests of Montanans. *Citizens United* forced both Rehberg and Tester—candidates deeply rooted in Montana and its culture—to look farther afield for the resources to fund their campaigns. Ironically, the decision in *Citizens United* put Montana's fate right back in the very hands of the people Montanans distrusted the most since gold was found in her hills: well-heeled outsiders who thought they knew best for Montana and her people.

---

# NOTES

1.  Rehberg, interview, August 22, 2011. Rehberg always acknowledged that Tester, as the incumbent, would outraise him.

2.  Preston Elliot, interview with author, December 20, 2012.

3.  Political entrepreneurs have always tested the limits of campaign finance law. The National Conservative Political Action Committee (NCPAC) formed in the 1970s did it shortly after the Supreme Court's decision in *Buckley v. Valeo,* as did Moveon.org and Swift Boat Veterans for Truth in the 2004 presidential campaign. Different in the post-*Citizens United* landscape is the plethora of organizational options available for individuals interested in electioneering and the possibility of spending vast sums of money that would never have to be disclosed publicly. See Parker 2008.

4.  Travis N. Ridout and Michael M. Franz, *The Power of Persuasive Campaign Advertising,* kindle edition, (Philadelphia, PA: Temple University Press, 2008), location 421.

5. James N. Druckman, "Priming the Vote: Campaign Effects in a U.S. Senate Election," *Political Psychology* 25, no. 4 (2004), 577–594; Jon A. Krosnick and Laura A. Brannon, "The Media and the Foundations of Presidential Support: George Bush and the Persian Gulf Conflict," *Journal of Social Issues* 49, no. 4 (1993), 167–182. In the case of Druckman's (2004) study, he finds that voters attentive to the campaign and media found themselves exposed to messages about integrity and Social Security. This increased exposure to these particular messages affected their vote choice after controlling for other factors

6. Shanto Iyengar, *Is Anyone Responsible? How Television Frames Political Issues* (Chicago, IL: University of Chicago Press, 1991).

7. The REAL ID act established stringent federal requirements for the issuance of driver's licenses in response to the 9–11 terrorist attacks. Liberals and conservatives blanched at what they perceived to be the development of a national identification card, and Montanans angrily pushed back against the law—led vocally by Democratic Governor Brian Schweitzer. See Josh Goodman, "Brian Schweitzer and the Politics of Real ID," *Governing Magazine,* March 21, 2008.

8. D. Iverson, interview.

9. Watch Rehberg's announcement on YouTube: http://www.youtube .com/watch?v=jP7TMVcCjhU.

10. Rehberg, interview, August 22, 2011.

11. Rehberg, interview with author, April 4, 2012. He returned to this theme during our September 7, 2012 visit. There is some evidence that in negative races with several candidates, voters will abandon those attacking the most for another alternative.

12. David C.W. Parker, "The Montana Senate Race: Who are these guys and what are their records?" *Big Sky Political Analysis,* posted February 29, 2012, http://bigskypolitics .blogspot.com/2012/02/montana-senate-race-who-are-these-guys.html.

13. Erik Iverson, interview with author, January 24, 2013.

14. Jake Eaton, interview with author, November 24, 2012.

15. Rehberg, interview, August 22, 2011.

16. Poll conducted of 625 Montana voters by Mason Dixon for Lee Newspapers, March 14–16, 2011. Margin of error is +/- four percent. In author's possession courtesy of Chuck Johnson.

17. The tagline became he voted with Barack Obama 95 percent of the time, which is the updated presidential support score calculated annually by CQ Press. See Chapter 8 for a detailed discussion.

18. Tom Lopach, interview with author, November 30, 2012.

19. Ibid.

20. Ibid.

21. Text of Tester's 2011 Mansfield-Metcalf remarks, in author's possession.

22. Andrew Maxfield, interview with author, January 7, 2013.

23. Lopach, interview, November 11, 2012.

24. Maxfield, interview.

25. Mansfield-Metcalf remarks, March 12, 2011.

26. Ibid.

27. Elliott, interview.

28. There was a seven point difference between *Denny* and *Dennis* in Tester's polling. Christie Roberts, interview with author, December 14, 2012. Roberts was Tester's director of research. Denny was not always known as Denny in statewide political circles as Pat Williams reminded me (Williams, interview). In 1996, he ran as *Dennis* and not *Denny* Rehberg against Max Baucus. Apparently, Dennis became *Denny* during his 2000 run for the open house seat. *Dennis* plainly irritated Rehberg's staffers. "The guy's name is Denny. His mom calls him Denny" said campaign chief of staff Jake Eaton (Eaton, interview).

29. Mansfield-Metcalf remarks, March 12, 2011.

30. Republican political consultant, interview with author, February 19, 2009.

31. Topline of Moore Information Poll conducted for Rehberg February 12–14, 2012 with a sample size of 500, margin of error +/- 4.4 percent. Obtained from Bob Moore via e-mail correspondence with the author after Congressman Rehberg provided permission.

32. Poll conducted by Mason Dixon for Lee Newspapers, March 14–16, 2011. See also Mike Dennison, "Majority Wants Repeal of Health-Reform Law," *Billings Gazette,* March 20, 2011.

33. Montana Chamber of Commerce P-Base Survey conducted November 14–18, 2011 with a sample of 600 Montanans, top lines and crosstabs in author's possession, 48 percent identified jobs, unemployment and wages as the number one issue, 64 percent of Montanans believed the national recovery was moving in the wrong direction. Interestingly, only 30 percent said the same about Montana's economy specifically. The numbers for 2010 were nearly identical.

34. Herbert B. Asher, *Polling and the Public: What Every Citizen Should Know,* 7th Edition, (Washington, DC: CQ Press, 2007); Frank Newport, "What's in a Name? Affordable Care Act vs. Obamacare," *Polling Matters,* Gallup, http://pollingmatters.gallup.com/2013/11/whats-in-name-affordable-care-act-vs.html.

35. Steve Liesman, "What's in a name? Lots when it comes to Obamacare/ACA," CNBC, September 26, 2013, http://www.cnbc.com/id/101064954.

36. Kaiser Health Tracking Poll conducted in November 10–15, 2011 using a random, representative sample of 1,209 adults, http://kaiserfamilyfoundation.files.wordpress.com/2013/01/8259-f.pdf.

37. Andrew Maxfield, e-mail correspondence with author, October 22, 2013.

38. Mason Dixon Poll, March 14–16, 2011.

39. Maxfield, e-mail correspondence.

40. Moore Poll, February 12–14, 2012.

41. Text of remarks, 2011.

42. Maxfield, interview.

43. This section is based upon my previously published book on campaign finance and congressional elections. See Parker 2008.

44. Scott Thomas, "The 'soft money' and 'issue ad' mess: How we got here, how Congress responded, and what the FEC is doing," Campaigns & Elections Election Law

Compliance Seminar, 2003: p. 6, http://www.fec.gov/members/former_members/ thomas/thomasarticle06.pdf.

45. *Colorado v. Federal Election Commission* (1996).

46. Michael M. Franz, "The *Citizens United* Election? Or Same As it Ever Was?" *The Forum: A Journal of Applied Research in Contemporary Politics* 8, no. 4, (2010), 3.

47. Franz, "The Citizens United Election"; Michael M. Franz, "Interest Groups in Electoral Politics: 2012 in Context," *The Forum: A Journal of Applied Research in Contemporary Politics* 10, no. 4, 62–79.

48. I first heard the ad on the car radio while driving my daughter to her ballet class and only later discovered that Environmental Defense Fund had also purchased television time.

49. Internal Revenue Service, "Social Welfare Organizations," http://www.irs.gov/ Charities-&-Non-Profits/Other-Non-Profits/Social-Welfare-Organizations.

50. One analysis of independent expenditures and broadcast advertising from the 2010 congressional campaign cycle—the first campaign cycle held under the new *Citizens United* regime—found that pro-Democratic groups spent about $30 million less than pro-Republican groups during the cycle. Republican groups spent about twice as much on television ads. When party and candidate money is added to the equation, however, any Democratic disadvantage disappears. Outside groups made Republicans more competitive financially in an environment where the incumbency advantage favored the Democratic Party. See Franz, "The *Citizens United* Election?."

51. Kenneth Goldstein, Sarah Niebler, Jacob Neiheisel, and Matthew Holleque, "Presidential, Congressional, and Gubernatorial Advertising, 2008," combined File [dataset], (Madison: The University of Wisconsin Advertising Project, the Department of Political Science at the University of Wisconsin-Madison, 2011). The data were obtained from a project of the University of Wisconsin Advertising Project that includes tracking data from TNSMI/Campaign Media Analysis Group in Washington, DC. The opinions expressed in this book are those of the author and do not necessarily reflect the views of the University of Wisconsin Advertising Project.

52. Information on airdates for the 2010 and 2012 cycle was obtained from Michael Franz, codirector of the Wesleyan Media Project. I analyzed aggregate data to determine the earliest air date in each contest and the sponsor of the ad. The Wesleyan Media Project "was established in 2010 to track advertising in federal elections, and it is a successor to the Wisconsin Advertising Project, which tracked political advertising between 1998 and 2008." The project acknowledges the generous support of The John S. and James L. Knight Foundation, the Rockefeller Brothers Fund, and Wesleyan University on their website. My analysis is mine alone, and does not reflect the views of either Wesleyan University, The Wesleyan Media Project, or their funders. You may visit the website at: http://mediaproject .wesleyan.edu/data-access/.

53. The first ad aired according to the Wesleyan Media Project was a Crossroads GPS ad called "Watch" on July 8, 2011. According to an e-mail exchange with Michael Franz and Erika Franklin Fowler at the Wesleyan Project, the organization collecting advertising data uses discovery markets to collect advertising data. When ads do not

appear in those discovery markets, CMAG's technology does not pick up on the ad. I used my collection of advertising buy sheets obtained directly from television stations in Montana to identify the date of the first ad aired in Montana. Importantly, however, is that the Wesleyan Media Project data are likely conservative estimates of when advertisements first hit media markets. One final point: Aaron Murphy, Tester's communications director, swears an ad was aired in November or December 2010 attacking Tester. I did not look at files from the 2010 campaign cycles when visiting television stations, so it is possible that the first ad aired even earlier in the 2012 Senate race than March 2, 2011.

54. Every television station is required by the Federal Communications Commission (FCC) to keep a political file where they include the advertising contracts and invoices for all candidate, party, and issue ads aired on their station during an election cycle. These files must be made available for public inspection during regular business hours. I travelled, multiple times, to every television station throughout Montana to record digital images of these advertising contracts. Some station managers also provided me with summary spending totals by group at the conclusion of the campaign. I used these contracts to develop spending totals for broadcast advertisements aired during the Senate race and the number of spots by broadcast month. This serves as the basis for analysis of campaign advertising for this and ensuing chapters.

55. Tester, interview, November 11, 2011. The senator further elaborated: "It's bad policy and he's for it now. My guess is he'll probably be against it later. It's bad policy because it allows one government agency to run over the top of other stuff. They've got an MOA . . . MOU right now, memo of understanding right now that works. Border patrol will tell you it works and yet he wants to try to make this. . . . He wants to try to do a land grab which is very interesting."

56. Entitled the National Security and Federal Lands Protection Act, the bill allowed "The Secretary of Homeland Security . . . immediate access to any public land managed by the Federal Government (including land managed by the Secretary of the Interior or the Secretary of Agriculture) for purposes of conducting activities that assist in securing the border (including access to maintain and construct roads, construct a fence, use vehicles to patrol, and set up monitoring equipment)." The bill was reported out of the Committee on Natural Resources and placed on the union calendar were it remained for the remainder of the 112th Congress. Rehberg cosponsored the bill about a month after it was introduced.

57. This is not inconsequential given the lowest unit rate rules established by the FCC effectively give candidates more buying power in the final days of the campaign. David D. Oxenford, "Political Broadcasting: Answering your Questions on the FCC's Rules and Policies," Davis, Wright, and Tremaine, LLP, December 17, 2007, http://www.dwt.com/advisories/Political_Broadcasting_Answering_Your_Questions_on_the_FCCs_Rules_and_Policies_12_17_2007/.

58. Tester had sponsored a failed amendment delaying the cap.

59. Remarks made by Denny Rehberg at Ash Grove Cement outside of Helena, Montana, April 4, 2012.

60. And yet Rehberg not only supported *Citizens United,* he knew that outside groups were essential to keeping him competitive in the money game during the campaign.

61. Aaron Murphy, interview.

62. Tester, interview, August 16, 2011.

63. E-mail from Preston Elliot to Campaign Supporters, July 29, 2011, in author's possession, emphasis in the original.

64. Tester's remarks made at the 2012 Mansfield-Metcalf dinner in Helena, in author's possession. Tester had a bad cold that night.

65. The Tester campaign attacked the messenger because it is effective. In 1980 radio and television advertisements sponsored by the National Conservative Political Action Committee (NCPAC) targeted nine liberal Democratic senators, seven of whom lost. Unlike other candidates, Eagleton was targeted late in the cycle and responded aggressively by tagging NCPAC as a Virginia-based group that had no business telling Missourians how to think. The strategy was so effective that the Eagleton campaign outlined their tactics in a memo that was circulated among Senate Democrats running for reelection in 1982.

66. Matt Gouras, "Hullabaloo over five-fingered Tester in attack ad," Associated Press, September 30, 2011. The ad, entitled "Jon Tester #1 in Lobbyist Money," is in author's possession.

67. See the Crossroads GPS Chanel on Youtube at: http://www.youtube.com/watch?v=1HtHY1qvizI.

68. "The Fall TV Season's Senate Air Wars" at FactCheck.org, posted on November 15, 2011, http://www.factcheck.org/2011/11/the-fall-tv-seasons-senate-air-wars/; Cameron Joseph, "Crossroads ad pulled off Montana cable network," *The Hill,* November 12, 2011, http://thehill.com/blogs/ballot-box/senate-races/193205-crossroads-ad-pulled-off-montana-cable-network.

69. Text of Tester's remarks, March 10, 2012.

70. SB 3628 was introduced in the 111th Congress and commonly known as the "DISCLOSE" Act.

71. Aaron Murphy said that the pledge came from Tester himself because Tester believed it was the right thing to do, Murphy, interview.

72. Dan Eggen, "Scott Brown, Elizabeth Warren Pledge to Curb Outside Campaign Spending," *Washington Post,* January 23, 2012.

73. Robin Bravender, "Dueling pledges face off in Montana Race," *Politico,* February 10, 2012. The article links to Rehberg's "Made in Montana Pledge" at http://images.politico.com/ global/2012/02/made_in_montana.html.

74. Open Secrets breaks down contributions by zip code as well as whether the contribution came from within the state or not. See http://www.opensecrets.org/races/geog.php?cycle=2012&id=MTS1&spec=N.

75. "Rehberg Rejects Tester's Plan to Keep Third-Party Ads Out of Montana," Tester Campaign Press Release, February 13, 2012. This begs the question of why Senator Tester's campaign offered a pledge to Rehberg in the first place if they sincerely believed he would simply violate it.

76. Rehberg, interview, April 4, 2012.

77. Ibid.

78. Michael M. Franz, "Interest Groups in Electoral Politics: 2012 in Context." The recent Supreme Court decision in *McCutcheon v. FEC* might change this dynamic and help invigorate party fundraising efforts.

# What Voters Know, How They Decide, and When Campaigns Matter

**N**ate Silver drew the attention of the political world for his uncannily accurate predictions of the 2008 presidential elections. Writing as "Poblano" for the blog fivethirtyeight.com, Silver used a sophisticated econometric model successfully to forecast the outcome of the Republican and Democratic presidential primaries. Ultimately, the baseball sabermetrician with an economics degree from the University of Chicago correctly projected the electoral college vote in forty-nine states and all thirty-five Senate races on the ballot that year.[1] In 2012, Silver got all fifty state electoral college votes correct and thirty-one out of thirty-three Senate races.[2] Silver claims that by thinking probabilistically, adapting one's forecast with new information, and looking for consensus makes predicting gubernatorial and Senate races relatively easy.[3] Pundits and journalists often fail in their predications because they get lost in the campaign narrative; in other words, they emphasize campaign moments and tactics at the expense of other empirical observations with more predictive value.[4]

In this chapter and the next, I demonstrate how and why the campaign between Tester and Rehberg mattered. Unlike the political pundits and journalists Silver scorns, however, I do not emphasize so-called "game-changing moments." In fact, in all the postelection interviews I conducted with Tester and Rehberg's campaign staff, nobody cited such a moment. Tester's campaign manager said flatly that there wasn't one. And, like the true Montanan Preston Elliott is, he referenced hunting: "My hunting instructor one time said when you walk up to a deer, make sure it's dead. And the best way to do that is to poke it in the eye. If it doesn't blink, you're done."[5] Preston thought the race could still be lost in the wee hours of Wednesday morning after Election Day because he had staff members watching ballots as they were counted in Yellowstone County, poking the deer in the eye. I asked Erik Iverson, Rehberg's campaign manager, when he knew they had lost. He said he thought they would win up until the actual results started rolling in.[6]

No one could identify a game-changing moment because there likely wasn't one. The Tester campaign won because of some key advantages he had as the incumbent senator, advantages likely not captured by Silver's model. And, just as important, the Tester campaign created some important informational advantages through its media outreach and advertising efforts that helped blunt the effects of outside spending pouring into the race. There's also the fact that Rehberg had represented Montana successfully for almost twice as long as Tester, which in retrospect, may have been a hindrance.

In this chapter, I discuss how voters make decisions in congressional campaigns. Using polling from the Rehberg campaign and a series of focus groups with Montanans, I demonstrate why running as a House member against a sitting senator—particularly in smaller states—puts the House member at a clear disadvantage. Furthermore, I stress how Rehberg faced an accomplishment deficit and favorability deficit among Montanans relative to Tester. I build on this in the following chapter; I show how Tester's media coverage, campaign advertisements, and the voter's preference for him personally helped Tester deflect a carefully orchestrated campaign attempting to tie him to an unpopular president and his policies. This was aided by an early informational advantage generated by Tester in spring of 2012, when his campaign dominated the airwaves with positive campaign ads stressing Tester's personality and relationship to the land. To understand how the events unfolded in Montana, one first needs to understand how voters make decisions in congressional elections. Once that has been accomplished, we can better see the advantages Senator Tester enjoyed relative to Congressman Rehberg and how individual reputations and representational relationships trumped the partisan considerations among Montana voters.

## HOW INDIVIDUALS MAKE VOTING DECISIONS IN CONGRESSIONAL ELECTIONS

As members of Congress do their work at home and in Washington, they wish to establish particular reputations among their constituents while earning their trust. That trust becomes the bedrock of their relationship with the people and place they represent, and if the constituents give their trust, they reelect the member of Congress. The hope for members is that by sponsoring legislation, helping constituents solve their problems, and communicating with constituents with newsletters and trips home, constituents will form lasting, positive impressions of them. Although the public has never particularly liked Congress as an institution, and trust has dipped to perilously low levels in recent years, constituents often report liking and trusting their member of Congress, which accounts in part for the high rate of reelection.[7]

Voters may like their members, but how they view the political world is rooted first in their partisanship. Political scientists have long known that party identification—whether an individual views himself as a Republican, Democrat, or Independent—acts as a filter through which people see the political world.[8]

Those identifying strongly with a party are more likely to participate politically. They are more likely to vote, to follow politics, and are generally more knowledgeable about current events.[9] They also tend to be more rooted in their political views, less amendable to persuasion, and express lower levels of approval of public officials from the opposing party.[10] Independents, alternatively, are less engaged politically, less knowledgeable about politics, and are more likely to be pulled in different partisan directions by competing political values—even if many independents typically lean consistently toward one of the parties.[11] Partisans who are weakly attached to their parties also often find themselves similarly "cross-pressured."

Partisanship is a powerful factor explaining whether and how somebody votes. Members of Congress, therefore, are evaluated by voters based not only on their own individual reputation or brand but on their party's brand.[12] For many voters, the party brand is the only cue needed. As a result, many congressional elections are dull, predictable affairs. This has become particularly true in House elections as the number of competitive House seats has declined dramatically over the past four decades.[13] There are many reasons for the rise of safe seats, including residential self-selection, redistricting, and the ideological sorting of voters over the past four decades.[14]

Although partisanship is the single best predictor of how individuals vote, the outcomes of congressional elections are not all preordained. Voters can and do defect from their party. Short-term factors move voters—especially those who are cross-pressured—away from their party.[15] In times of economic despair, members of Congress representing the majority party are punished by voters eager for change. Presidential campaigns have a tendency to bring younger and less politically engaged voters to the polls because the information environment reduces the costs of voting.[16] Similarly, midterm elections often attract an older—and generally more conservative—electorate to the polls.[17] In these ways, forces often outside the control of an individual member of Congress affect how voters perceive them and sometimes can put a relatively safe member of Congress who has developed an otherwise strong relationship with their constituency in political peril.

Other times, short-term forces affecting a congressional election have everything to do with the member and his reputation. In their work on Senate elections, Alan Abramowitz and Jeffery Segal found that incumbent senators who are involved in scandal, controversy, or have health issues earn a lower share of the vote than colleagues without these personal problems.[18] It was a scandal that undercut Senator Burns's reputation for honesty among Montana voters, which created an opportunity for a talented candidate like Jon Tester to ride narrowly to victory in 2006. Events *can* change the voting calculus of constituents. The central goal of any congressional campaign is to understand the electoral environment facing its candidate and develop an argument resonating with enough voters to win come Election Day. This means understanding not only what makes voters tick but also comprehending the full set of assets and liabilities both candidates bring to the table.

Generally speaking, incumbents are heavily advantaged in any congressional campaign. Thinking about elections as a choice made by voters in an information environment helps understand the incumbency advantage. Incumbents have a tremendous advantage in controlling the flow of information constituents receive. Constituents see them on the television, read about them in the newspaper, receive newsletters from them in their mailboxes or inboxes extolling the members' virtues, and meet them at forums as they travel their states and districts. It is well-documented that incumbents in both the House and Senate are better known than the candidates challenging them—if they receive a challenger at all.[19] A substantial portion of House members win reelection overwhelmingly because they enjoy large information advantages. In 2012, 66 percent of House races had margins of victory greater than 20 percent.[20]

Senators have similar information advantages over challengers, but they are not as great as their House colleagues. All things being equal, an ambitious politician would rather serve in the Senate. Senators exert more institutional power than House members, the job is more prestigious, and they serve longer terms. As a result, incumbent senators are more likely to draw a quality challenger that has successfully run and served in office, meaning they have established their own reputation and relationship with a set of constituents. According to political scientist Gary Jacobson, only 19 percent of House incumbents running for reelection faced a quality challenger between 1946 and 2010.[21] Using data collected for another project and applying Jacobson's standard of quality, I find that 55 percent of incumbent senators drew a quality challenger between 1946 and 2008.[22] The fact that senators have less substantial information advantages over their challengers is one (but not the only) reason they find themselves less electorally secure. Despite the widespread belief that House members by dint of their running every two years for reelection and often representing smaller constituencies are closer to their constituents, constituents report higher rates of contact with senators than their representatives in states with fewer than four House members and similar rates of contact in states with fewer than nine House members. Only in the largest states do constituents indicate a closer relationship with their House member.[23]

When voters do defect from their party, they are more likely to defect to an incumbent. When voters cast their ballots, they have two pieces of information in front of them: the names of the candidates and their party affiliations.

Absent any external information, the voter is most likely to vote party. A defection is more likely when the voter recognizes the names of the candidates and knows something about them; more often than not, the voter will have more information about the incumbent. Jacobson assembled five decades' worth of data from the National Election Studies and the Cooperative Congressional Election Study showing that defections overwhelmingly favor incumbents in House elections. Senate incumbents also have an advantage, although their defection advantage over challengers is smaller.[24] The power of incumbency begins with this information advantage, which often discourages quality challengers from emerging. In absence of either national forces placing the incumbent's party at a disadvantage or a series of events tarnishing the incumbent's reputation that serves to undercut his information advantage, the best candidates steer clear of running against incumbents. They wait instead to run in an open seat when the incumbent information advantage is no longer relevant. A big reason why Senate races tend to be more competitive is because the quality of the challenger diminishes the informational advantages enjoyed by incumbents.

## MONTANA: INDEPENDENT VOTERS FACING A RICH INFORMATION ENVIRONMENT

In the 2012 Montana Senate race, a number of factors initially eroded Senator Tester's information advantage over his challenger, Congressman Rehberg. For one, Senator Tester began the election at a disadvantage simply because he was a Democrat representing a reddish state—a state that already had one quite senior Democratic senator. His partisan base was smaller than Rehberg's. Assuming both Tester and Rehberg maintained their bases, Tester would have to draw a disproportionate share of independents—many of whom described themselves as conservative. The silver lining for Tester was that Montana, given its large segment of independent voters, had a substantial number of voters who were potentially cross-pressured. Montana voters are also willing to split their tickets—suggesting weak partisan attachments. According to one recent analysis, Montana voters split their tickets with a higher degree of frequency than voters in any other state.[25] As an incumbent running for reelection, Tester could expand his small partisan base given that defections often advantage incumbents.

Unfortunately for Tester, the information environment did not necessarily advantage him in 2012. Rehberg was not the typical challenger many senators face when running for reelection. Rehberg was a quality challenger who was also well-known and had developed his own brand. As the state's lone congressman, he served the same geographic constituency as Tester. If anyone could eat into Senator Tester's information advantage, it was Rehberg. Furthermore, given Rehberg had represented Montana far longer than Senator Tester, it was likely that party defections would split about equally between the two candidates. Given the Republican and conservative tilt of the electorate, the odds favored Rehberg.

Or did they? Although Rehberg and Tester were both well-known, Tester—as the sitting senator—may still have had the informational and reputational edge over the congressman. True, Tester and Rehberg share the same representational space. But Tester, as a senator, had more official resources at his command. Tester's official office allowance—which includes money with which to pay staff salaries, franked communications, travel back to the state, and rent for office space—was about twice that of Rehberg's. The result was far greater opportunity to contact constituents on a daily basis. Tester had eight offices scattered throughout the state; Rehberg, four. Tester had twice the staff. In addition, as Lee and Oppenheimer note, constituents in smaller states are more likely to contact their senator than their House member to resolve an issue or to voice an opinion on an issue.[26] Why? A member of a focus group conducted during the heat of the Senate race put it plainly: "I think they have better constituent services. They have more offices. More staff. More power."[27] In a battle of incumbents, particularly when sharing a representational space, Senator Tester's resource advantage proved critical.

## REPRESENTATIONAL RELATIONSHIPS: WHAT DID MONTANANS KNOW AND WHEN DID THEY KNOW IT?

Despite a substantial number of advertising spots dumped on Montanans between March 2011 and February 2012, views of Senator Tester and Congressman Rehberg changed hardly at all. In April 2011, shortly after Rehberg officially announced his bid, Bob Moore went into the field to do an extensive benchmark poll. He found the race tied at 45 percent.[28] Ten months later, his polling showed the race again dead even at 45 percent. Public polling also indicated little movement.[29] Public Policy Polling (PPP) showed Rehberg with 48 percent in November 2010 and 47 percent in June and November of 2011. In those same polls, Tester polled at 46, 45, and 45 percent, respectively.[30]

Unlike most congressional campaigns, both candidates enjoyed near universal name recognition given their statewide service. Fewer than five percent of voters indicated they had never heard of either Jon Tester or Denny Rehberg when asked whether they approved of the jobs they were doing in Congress.[31] Generally speaking, both candidates were viewed positively. In Rehberg's April 2011 survey, 52 percent of respondents indicated they had a favorable impression of the congressman while 57 percent said the same of Tester. When asked about whether they approved of the jobs both were doing in Congress, 55 percent approved of Tester's job in the Senate while 48 percent said the same of Rehberg.[32] In PPP's poll in late 2010, Tester's approval rating sat at 50 percent and Rehberg's at 49.[33] Little had changed in the ensuing five months. These numbers put both Tester and Rehberg in a good position electorally. Neither was underwater—meaning neither found themselves with more voters disapproving of their job performance or viewing them unfavorably. PPP, in fact, indicated that Tester's approval rating in November was among the top ten of senators in races they had surveyed.[34]

The strength of both Rehberg's and Tester's relationships with Montanans is underscored when looking at how Montanans viewed President Obama and Montana's senior senator, Max Baucus. Only 43 percent of Montanans had a favorable impression of President Obama, and 42 percent disapproved of his job as president.[35] And although 52 percent of respondents in the April 2011 poll viewed Baucus favorably (midway between Tester and Rehberg), Baucus was well underwater in terms of job approval in other public polling conducted throughout 2010 and 2011. Between 38 and 41 percent of Montanans in these polls indicated that they were unsatisfied with Baucus's performance.[36] Generally speaking, one gets the impression that by early 2012, Montanans would have a difficult choice between two well-regarded politicians. Many Montanans preferred not making a choice. They wanted Tester to stay in the Senate and Rehberg to keep serving as a member of the powerful House Appropriations Committee. At least, that's what I heard over and over again from regular Montanans I encountered in my travels.

Nonetheless, voters would have to make a choice and the candidates certainly wanted to make sure they made the right one by framing the campaign in terms most favorable to them. Part of this framing, as discussed in the last chapter, begins with how candidates positioned themselves and communicated accomplishments to voters. Senator Tester wanted voters to believe that he was working hard for them in the United States Senate, and that he had achieved some tangible, bipartisan legislative accomplishments in an increasingly rancorous political environment. Tester also wanted to be sure that he, not Rehberg, was seen as most "one of us" by Montana voters—that Rehberg was nothing more than a career politician associated with all the ills of Congress. Congressman Rehberg, alternatively, hoped that Montanans knew that he was the real conservative in the race who was closer ideologically to the average Montanan. Tester, unlike Rehberg, was a close associate of President Obama and the administration's "failed" policies that had foisted an unpopular health reform on Montanans while hindering the economic recovery from one of the worst depressions in U.S. history. In terms of how political scientists think of elections, Tester hoped to localize the election while Rehberg hoped to nationalize it.

The competing personal reputations and relationships established by both Rehberg and Tester lay at the core of each campaign's ability to win the hearts and minds of voters. Who had established the stronger relationship with Montanans during their time in office, and, as important, which candidate had the more distinctive brand? One question that academics often ask to get at the reputational relationship established by members of Congress is an open-ended one allowing voters to give their "off the top of their head" impressions. In the National Election Studies conducted since 1978, respondents are asked if they have any like or dislike about their member of Congress and, if so, what is it?[37] About 60 percent of constituents can express at least one like or dislike about their incumbent senator or House member according to recent research.[38] Gary Jacobson's analysis of patterns in the likes/dislikes expressed about House candidates demonstrates that since the 1970s, the number of comments "about candidates' personal characteristics, performance, and district services fell, while the proportion of comments concerning party, ideology, and policy grew."[39] Jacobson argues that the shift from personal qualities to political characteristics has made incumbents more vulnerable because a focus on ideology or policy has the ability to "repel" as well as to "attract."[40] As the political environment has become increasingly polarized, incumbents have found it harder to capitalize on informational advantages built upon constituent service, casework, and their personal relationships with voters. If this is the case, Tester faced a substantial challenge in persuading Montanans to make their decisions based upon his personal relationship with them.

Moore asked a similar question on seven of the nine surveys I obtained and which he conducted for Rehberg. Instead of asking whether the respondent had a like or dislike about Rehberg or Tester, Moore asked whether the respondent had seen, read, or heard anything about Rehberg or Tester. If the respondent answered yes, the interviewer asked what specifically the respondent recalled. Half of the respondents remembered something about Rehberg, while 58 percent said the same about Tester in February of 2012.[41] Interestingly, the gap in voter recollection about specific information about Congressman Rehberg and Senator Tester had increased from one percentage point to eight in less than a year. Voters from February 2012 through late September of 2012 would consistently say they recalled more specifically about Senator Tester than Congressman Rehberg. This gap would grow to as much as sixteen points in April 2012 and shrink to as little as three in early August of 2012. How and why this information advantage occurred explains much of what happened during the ensuing campaign.

Voters knew a little bit more specifically about Senator Tester than Congressman Rehberg when pressed: 47 percent versus 42 percent, respectively. Their impressions of both in the early days of the campaign are telling. To interpret meaningfully the wide-ranging, open-ended responses, I categorized useable responses into four content areas: whether the comment mentioned an issue, a personality trait or characteristic, the political party, or, if I could not code into any of these categories, as miscellaneous. Finally, responses of less than 0.5 percent were not tabulated by Moore, so these are classified as noncodeable. I also classified each comment as either negative, positive, or neutral. Using this scheme, we gain insight into what voters knew about Senator Tester and Congressman Rehberg and whether these impressions were helpful to the brand cultivated by each as they began electioneering in earnest.

## TABLE 7.1

*What Respondents Recalled Hearing or Reading About Senator Tester and Congressman Rehberg, February 2012*

A. Open-Ended Comments by Category

|  | Rehberg | | Tester | |
|---|---|---|---|---|
|  | Number of Comments | Percentage | Number of Comments | Percentage |
| Personal | 12 | 31% | 13 | 33% |
| Issue | 17 | 44% | 19 | 48% |
| Misc | 9 | 23% | 5 | 13% |
| Partisan | 1 | 3% | 3 | 8% |
| Total | 39 |  | 40 |  |

B. Open-Ended Responses by Tone

|  | Rehberg | | Tester | |
|---|---|---|---|---|
|  | Number of Comments | Percentage | Number of Comments | Percentage |
| Positive | 11 | 28% | 13 | 33% |
| Neutral | 13 | 33% | 14 | 35% |
| Negative | 15 | 38% | 13 | 33% |
| Total | 39 |  | 40 |  |

*Source*: Analysis based on poll conducted by Moore Information on behalf of the Rehberg campaign in February 2012. Poll obtained with permission of Congressman Rehberg and in author's possession.

The results are reported in Table 7.1. A plurality of comments made by voters was neutral and centered on policy. Generally, most of the issue-based comments were coded as neutral because it was not clear if the voter perceived the stance taken by the member as positive or negative. What is striking about the issue-based comments, however, is the fact that neither Tester nor Rehberg garnered many negative comments about their policy positions. Furthermore, the positive ways in which Tester and Rehberg are associated with issues in the minds of respondents are exactly as the campaigns would want. Three percent of respondents made mention of Tester's work with veterans, and another three percent mentioned his Forest Jobs and Recreation Act.[42] These are two legislative accomplishments Tester and his staff worked hard to promote, and their efforts to disseminate information about them yielded positive results.

Montanans made no negative comments about Congressman Rehberg's position on issues, and even though nearly half of the issue-based comments were positive ones about Rehberg, voters had trouble linking Rehberg to specific accomplishments. The only comment made above the 0.5 percent threshold about Rehberg's work in the House concerned his efforts to keep the U.S. Forest Service from removing a 67-year-old statue of Jesus at the top of Big Mountain in Whitefish. The statue remained at the center of a dispute with Freedom from Religion Foundation which had filed suit to remove the statue from national forest land.[43] Two percent of respondents recalled Rehberg's efforts to keep Jesus watching over skiers and other resort visitors.

In general, voters had only faint impressions of the Washington work in which both members engaged. But Montanans had a better idea of Tester's accomplishments. This matched what Tester's pollster had found: Some Montanans had an idea about Jon's legislative work and "many of the things he'd accomplished were actually quite positive," particularly his efforts on behalf of veterans. Still, many had not yet heard about them. Maxfield was unfazed. It "takes campaigns for voters to get reacquainted with their elected officials" he told me in early January after the race had concluded.[44]

More striking, however, is how the candidates were viewed personally by voters. One-third of voters made a comment about Tester or Rehberg as individuals, and on balance, Rehberg was perceived adversely. More than 90 percent of these individual comments volunteered about Rehberg as an individual were negative, compared to a little less than half of those about Tester. People noted that they had met Tester, knew he was a farmer, and that he was accessible. Negative comments about Tester were generally vague.

Rehberg, on the other hand, suffered from some negative impressions respondents had about him personally. The single most common comment made about

Rehberg by Montanans concerned his wealth: Four percent elicited this response when probed. Three percent mentioned a lawsuit the Congressman and his wife had filed against the City of Billings concerning damages sustained in a brush fire that, according to the Rehbergs, the city had not sufficiently contained.[45] One source described the lawsuit as a "business decision."[46] He told me that "The value of their land went from $35 million to $5 million; it was substantial in terms of valuation. And the only way they could recover something if insurance turned them down was to get the fire department to be negligent."[47] The lawsuit eventually was dropped by the Rehbergs after much negative publicity throughout the state but particularly in Billings.

Another one percent mentioned a terrible boating accident on Flathead Lake that left Rehberg with bruised ribs and a fractured ankle.[48] Rehberg's state director, Dustin Frost, was in a coma for over a week after the wreck.[49] It was later determined that the operator of the boat, Republican State Senator Greg Barkus of Kalispell, had been intoxicated.[50] A segment of Montanans thought poorly about Rehberg personally but agreed with him on a number of issues. More Montanans, according to Rehberg's February poll, agreed with the statement that Republicans had the best plan to help the economy grow (51 percent) and

Rehberg Ranch Estates in 2012, a subdivision which sits on land developed by Congressman Rehberg and his wife Jan. It was grassland to the north of the development that caught fire on July 4, 2008, which became subject of a lawsuit between the Rehbergs and the City of Billings in 2010.

Photo taken by Larry Mayer and reprinted here courtesy of the *Billings Gazette*.

indicated a wish to support a Republican "who will be a check and balance on President Obama's agenda" (54 percent).[51]

## TALKING POLITICS: THE BOZEMAN FOCUS GROUPS

To provide additional insight into what Montana voters thought about the role of members of Congress generally and their impressions of Senator Tester and Congressman Rehberg, I conducted three focus groups with Montana voters in Gallatin County between June and mid-August of 2012. Gallatin County happens to be one of the more populous and fastest-growing counties in the state. It is also quite politically diverse. The size of the focus groups varied between seven and nine individuals, and the sessions were conducted in the homes of Bozemanites who recruited individuals from a range of political and professional backgrounds. The age of participants ranged between 22 and 68, with a median age of 49. The groups were mostly male: Only 28 percent of the participants were women. As a result, the groups skewed conservative. One focus group consisted primarily of Democrats, another of Independents, and one almost exclusively of Republicans. I crafted a short list of questions to guide the discussion, and we spent between sixty and ninety minutes talking about the ongoing Senate campaign and representation.[52] In return for their participation, I guaranteed anonymity and changed names to protect identities.

Three key findings emerged from the focus groups confirming not only much of what the Rehberg campaign uncovered in polling but also what political scientists know about voters and their perceptions of members of Congress. First, the participants all saw the process of representation as political scientists might explain it to undergraduates: It is a mix of reflecting the values of constituents as delegates and using wisdom and judgment as trustees to do what is right even if it goes against majority will. Edward, a 40-something contractor who described himself politically as "pissed off at both parties" suggested this delicate balance when I asked the group how they saw the primary responsibility of a member of Congress: "I want them to be trying as hard as I do to do the right thing. . . . I'm hoping that my congressman and my senator are way smarter than me as I am smarter than my employees . . . because . . . if I acted according to their whims we would have gone bankrupt a long time ago."[53]

Nicholas, a 60-year old retired policeman newly relocated to Montana, echoed this perspective: "I don't think that my legislators should always vote the same as polls would indicate."[54] Another recurring theme was a desire for statesmanship. Participants wanted candidates and legislators who would "say what they mean . . . [and] actually have a set of values and beliefs that's real."[55] Michael, a conservative Republican: "They need to do what's best for their state but they also need to represent their state ... in the bigger picture."[56] They want their congressmen to listen to constituents, use their judgment, and then represent the state as a whole in the halls of national government.

It was less clear that the folks I interviewed had a distinct vision of what a member of Congress should do for them. Thinking about the classic roles Fenno uses to describe legislators (constituent servant, policy expert, and "one of us"), participants in the Republican focus group adamantly rejected the notion that their representatives and senators should primarily pass legislation or bring back pork to the state. Small business owner Samuel bluntly said that earmarking and pork barreling were not part of their job.[57] When I asked them to evaluate the argument that passing legislation was a sign of effectiveness, Adam scoffed: "Yeah, we don't have enough laws, do we? Yeah, pass more laws, oh yeah."[58] One got the sense from the conservative Republicans that the job of their representative was to either repeal laws or, failing that, stop government from expanding. Obstructionism, said Zach, a middle-aged conservative salesman who had voted for Ross Perot twice and regretted it, was "great. Gridlock is good for us in Montana. The closer we are to bipartisanship, you can just feel the dollars flee from your pocket and run scared to Washington."[59]

Democrats and some Independents, alternatively, did believe that earmarking was an important function in which their members should engage. Self-identified Independent Barbara chimed in, objecting to calling such spending "pork." She noted that "the reality is that our government spends a ton of money ... and the public [through their representative] has a role in pushing projects in good directions."[60] Rehberg, the appropriator, had a problem because while Democrats and Independents appreciated earmarking, his conservative base most definitely did not.

If there was little agreement on what precisely a member should do to demonstrate effectiveness other than visit and listen to constituents while balancing judgment with majority consensus, there was some sense that the roles of senators and House members differed and, perhaps, the Senate required a particular temperament and skill set. Participants saw the jobs as varying tremendously in their power. Here's Harold's response: "Our one representative has little to no impact whatsoever ... He's got very little power. And so, least with the Senate, we have as much say as the rest of the country."[61] The Senate is seen as more prestigious with greater responsibilities, suggesting the need for someone cut from a different cloth. "I tend," said Nicholas, to "see a senator as having the potential to be in the role as a statesperson much more than a representative."[62] Senators could "get something done" because the House members are "one person in a sea." Not only would the Senate get more done but it would be more careful, "more considerate. [They] will more thoroughly look at something, be more educated on the topic. Representatives are going to be quicker and want to talk about money," said Albert.[63] During the discussions, nearly no one mentioned that their senator should look like Montanans—be "one of us," and casework or helping constituents hardly came up. Deliberation and developing policy expertise received the most emphasis.

After asking about their perceptions of members of Congress and the differences between the two chambers, we zeroed in on how they felt about Tester and Rehberg specifically. Republican participants predictably dismissed Tester as representing the national party's interests. "Tester's proven when it comes to a national party decision, he votes a national party line. He must, or they will not give him his chairmanship, they will not give him his funding. So you have to choose in this Senate race the party that has the least chance of increasing taxes" said Zach.[64] Democrats, if they had complaints about Tester, wanted him to be more liberal. Independents had the least developed impressions of all, as one might expect of a segment of voters that tends to be cross-pressured and less interested in politics.

Nevertheless, the deviations from this general story hinted at some of Tester's strengths and some of the hurdles Rehberg would have to overcome during the summer and fall. More than once, Tester was described as a "one of us" representative even if the groups didn't associate "one of us" with senators more generally. Walter, the self-described but cross-pressured Republican, believed that Tester looked like most Montanans and reflected their values. He approved of the job that Tester was doing but didn't think he could vote for him. He was torn: "If I could vote for Tester on a social perspective, I would vote for him. However, the National Federation of Independent Businesses and the National Association of Homebuilders both are supportive of Rehberg, and I figure my ultra-small social circle will benefit more from me being able to make a little more money so that my kids can get a little bit more education."[65]

Republican Blair, a realtor in her mid-sixties who had lived in Montana for thirty years, liked what Tester was doing despite the fact she expressed support for budget cuts and a concern over the federal deficit. Why? Because of Tester's constituent service, an impression often associated with House members in larger states: "The reason why I will approve of Tester is because he's the only one between him and Rehberg who have made any contact with realtors. Who has asked about any issue with water rights? Who has asked about any issues with private property rights? . . . Who has paid attention to the housing industry? We have not heard one word from Rehberg at all."[66] For Blair, Tester had gotten stuff done for her industry. That might have tipped the balance.

Edward aired the typical complaint about Congress, but in so doing, demonstrated why Tester may have had an advantage among Independents like him who are a less politically sophisticated group of voters: "I think all 600 of them should be strung up. . . . The only thing that comes to mind when you ask me what do I think about Tester or Rehberg is a commercial with Tester where I was inspired to like him. He's on a tractor, he's up in Great Falls or up on the Hi-Line and that's good whatever he said. Do I know what he said? No. And then Rehberg? He's drunk and he wrecks his boat on Flathead Lake. Those are the two overwhelming moments and that's the indication of what these guys mean to me. *American Idol*'s more real."[67] He knew very little about either candidate, but what little he did know drew him closer to Tester and away from Rehberg.

Democrats and Independents mentioned Tester's work as a farmer, his evenhandedness, and the fact that he would come back and listen to voters frequently. They also believed, because of this, he had not been consumed by Washington, DC. Ethel had lived in the nation's capital for ten years before moving to Bozeman. A 59-year-old Democrat, she said Tester was "doing a good job" because she believed he was "a fair player, that he wants to listen, that he wants to do the right things . . . [Tester's] done a pretty good job of not becoming corrupted by the 'ugly beast' of Washington, DC."[68] Even conservative Republicans unlikely to vote for Tester begrudgingly gave him marks for looking "like a farmer" and the fact he was from a rural community.[69]

When the conversation turned to Rehberg, little enthusiasm emerged. The lawsuit came up, as did the boat crash on Flathead Lake. Democrats, Republicans, and Independents all made comments about Rehberg's "personal problems" as they put it. Republicans also mentioned concerns with Rehberg's votes for Real ID and the Patriot Act. This perhaps provides some evidence that the early spending by Montana Hunters and Anglers in the fall criticizing Rehberg's support for a bill granting more authority to the Department of Homeland Security to operate on public lands may have reignited long-standing conservative concerns with Rehberg on privacy issues. Blair, the realtor who had been impressed with Tester and his office staff in Butte, was blunt: "I'm really split with that man. . . . He's been there a long time, and I listen to his ads now and I think, bucko, you've been there a hell of a long time. Why the hell haven't you done that already?"[70] I asked the Republican group if anyone was enthusiastic about Rehberg. Michael said, "Nobody loves Denny Rehberg, but my God, he's not Jon Tester."[71] Blair jumped in, saying that Rehberg had "filed a lawsuit against his own hometown, for crying out loud."[72] Harold, who was a self-identified Republican and pro-life, said he'd be "voting party" but added that "if there was a different Republican I could vote for, I'd vote for him."[73]

If the Republicans could point to legislation Rehberg had supported they didn't like, Independents and Democrats had a hard time associating Rehberg with any accomplishments. Ethel believed that Rehberg piloted on "cruise control.

He's had that seat, he cruises along, [and] I don't see what he's done for Montana so far, and I don't hear him telling me what he's going to do for Montana. I'm very unimpressed, and I don't understand why he gets reelected."[74] William, a 67-year-old environmental consultant, called him "lazy . . . He's introduced virtually no legislative proposals in all the years he's been in Congress. He is arrogant. He seems to be very self-centered."[75] We see across focus group participants from a variety of backgrounds evidence confirming what the polls showed in February 2012: Rehberg had not connected with Montanans personally, and they had little sense about what he had done for them while serving in Congress over the past decade. Given the consensus among group participants that the Senate needed people with an even temper and an ability to build bridges, the path forward for Rehberg seemed challenging.

Between the polls conducted by Bob Moore and the Bozeman focus groups, one senses that on the issues, Rehberg seemed a better fit with Montanans, but that Tester had done a better job connecting. In addition, impressions of Tester had developed based upon his constituent service. Voters also could associate his name with work he had done on behalf of veterans (in Moore's poll, 44 percent of voters agreed that Tester was more concerned with veterans while only 27 percent said Rehberg was), and his labors on behalf of the Forest Jobs and Recreation Act.[76] This work, particularly Tester's constituent outreach, impressed some independent and conservative-leaning Republicans. For Tester, the path forward seemed clear: Bring more awareness to these types of accomplishments and continue building his strong personal relationship with Montana voters.

Yet Rehberg, in some respects, had an easier path forward. Given the partisan leanings of the state, if he could make the election about Tester's support for the national Democratic Party platform and an unpopular President Obama, he might win despite the fact that he wasn't Mr. Congeniality. Even so, the smart bet would be to rehabilitate his image among Montanans, especially because it was a weakness that Tester and his allies likely would exploit throughout the summer and fall.

The problem for Rehberg, however, was the fact that voters did not necessarily see Tester as a liberal clone of Barack Obama—at least not in the early days of 2012. Despite a year's worth of outside spending, much of it connecting Tester to Obama and his policies, there was almost no change in how Montanans viewed Tester ideologically. In April 2011, 52 percent identified Tester as a moderate or conservative. That number actually increased to 55 percent in February 2012. Digging deeper, 45 percent of Montanans when prompted agreed that Tester had sided too much with Obama, but an identical number believed that Tester had been an Independent senator.[77]

To frame Tester as a national Democrat, Rehberg and his allies relied on an obscure statistic favored by academics: The *CQ* Presidential Support Score. Each member's presidential support score is the percentage of times they vote for legislation on which the administration has taken a public position as calculated by the editors of *Congressional Quarterly*. Higher scores indicate more support for the administration; lower scores, less support. Traditionally, administrations receive the bulk of their support from their copartisans—with support for the administration's positions from the opposition declining in recent decades. Congressional Democrats support Democratic administrations, and Congressional Republicans support Republican administrations. According to the Rehberg campaign's claims, Senator Tester supported President Obama 95 percent of the time—the average of his voting record as compiled by *CQ* between 2009 and 2011. The Rehberg campaign constantly linked Tester to the Obama administration in press releases and social media. Chris Bond, the Rehberg campaign's press secretary, linked Tester to Obama or attacked the administration in 40 percent of tweets sent between November 2011 and the end of March 2012. Early advertisements by outside groups did not use the 95 percent number but highlighted Tester's support for unpopular administration initiatives. Crossroads GPS launched more than 800 ads in June and July of 2011 focusing on Tester's support for "Obamacare," the failed stimulus, and increased taxes.[78] The 1,300 advertisements aired by the U.S. Chamber of Commerce in November similarly focused on higher taxes and Tester's vote for the president's healthcare policy.[79] The constant drumbeat linking Tester to Obama was an effort to make Montanans, who leaned conservative, to cast their Senate vote as a protest of the presidential administration.

The presidential support score is not "a random number made up in Washington" as Tester Communications Director Aaron Murphy dismissed it when drawing attention to Tester's record as an independent-minded senator not beholden to the administration.[80] Notwithstanding the presidential support score, however, Tester could not easily be painted as a liberal, Obama supporter. First, Tester's scores approximated the average for Senate Democrats and generally reflect the support given an administration by copartisans in the Senate. Second, the score does not reflect a senator's complete body of work, just roll call votes. There are a host of other ways a member of Congress can signal independence from an administration, in particular by writing letters and holding hearings to object to rules promulgated by an administration. Given how difficult it is to pass legislation, much of what is accomplished in Washington is done by agencies writing rules. Tester, like any member of Congress, routinely lodges complaints against regulations problematic for his state and its interests. For example, Tester and Rehberg both made it known they opposed Department of

Labor regulations concerning child labor on family farms, and their actions were instrumental in halting the implementation of those regulations.[81] These types of activities are frequent and do not get recorded in the presidential support score based exclusively on roll call votes.

More problematic is that a number of noncontroversial votes receiving bipartisan support are included in the total, including a sizeable number of judicial appointments to the federal district and appellate benches. These votes inflate the support a member gives an administration. I recalculated the presidential support scores for the Montana congressional delegation in 2009, 2010, and 2011 by dropping all votes receiving more than 80 percent support for or against the president's position.[82] The result is presented in Table 7.2 along with the Presidential Support score as calculated by *CQ*. No matter how you slice it, Rehberg was a persistent foe of the administration. His adjusted score is similar, mostly because the House does not vote on judicial nominations so there are comparably fewer noncontroversial votes to drop. Tester's score, however, changes substantially in 2010 and 2011: from 97 to 83 and 90 to 84 percent, respectively. On average, Tester supported the administration only 88 percent of the time during those three years, which is two percentage points less than the average Senate Democrat. The *CQ* score, however, shows Tester mirroring Senate Democrats. Given that there is little variance in the scores, the two percentage point difference is an important indicator that Tester does not vote lock step with the administration or his party. Other evidence points to his centrist tendencies ideologically, in particular the fact that he was the 17th most conservative of the 63 Democrats serving in the 111th Congress according to an analysis

TABLE 7.2

*Measuring Support for President Obama in the Senate and the House, 2009 to 2011*

| | 2009 | | 2010 | | 2011 | |
|---|---|---|---|---|---|---|
| | CQ Support Score | Adjusted Score | CQ Support Score | Adjusted Score | CQ Support Score | Adjusted Score |
| Tester | 97% | 96% | 97% | 83% | 90% | 84% |
| Baucus | 96% | 93% | 97% | 93% | 95% | 95% |
| Senate Dems | 92% | 94% | 94% | 83% | 92% | 93% |
| Rehberg | 26% | 14% | 26% | 14% | 22% | 22% |
| House GOP | 26% | 17% | 29% | 19% | 22% | 22% |

*Source*: CQ Support scores obtained from *Congressional Quarterly*'s annually published Voting Studies. Adjusted scores calculated by the author by removing all votes where members voted 80 percent or more for or against the measure.

of NOMINATE scores.[83] Could Rehberg and his allies make the 95 percent number stick, and would impressions of Tester change? Alternatively, could Tester demonstrate that the number did not reflect his record and, more importantly, remind voters that they liked him more than Rehberg—even if they identified with a different party? The election would turn ultimately on the answers to these questions.

## REINFORCING AN INFORMATION ADVANTAGE

Senator Tester had three formidable advantages in the spring of 2012 as the campaign geared up for the big push. First, he had an information advantage because, as a senator, he had a clear resource advantage over the state's lone House member. He had more staff, more offices, and a larger operation devoted to press attention than the congressman. His larger staff put out more press releases and gained more free press. Between 2007 and March 2012, Tester's Senate staff released more than 1,300 press releases compared to 600 for Rehberg. *Billings Gazette* coverage also favored Tester over the same period: 966 articles mentioned the junior senator versus 718 mentioning the congressman.[84] Tester could also use his resources to do more constituent service and casework than the congressman, and given that constituents in small states have equal or even better access to their senator than their congressman, his informational advantage was magnified. Although many individuals in my focus groups had contacted both Tester and Rehberg about a concern, it would not surprise me if more constituents had personal interaction with Tester and Baucus than Rehberg given the resource disparity and the fact that constituents report more contact with senators than House members in small states.

Second, Tester could simply do more legislatively than Rehberg, and Rehberg was unable to draw attention to the work he had done in the House as an appropriator. It is virtually impossible for House members to draw attention to their legislative accomplishments until they become quite senior and obtain a committee chairmanship. Even affecting the shape of legislation is difficult because as the House has become more polarized, less legislation reaches the floor, and the legislation that does is typically considered under a closed rule restricting amendments considerably. Senators, however, can make their mark in a chamber with fewer restrictions on legislative entrepreneurship. In Chapter 5, I note Tester's success as a freshman in amending legislation. Constituents could recall Tester's work for veterans and even his Forest Jobs and Recreation Act—a bill which Tester had drafted but that hadn't even received a committee vote at that point. It was no surprise that no one in the focus groups or in Moore's polls mentioned Rehberg's extensive work bringing appropriations dollars back to the state given his deemphasizing these accomplishments with the concurrent rise of the Tea Party. As a result, voters could more clearly discern that Tester was doing something for them, while Rehberg seemed comparatively ineffective.

Third, voters liked Tester more than Rehberg personally, and they perceived Tester as ideologically moderate. In both polls and focus groups, almost nothing came to light placing Tester in a negative light personally. The top mentions about Rehberg in Moore's polls when asked, however, concerned his personal wealth and his lawsuit against the City of Billings. After nearly a year of advertising (March 2011 through January 2012) in which pro-Rehberg allies aired 4,200 spots to the 4,400 television ads sponsored by pro-Tester groups, respondents didn't seem to like Tester less or Rehberg more. Figure 7.1 displays the spots aired by month between March 2011 and through April 2012 by whether the sponsor was opposing Tester or Rehberg. Figure 7.2 shows the same data but indicates which side had the advantage in the number of spots aired.[85]

## FIGURE 7.1
*The Early Advertising Wars, March 2011 to April 2012*

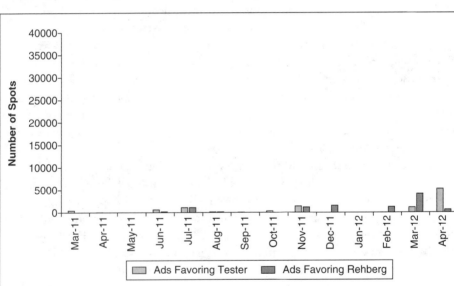

*Source*: Advertising spot data calculated by author from advertising contracts and invoices available in the public political files of Montana's television stations per Federal Communications Commission regulations. Spots aired by outside groups that either take a position for the candidate, an issue favoring the candidate, or attacking the candidate's opponent are coded as favoring a candidate. Candidate ads are coded as favoring the candidate sponsoring them. Light gray indicates ads favoring Tester, darker gray ads favoring Rehberg.

**FIGURE 7.2**

*Advertising Advantage in Spots, March 2011 to April 2012*

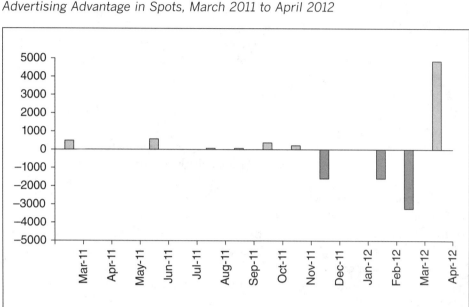

*Source*: Advertising advantage calculated as the total number of spots aired by Tester and his allies. Darker gray and negative values indicate a Rehberg advantage, while positive, lighter gray values indicate a Tester advantage. Advertising spot data calculated by author from advertising contracts and invoices available in the public political files of Montana's television stations per Federal Communications Commission regulations.

Did the ads work? In their book about the 2012 presidential campaign, Lynn Vavreck and John Sides note that one of the reasons why the outcome between Mitt Romney and Barack Obama seemed pre-ordained was not because the efforts of the campaigns did not matter but because they largely cancelled each other out over the long haul.[86] They characterized the advertising campaign between the two sides as a tug of war that ended in a draw. As neither side gained an informational advantage, fundamental factors favoring the president including positive economic growth put Obama over the edge in a close election. Through 2011 and early 2012, outside spending in the Montana Senate race was largely even between the two sides. Through March 2011 and January 2012, 51 percent of all advertising spots favored Jon Tester, and 49 percent favored Congressman Rehberg. Nearly all, excepting some spots by AARP and the Electronic Banking Coalition, were negative.

In February and March, this changed. Eighty-two percent of the spots aired by outside groups blasted Senator Tester and created an informational advantage for Rehberg. It would not last long. The final ace in Tester's hole was his fundraising advantage: Through the close of the first quarter of 2012, Tester had $4.3 million cash on hand compared to Rehberg's $2.7 million.[87] Tester could quickly turn this financial advantage into an informational advantage. Most importantly, he could control his message. If the *Citizens United* era had moved the advertising calendar for outside groups, it did the same for the candidates' own advertising efforts.

The Tester campaign decided to go up with advertising in late March—incredibly early in the pre-*Citizens United* era, but seemingly par for the course compared to other competitive Senate campaigns that year and in 2010.[88] In April, the Tester campaign aired a whopping 4,700 spots—more than half the number of ads that had been aired in the campaign's first twelve months. In combination with interest group spending, Tester and his allies aired 88 percent of the spots in April of 2012, creating by far the largest information advantage to date on the airwaves for either candidate.

Tester's ads capitalized on his personal strengths and the perception among voters that he was a moderate despite efforts to characterize him otherwise. "Combine" featured Tester on his tractor in his wheat field, talking to the camera about cutting government waste, the silly partisanship paralyzing Washington, and the fact that Montanans don't care about which party gets the credit for accomplishments—just that something gets done.[89] Another ad reminded Montanans of all the work Tester had done fighting for veterans. Perhaps the best of the lot is "Montana Beef," which shows Jon Tester packing up a suitcase of Montana beef, carrying it to Washington, and sitting down to eat a burger with his wife Sharla who had cooked it up on their electric range in their Washington townhouse.[90] In all three cases, the ads reminded Montanans that they liked Tester, he was "one of us," and he was just a regular guy who happened to be their senator. He was also depicted as nonpartisan and working to help out a sizeable group of the Montanans; veterans, whom everyone believes deserve attention and help as America's protectors. Political scientists call these types of ads "valence advertisements" because they hit on issues that are nearly universal in their support. If you love Montana, which all Montanans do, how can you not love Mr. Montana, Jon Tester?

Did the information advantage created by the Tester campaign's early advertisements generate any effect? The Rehberg campaign conducted a poll in the last two days of April 2012.[91] Although the job approval ratings for Rehberg and Tester hardly budged, two things leapt out. First, the number of respondents indicating they had heard or read anything about Jon Tester jumped from 58 percent in the February poll to 71 percent. And, perhaps more importantly, for the only time in all of Moore's polls, Jon Tester had developed a lead just barely outside the margin of error: 44 to 38 percent. Voters were learning a lot about Jon Tester, less about Rehberg, and it seemed to be translating into additional support. The question for the Rehberg campaign was what to do about it.

## CONCLUSION

Campaigns are fundamentally about an information environment: incumbents win reelection often because voters know more about them than their challengers. "You can't beat somebody with nobody," goes the old political saying, and half the battle facing a challenger is simply becoming known and then becoming an acceptable alternative to the incumbent. In the 2012 Montana Senate race, the challenger was well-known and recognized by Montanans. By his service in the House over the past decade, Congressman Rehberg had overcome the first hurdle facing a challenger. The remaining question for Rehberg was whether he could become an acceptable replacement for the incumbent, Jon Tester. He believed yes: If Montanans voted on partisanship and issues, they would turn Tester out. Rehberg was conservative, Tester was not; Rehberg opposed the administration on all key initiatives, Tester had not. Rehberg voted against the administration relatively consistently; Tester voted with Obama "95 percent" of the time. The Rehberg campaign believed that this singular fact would minimize Republican and Independent defections to Senator Tester, making Rehberg Montana's next senator.

The fundamental problem Rehberg faced, however, was that Montanans had concerns about Rehberg personally while simultaneously had difficulty associating him with any concrete accomplishments during his decade of service in the House. The Rehberg campaign compounded the problem by deemphasizing the congressman's work as an appropriator. Alternatively, Tester was associated in the minds of Montanans not only with some key legislative accomplishments, in particular his work with veterans, but they also felt warmly toward him and his association with the land as an active farmer. The Tester campaign then used its substantial financial resources to generate a critical information advantage early in the campaign that had the potential to pull him out of his statistical tie with Rehberg. Whether the effects of the early advertising advantage would linger remained to be seen and will be examined next.

# NOTES

1. FiveThirtyEight, http://en.wikipedia.org/wiki/FiveThirtyEight.

2. Nate Silver, "Five Thirty Eight's 2012 Forecast," *The New York Times,* November 6, 2012, http://fivethirtyeight.blogs.nytimes.com/fivethirtyeights-2012-forecast/.

3. Ibid., p.69.

4. Nate Silver, *The Signal and the Noise: Why so Many Predictions Fail—But Some Don't.* (New York, NY: The Penguin Press, 2012).

5. Elliot, interview.

6. E. Iverson, interview.

7. This is known as Fenno's Paradox. John R. Hibbing, "Appreciating Congress," in Joseph Cooper, ed. *Congress and the Decline of Public Trust,* (Boulder, CO: Westview Press, 1999).

8. Campbell et al., *The American Voter.*

9. Campbell et al., *The American Voter;* William H. Flanigan and Nancy H. Zingale, *Political Behavior of the American Electorate,* 9th ed. (Washington, DC: CQ Press, 1998); Sidney Verba and Norman H. Nie, *Participation in America: Political Democracy and Social Equality,* (Chicago, IL: University of Chicago Press, 1987).

10. John Sides and Lynn Vavreck, *The Gamble: Choice and Chance in the 2012 Presidential Election.* (Princeton, NJ: Princeton University Press, 2013), 23, and 180–187; Gary Jacobson, *A Divider, not a Uniter: George W. Bush and the American People.* (New York, NY: Pearson Longman, 2006).

11. Campbell et al., *The American Voter;* Verba and Nie, *Participation in America;* Bruce E. Keith, David B. Magleby, Candice J. Nelson, Elizabeth A. Orr, Mark C. Westlye, and Raymond Wolfinger, *The Myth of the Independent Voter.* (Berkeley: University of California Press, 1992).

12. Gary W. Cox and Mathew D. McCubbins, *Legislative Leviathan: Party Government in the House.* (Berkeley: University of California Press, 1993); Parker, *The Power of Money in Congressional Campaigns.*

13. Wasserman, "Introducing the 2014 Cook Political Report Partisan Voter Index." See also Chapter 1.

14. Theriault, *Party Polarization in Congress;* David C.W. Parker, "The Tangled Roots of Polarization," *Symposium Magazine,* November 2013, http://www.symposium-magazine.com/the-tangled-roots-of-polarization. Recent work suggests residential sorting is less important than previously thought as an explanation for polarization. See Clayton Nall and Jonathan Mummolo, "Why Partisans Don't Sort: How Neighborhood Quality Concerns Limit Americans' Pursuit of Like-Minded Neighbors." Working Paper, November 5, 2013 draft, http://www.nallresearch.com/partisanship-and-residential-preference.html.

15. Gary C. Jacobson, *The Politics of Congressional Elections,* 8th ed. (Boston, MA: Pearson, 2013), 166–176; Flanigan and Zingale, *Political Behavior of the American Electorate;* John R. Petrocik and Scott W. Desposato, "Incumbency and Short-Term Influences on Voters," *Political Research Quarterly* 57, no. 3 (2004), 363–373.

16. Jacobson, *The Politics of Congressional Elections*, 167–8; James E. Campbell, "The Revised Theory of Surge and Decline," *American Journal of Political Science* 31, no. 4 (1987), 965–979.

17. Wasserman, "Introducing the 2014 Cook Political Report Partisan Voter Index."

18. Alan I. Abramowitz and Jeffrey A. Segal, *Senate Elections*. (Ann Arbor: University of Michigan Press, 1992), 109–115.

19. Jacobson, *The Politics of Congressional Elections*, 130–137.

20. "United States Congress," *Ballotpedia*, http://ballotpedia.org/United_States_Congress_elections,_2012.

21. Jacobson, *The Politics of Congressional Elections*, 48, table 3–4.

22. Analysis of all incumbent senators seeking reelection from 1946 through 2008. Analysis available from author upon request.

23. Lee and Oppenheimer, *Sizing Up the Senate*, 53. See Table 3.1.

24. Jacobson, *The Politics of Congressional Elections*, 129–130. The data for senators is from 1978 through 2010 and from 1958 through 2010 for House members.

25. Eric Ostermeier, "Iceberg: Split-Ticket Voting Leaves GOPers Cold in Two Northern US Senate Races," *Smart Politics Blog*, November 21, 2012, http://blog.lib.umn.edu/cspg/smartpolitics/2012/11/iceberg_split-ticket_voting_le.php.

26. Lee and Oppenheimer, *Sizing Up the Senate*, 56.

27. Focus Group, June 28, 2012.

28. Poll of Montana Voters conducted by Moore Information in April 2011 for Montanans for Rehberg. The poll consisted of 450 registered voters with a margin of error of 4.6 percent.

29. Poll of Montana Voters conducted by Moore Information February 12–14, 2012 for Montanans for Rehberg. The poll consisted of 500 registered voters with a margin of error of 4.4 percent.

30. Press release, "Rehberg, Tester close in early 2012 Montana Senate," Public Policy Polling, November 16, 2010; Press release, "Rehberg maintains slim lead over Tester in Big Sky Country," Public Policy Polling, June 21, 2011; Press release, "Rehberg still leads Tester by two," Public Policy Polling, December 1, 2011, http://publicpolicypolling.com.

31. From Moore Information polls in April 2011 and February 2012.

32. Moore Information poll, April 2011.

33. Press Release, "Rehberg, Tester close in early 2012 Montana Senate."

34. Ibid.

35. Moore Information Poll, April 2011.

36. "Rehberg, Tester close in early 2012 Montana Senate"; "Rehberg maintains slim lead over Tester in Big Sky Country."

37. The American National Election Study, http://www.electionstudies.org/studypages/cdf/cdf.htm.

38. Parker and Goodman, "Making a Good Impression"; Parker and Goodman, "Our State's Never had Better Friends." Analysis is based upon the 1996, 1998, and 2000 ANES for House members and the 1988, 1990, and 1992 Senate Election Studies.

39. Jacobson, *The Politics of Congressional Elections*, 152.

40. Ibid.

41. Moore Information Poll, February 12–14, 2012.

42. Ibid., 6.

43. Tristan Scott, "Rehberg promises to stand watch over Jesus statue," *Missoulian,* July 16, 2012.

44. Maxfield, interview.

45. Associated Press, "Rehberg Ranch Estates sues city of Billings," *Billings Gazette,* July 4, 2010. He and his wife Jan dropped the lawsuit in November of 2011. Associated Press, "Rehberg to Drop Fire Lawsuit," *Billings Gazette,* November 10, 2011.

46. Burns staffer.

47. Ibid.

48. Vince Devlin and Michael Jamison, "Rehberg undergoes surgery following serious Boating Accident on Flathead Lake," *Missoulian,* August 28, 2009.

49. Associated Press, "Frost Leaving Rehberg's Staff," *Billings Gazette,* March 1, 2010.

50. Tristan Scott, "Judge Rejects Plea Deal in Greg Barkus Boat Crash Case," *Missoulian,* January 20, 2011.

51. Moore Information Poll, February 12–14, 2012.

52. For those who are interested, the questions are available at the online appendix to the book.

53. Focus Group conducted by author on July 25, 2012 in Bozeman, Montana.

54. Ibid.

55. Ibid.

56. Focus Group conducted by author on August 21, 2012 in Bozeman, Montana.

57. Ibid.

58. Ibid.

59. Ibid.

60. Ibid.

61. Focus Group, July 25, 2012.

62. Ibid.

63. Focus group, June 28, 2012.

64. Focus Group, August 21, 2012.

65. Focus Group, July 25, 2012.

66. Focus Group August, 21, 2012.

67. Focus Group, July 25, 2012.

68. Focus Group, June 28, 2012.

69. Focus Group, August 21, 2012.

70. Focus Group, August 21, 2012.

71. Ibid.

72. Ibid.

73. Focus Group July 25, 2013.

74. Focus Group, June 28, 2012.

75. Ibid.

76. Moore Information poll, February 12–14, 2012.

77. Moore Information polls, April 2011 and February 12–14, 2012.

78. Spot data based on advertising contracts and invoices obtained by author from Montana's television stations. See Chapter 6, Footnote 54. The ad was titled "Watch," http://www.youtube.com/watch?v=q3jHDElOQqI.

79. "Real Effects," http://usatoday30.usatoday.com/news/politics/political-ad-tracker/video/786809/u-s-chamber-of-commerce-is-jon-tester-listening.

80. Mike Dennison, "U.S. Senate Race: How Often do Rehberg, Tester Vote with the President?" *The Missoulian*, March 4, 2012.

81. Press release, "Tester to Labor Dept.: Back off Proposal to Restrict Family Farms," December 21, 2011, http://www.tester.senate.gov/?p=press_release&id=1702; Press Release, "Rehberg Questions Labor Secretary Solis on Youth Ag Rule," March 28, 2012. Available from author.

82. See Jon R. Bond, Richard Fleisher, and Michael Northrup, "Public Opinion and Presidential Support," *Annals of the American Academy of Political and Social Science,* (1992) 499: 47.

83. Baucus was the 5th most conservative. In the 110th Congress, Tester and Baucus were the 13th and 4th most conservative Democrats. Analysis available from author. Also see http://bigskypolitics.blogspot.com/2012/02/montana-senate-race-who-are-these-guys.html. For an historical perspective of the Montana congressional delegation ideologically, see http://bigskypolitics.blogspot.com/2013/07/montana-congressional-delegation.html.

84. I simply searched the *Billings Gazette* electronically for all articles mentioning either Rehberg, Baucus, or Tester. Articles were then discarded that did not deal with the congressman or Montana's two senators. In particular, a number of articles mentioning Rehberg Way in Billings were discarded.

85. Data collected from advertising contracts and invoices obtained by author from Montana's television stations. See Chapter 6, Footnote 54 for further detail.

86. Sides and Vavrek, *The Gamble*.

87. Cash on hand numbers obtained from quarterly reports filed to the Federal Election Commission by the candidates, http://fec.gov/finance/disclosure/candcmte_info.shtml.

88. See Chapter 6, 125–126.

89. "Combine," http://www.youtube.com/watch?v=e5VKAzKLnCg.

90. "Montana Beef—Montana Proud," http://www.youtube.com/watch?v=J1pteKuWCEI.

91. Moore Information Poll conducted for Montanans for Rehberg, April 29–30, 2012. The poll included a sample of 400 registered voters with a margin of error of 4.9 percent.

# The Message Matters: The Politics of Personality and Issues

I f election outcomes are so easily predicted, then what effect—if any—do campaigns have? Political scientists Andrew Gelman and Gary King explain how campaigns affect election outcomes even though the end result is often known in advance with a high level of certainty. They claim that presidential campaigns are fairly balanced informational affairs.[1] With both candidates having similar financial resources, it is difficult for either to sustain an edge in advertising or organizational outreach for very long. Gelman and King argue that a campaign and its communication efforts "enlighten" the preferences of voters by informing them about the ideologies of the candidates and their issue positions. In highly balanced campaigns—the feature of most competitive elections—voters "improve their knowledge about the fundamental variables and have sufficient information on Election Day" to cast their ballots in line with preexisting preferences.[2] Voters may learn during campaigns, but campaigns don't so much as move voters to or away from a candidate. Rather they amplify existing inclinations. Gelman and King call their theoretical account the "enlightened preference" model.[3]

Campaigns matter but not as journalists believe. Game-changing moments emerge rarely to shift the impact of fundamental factors on an election outcome. When such moments do happen, they do so in unbalanced, low-information environments—which is not the type of information environment Montanans faced in 2012. The 2012 Montana Senate race qualifies as a high-information environment for voters. Both candidates had near-universal name recognition, and half of the voters polled in February of 2012 said they could recall reading or hearing something about either candidate from the news. Nearly 170,000 ads aired in Montana's six media markets during the race beginning in March 2011 through Election Day 2012.[4] Compare this to the number of ads aired by the presidential campaign and their allies in the top five states: "Ohio (219,414 ads), Florida (197,603), Virginia (163,740), Iowa (132, 911), [and] Colorado (114, 876)."[5] The environment in Montana was primed for voter learning. The sheer volume of ads also raised the probability of low-information-voter persuasion.

In this chapter, I demonstrate how the information environment on television and in the media shaped the outcome in the Tester-Rehberg race. As predicted by political scientists, voters learned more about the candidates as the campaign intensified through the summer and fall of 2012. The information environment on the airwaves—dominated by Rehberg and Republican allies in the closing days of the race—did not produce the expected result, however. Despite repeated efforts by the Rehberg campaign and his allies to enlighten Montanans about the fundamentals with a well-orchestrated negative and contrast campaign, Tester managed to eke out a win. Tester's success lay in several important developments: his campaign's decision to advertise early, Rehberg's response, the substance of Tester and his allies' negative attacks, and an edge established by Tester over Rehberg in newspaper coverage of the race. The messages each campaign adopted throughout the course of the summer and fall mattered as much—if not more so—than the informational advantage enjoyed by Rehberg and his allies in the closing days of the campaign.

I focus on television advertisements, the decisions candidates made concerning the messages aired, and the private polls conducted by the Rehberg campaign as well as those made publicly available during the campaign. Although a considerable amount of attention has been given in recent years to online media and to the sophisticated get-out-the-vote efforts of campaigns, television still represents the single largest means by which Senate and presidential campaigns communicate with voters.[6] The messages used in these advertisements reflect those emphasized by the campaigns in their press releases and online communications; indeed, campaigns often post their ads on Facebook and Twitter to give them additional exposure. The emphasis on television advertising does not mean voter mobilization using sophisticated statistical techniques, experiments, personal contacts, and mail did not matter. There is some evidence that they did, and that they helped the Democrats. But the conclusions I draw on new media rest mostly on personal impressions gleaned from a few observations and postelection interviews. I do discuss the importance and possible effects of these efforts briefly in this chapter and consider the likely importance of voter targeting and mobilization efforts in the next chapter. Much more can be learned about why and how Senator Tester defied theory-based expectations by focusing on how the air wars affected the impressions of Montanans. I again demonstrate how Senator Tester's considerable advantages as an incumbent senator facing an incumbent House member provided an additional bonus in earned media. I close with a final visit with the candidates on the campaign trail which further illustrates the advantages and disadvantages each candidate faced in the closing days of the campaign.

## DO CAMPAIGNS MATTER? WHAT POLITICAL SCIENCE SAYS

Political science research suggests that the primary effects of campaigns are not so much in persuasion but in learning, reminding, and mobilizing.[7] According to Congress scholar Gary Jacobson, roughly half of a congressional campaign's budget is spent on mass market advertising such as television, radio, and online advertisements.[8] This is geared to make voters aware of fundamental factors: the partisan leanings of the candidates, the state of the economy, the candidate's positions on issues, and personal biographies. As voters learn, they should become steadfast in their initial leanings and justify their increasing support of the candidate reflecting their preexisting inclinations with information provided by the campaign's media efforts. Once voters have learned and been reminded of their commitments, campaigns then switch their efforts to mobilizing them to vote.

This is not to say that persuasion doesn't happen in campaigns; rather persuasion is difficult to accomplish. As has long been known by political scientists, campaign advertisements have limited effects on moving voters to the candidate of a different party because voters already have long-standing partisan commitments.[9] Strong partisans, who tend to be the most engaged and knowledgeable about politics, should be the least likely to be influenced by campaign advertisements aired by candidates of the other party because their own pre-existing beliefs make it less likely they will receive the information.[10] Political psychologists call this cognitive dissonance: When faced with a message conflicting with prior values, people discard it in favor of information reinforcing their existing beliefs.[11] The end result is that many voters simply come home—as Lazarsfeld, Berlson, and Gaudet found in one of the foundational studies of elections in the 1940s. Most campaign advertisements, if they have an effect, remind and do not persuade.[12]

If persuasion is difficult, under what conditions is it most likely to occur and among whom? Voters most susceptible to the persuasive effects of campaigns are those lacking strong partisan commitments who know less about politics: either weakly attached partisans or independent voters.[13] Campaigns with intense information environments, such as presidential elections in battleground states or competitive Senate elections like the 2012 race in Montana, are more likely to reach these persuadable voters.[14] When that information environment is unbalanced, providing one campaign with a clear advantage in campaign communications, persuasive efforts are even more likely to be successful.[15] Finally, recent research also suggests that messages aired late in the campaign are most likely to persuade because the effect of advertising is relatively short-lived and decays quickly.[16] Late advertising, therefore, is better than early advertising, and informational advantages in the final months of a campaign should have greater consequences than those aired earlier in the campaign.[17]

Finally, there is the question of advertising tone. Americans make known, loudly and often, their disgust with the ubiquity of campaign ads during election season. Their harshest language is reserved for negative advertisements that dominate campaign discourse.[18] Political observers and campaign consultants believe that negative ads simply work better than positive ads. Political science research is mixed. Some research shows that negative advertisements depress voter turnout; other research says the opposite.[19] Still more findings indicate that negative ads lower support for the candidate attacked.[20] And other studies find that negative advertisements can depress support for the candidate sponsoring the attack.[21] Perhaps the most complete study of the effects of campaign advertisements found that while negative ads stimulate more knowledge and are more memorable, overall, they are no more effective than positive advertisements.[22] The state of the research on advertising tone and learning suggests, at best, that advertisements aid in voter learning regardless of tone and best persuade low-information voters in the final days of a campaign when one side dominates the airwaves.

## REHBERG'S DECISION

By pure happenstance, I travelled with Congressman Rehberg in early April 2012 shortly after Senator Tester decided to launch his own television advertising effort. Congressman Rehberg and I discussed the merits of Tester's decision and how it would affect his own strategy moving forward. He had two concerns about Tester's early spending. He admitted that Tester had more cash available which meant that Tester could sustain a heavier and longer advertising effort. If Rehberg went up too early, he might not be able to sustain his advertising at an optimal level in the fall. As he often did, Rehberg used an example from a recent race: the 2004 Thune-Daschle race in South Dakota. Like Montana, South Dakota has one representative for the entire state. Rehberg noted that "Thune . . . saved all of his money 'til the end, didn't go up until August [of 2004]. And then when he went up, he stayed up and he stayed up heavy. But he resisted jumping in early. In that way you can control your message."[23] Like much of the conventional campaign wisdom and political science research, Rehberg believed that late and heavy advertising was critical to communicating with voters. Just as important, Rehberg wanted message control. The decision to hold out for as long as possible had "everything to do with having my own money for my own message and not having to rely . . . on third parties hopefully having the right message," he finished before we hopped in the car to make our next appointment.[24]

As Team Tester was dominating the airwaves with feel good spots about the senator, Republican-allied groups disappeared from television. In March, two Republican-allied organizations—the nonprofit 501(c)4 60 Plus Association and the United States Chamber of Commerce organized under the tax code as a nonprofit business association (a 501(c)6)—had dominated Montana television with a series of attacks on Senator Tester. The ads focused on Obamacare, with the Chamber's "Jon Tester's Way—The Wrong Way" emphasizing tax increases associated with the healthcare law. The 60 Plus Association ad, narrated by aging pop singer Pat Boone, stressed how the Affordable Care Act would cut Medicare by $500 million and create a panel of "unelected bureaucrats" that would "ration" healthcare.[25] But by April, these spots had been pulled. Why? It is unclear.

Tester and his allies had the airwaves to themselves. Another Democratic group, Citizens for Strength and Security (CSS), attacked Rehberg's personal shortcomings. The ad called Rehberg one of the wealthiest members of Congress and blasted him for accepting pay raises and wasting taxpayer dollars for the rental of an SUV. The Tester campaign had been publically circulating information on Rehberg's pay raises since December. And later, they circulated information claiming Rehberg broke a promise he made never to accept pay raises during this race for the Senate against Max Baucus in 1996.[26] This information then became the basis for the CSS spots. (Rehberg responded that the SUV was for his eastern Montana field representative JT Korkow to use in his travels across the region in lieu of paying for an additional office space.[27] And while Rehberg did say he would refuse any pay raises more than 15 years ago, annual cost of living adjustments to congressional pay are automatic per the 1989 amendments to the Ethics in Government Act.[28] These automatic increases are wrapped into "must-pass" appropriations legislation which fund large parts of government. Nevertheless, attacking a member's vote in this manner works because it plays into the negative impressions and stereotypes the public has of politicians generally and of Congress the institution. In fact, the public generally thinks that members of Congress are overpaid while at the same time grossly underestimating their actual pay.[29])

Some voters already had a sense of Rehberg's personal wealth, and others believed he had some personal failings as illustrated by their recall of the incident on Flathead Lake and the Billings lawsuit. These advertisements hoped to tap into those nascent negative impressions and the broader narrative the Tester campaign had established about Rehberg from the beginning.[30] As Christie Roberts, Tester's research director put it, "we pushed really hard to just always have the conversation be about what Rehberg had been doing in Congress that wasn't good for Montana."[31] Out of the 236 official press releases I received from Montanans for Tester, 69—or 29 percent—used the word *irresponsible* in reference to Congressman Rehberg or Republicans.[32]

After six weeks of Tester ads and attacks on Rehberg's vote for pay increases, did voter impressions of the two candidates shift meaningfully? Rehberg's campaign manager Erik Iverson admitted that the pay raise and SUV ads caused some concern at the time. I asked him after the campaign where Rehberg and

Tester stood in terms of favorability ratings with Montanans throughout the campaign. He said that they were fairly "similar" at the get-go, but "when the attack ads started on whatever it was, March 8th, it began to take its toll right out of the gate on Denny and that's when the Baucus and union-funded CSS ads started up about the pay raise and the car lease and all that stuff. You know, you put that kind of money behind a message in March with nothing else up there except for Tester's positive stuff, it can take a toll, and it did on Denny."[33] Still, looking at his own internal polls, there was no appreciable shift in Rehberg's favorability ratings by the end of April 2012. And voters did not suddenly think more favorably of Tester even with the advertising advantage his campaign had throughout April. What did change, however, was the information voters reported hearing, seeing, or reading about the two candidates. As noted at the close of Chapter 7, Tester had developed a clear advantage in that voters saw and heard more about him than Rehberg.[34]

Most important, among respondents who had encountered information about the candidates, 39 percent were more likely to vote for Tester as a result of that information with 35 percent less likely (the balance indicating they didn't know). Most worrisome for the Rehberg campaign was that in February, 40 percent indicated the information they had encountered would make them more likely to vote for the congressman. In April, only 31 percent said that, and 42 percent said it made them *less likely* to vote for him. Tester had another information advantage.

An analysis of exactly what voters had heard, seen, or read about the two candidates uncovers other troubling signs for Rehberg. Using the same approach as Chapter 7, I classified comments made by voters about the candidates as positive, neutral, or negative. Thirty-nine percent made positive comments about Tester in terms of what they recalled, 24 percent negative, with the balance neutral. Rehberg was upside down: 24 percent of what voters recalled was negative and only 16 percent positive. And while comments about Tester were a mix of issues and personal characteristics, recollections about Rehberg were mostly personal and negative: 43 percent of comments concerned Rehberg personally, and 63 percent of those comments were negative. Fully five percent of respondents either mentioned Rehberg's pay raises or the SUV.

The allegations of Rehberg's pay, combined with Tester's large early advertising buy, meant the Rehberg campaign had to make two decisions: First, should they try to close the information gap on television by going up earlier than they would have liked with their own ads? Second, if they did decide to air ads, what should the message be?

The Rehberg campaign did put up their own ads, airing nearly 2,000 spots that May in every media market save Glendive.[35] Despite this initial investment,

Tester and his allies maintained a clear advantage in advertising spots. All told, Tester and Democratic-groups aired almost 2,500 more spots than Rehberg and his supporters. Put into context, 88 percent of all the spots aired in April were sponsored by Tester and his allies. In May, that percentage fell to 64 percent.

Most repeat campaigns choose to reestablish their candidate's reputation among voters with a series of positive spots in the early going. These ads remind voters of why they supported the candidate in the past, what the candidate has done for them since, and work on "enlightening preferences." This was the path chosen by Tester. The Rehberg campaign, however, chose otherwise. The first spot they aired, "Honest," is what some political scientists call a contrast ad. It began with an attack on Tester and finished by contrasting with Rehberg's record. The clip starts with grainy footage of Tester in 2006 saying Montana needs "honest leadership," and with a female narrator ticking off all the ways Tester had provided anything but. She intones that Tester voted for higher taxes, raised his own pay, provided bonuses for Wall Street, and supported President Obama 95 percent of the time. Rehberg, conversely, cut taxes, opposed the bailouts of Wall Street and the auto industry, and voted against pay raises.[36] The advertisement focused largely on the narrative already established by outside Republican groups but explicitly linked Rehberg to issue positions many Montanans favored.

Why did Rehberg go with a contrast ad instead of focusing on his own biography in a series of positive spots? Erik Iverson stated that there was no other choice:

The race was tied, we were a point or two up when they launched 3,000 gross ratings points of SUV leases and pay raises. We went from plus two to minus four, minus five in the span of about four-and-a-half weeks. And we knew we were getting outspent. Our outside groups were nowhere to be found, Tester is sitting on a pile of cash, and our belief at that point was we need to rebut some of this stuff, we need to show a contrast and try to stabilize this thing because we are hemorrhaging and what some of our guys who have a lot of experience running races and were advisors and consultants and stuff were saying [was] this is right out of the DSCC playbook. 'They are going to spend a shit ton of money upfront, they are going to get you down early, and they are going to spend the rest of the campaign shooting arrows at you downhill.'[37]

Rehberg echoed Iverson's sentiments, suggesting that he would have liked other groups to "carry a coordinated negative message against [Tester] . . . [so] I would have had the opportunity to build up my foundation. I was not able to do that because you have to make a decision [based upon the resources at your command]. When they're attacking you, you gotta attack back."[38] Although the Rehberg campaign did air some spots over the summer putting a softer face on Rehberg, they were not sustained for long. Instead, most of the ads aired by the campaign were contrast or negative pieces on Tester and his record. Again, Erik Iverson: "We felt like Denny was just getting so badly throttled on issues . . . we felt like we could go a few weeks trying to do some [positive, personal] stuff, but then we would have to pivot and defend because the numbers would start to bleed on us."[39]

Rehberg's decision to forgo the traditional path of reestablishing himself for a sustained assault on Tester would have important implications later. If there was a moment during the campaign that may have been a game changer, it was a decision made at campaign headquarters based upon solid, empirical data—and not a gaffe made publicly on the campaign trail or during a debate. As the informational environment evolved, it became clearer that although this decision may not have lost the election for Rehberg, it did make winning harder.

## INFORMATION ADVANTAGES AND VOTER LEARNING: HOW PERSONALITY TRUMPED ISSUES AND RESOURCES

By the end of May, more than 30,000 ads had been shown on Montana's airwaves, most of them sponsored by various 501(c)4, c(5), and c(6) organizations operating under the newly permissive guidelines established in the post-*Citizens United* world of campaigning. Sixteen different groups had paid for advertisements, ranging from the conservative 60 Plus Association fighting against the new healthcare law to the liberal Patriot Majority, a group self-professed as advancing "economic solutions" and focusing on "nonpartisan empowerment."[40] More than 60 percent of spots aired were sponsored by these groups through May of 2012, with the balance aired mostly by Tester. This only heralded the beginning of an aggressive and sustained enrichment of the informational environment that would build throughout the summer and peak in November. Figure 8.1 depicts the number of advertising spots aired in Montana by month beginning in March 2011. Through May 2012, the 30,000-plus ads aired only represented 18 percent of the total number of spots that would be aired during the entire campaign. Montanans would be treated to nearly 170,000 airings of campaign ads during the campaign, which ramped up after May. From May to June, the number of spots increased by seven percent and then shot upward. From June to July, spots aired increased by 79 percent, the following month, 22 percent, and then between August and September, by 98 percent. Clearly, the candidates, parties, and interest groups believed that later advertising was most effective.

## FIGURE 8.1

*Television Advertising Spots in the 2012 Montana Senate Race, March 2011 to November 2012*

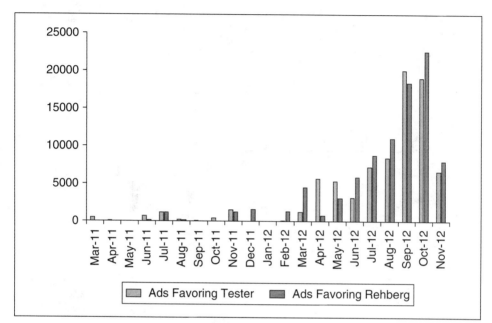

*Source*: Advertising spot data calculated by author from advertising contracts and invoices available in the public political files of Montana's television stations per Federal Communications Commission regulations. Spots aired by outside groups that either take a position for the candidate, an issue favoring the candidate, or attacking the candidate's opponent are coded as favoring a candidate. Candidate ads are coded as favoring the candidate sponsoring them. Light gray indicates ads favoring Tester, darker gray ads favoring Rehberg.

Figure 8.2 shows the advantage each side enjoyed in the number of spots and when. The Democratic advantage built by Tester's advertising in the spring quickly evaporated as Rehberg and his Republican allies joined the race in earnest. From June through the first week of November, Tester and groups supporting his campaign enjoyed an edge in the number of advertisements aired only in September.[41] In June, 65 percent of spots aired supported Rehberg's candidacy. Although Republicans never enjoyed such a considerable advantage again in the ensuing months, no less than 54 percent of all spots were sponsored by the Republican Party, Congressman Rehberg's campaign, or various 501(c) organizations supporting Rehberg (except September, of course, when Democrats sponsored 52 percent of all spots aired on television).

Reviewing television ads helps us understand the delicate balancing act between establishing partisan and individual candidate brands. Throughout the course of the campaign and in the weeks shortly after its conclusion, I collected

## FIGURE 8.2
*Spot Advantage on Television in the Montana Senate Race, March 2011 to November 2012*

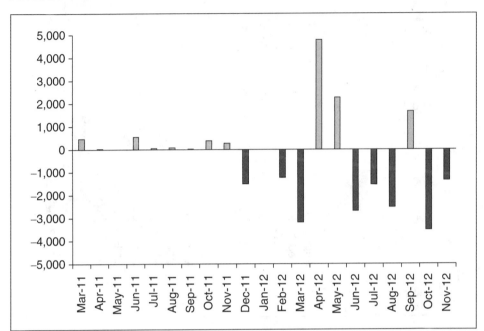

*Source*: Advertising advantage calculated in the number of spots aired by adding the number of spots sponsored by Tester and allied groups and subtracting spots aired by Rehberg and his allies. Negative, dark gray values indicate a Rehberg advantage, while positive, light gray values indicate a Tester advantage. Advertising spot data calculated by author from advertising contracts and invoices available in the public political files of Montana's television stations per Federal Communications Commission regulations.

ads aired on television by 23 interest groups, four party organizations, and the two candidates. I exclude from my review ads that aired exclusively on the Internet or spots from organizations that I could not verify as having actually aired on television.[42] Many ads were downloaded from YouTube, others were given to me by television station sales managers, and the campaigns gave me still more. I then coded these ads for the prominent campaign issues, themes, and frames articulated throughout the 20-month-long campaign. Finally, I classified the advertisements by tone using the same convention adopted by the Wisconsin and Wesleyan Media Projects.[43] Advertisements mentioning only the sponsored candidate or an issue are positive, those mentioning the opposing candidate exclusively are negative, and ads which mention both candidates are contrast ads. The results are presented in Table 8.1. To be clear, I code individual spots, not the number of airings of spots as I do not have access to all of these data.[44]

## TABLE 8.1

*Tone of Campaign Ads in Montana Senate Race by Ad Sponsor*

| Sponsor | Ad Tone | | | |
|---|---|---|---|---|
| | Positive | Negative | Contrast | Total |
| Tester | 48% | 38% | 14% | 100% |
| *Total Tester Ads* | *(10)* | *(8)* | *(3)* | *(21)* |
| Democratic IG | 10% | 90% | 0% | 100% |
| *Total Democrats IG Ads* | *(3)* | *(26)* | *(0)* | *(29)* |
| Democratic Party | 0% | 100% | 0% | 100% |
| *Total Democratic Party Ads* | *(0)* | *(11)* | *(0)* | *(11)* |
| All Pro-Tester | 21% | 74% | 5% | 100% |
| *Total Pro-Tester Ads* | *(13)* | *(45)* | *(3)* | *(61)* |
| Rehberg | 26% | 26% | 48% | 100% |
| *Total Rehberg Ads* | *(6)* | *(6)* | *(11)* | *(23)* |
| Republican IG | 0% | 100% | 0% | 100% |
| *Total Republican IG Ads* | *(0)* | *(28)* | *(0)* | *(28)* |
| Republican Party | 9% | 64% | 27% | 100% |
| *Total Republican Party Ads* | *(1)* | *(7)* | *(3)* | *(11)* |
| All Pro-Rehberg | 11% | 66% | 23% | 100% |
| *Total Pro-Rehberg Ads* | *(7)* | *(41)* | *(14)* | *(62)* |
| **All Ads** | 17% | 70% | 13% | 100% |
| **Total Ads** | **(20)** | **(86)** | **(17)** | **(123)** |

*Source*: Advertisements collected during the campaign by the author. Ads mentioning only favored candidate are positive; ads mentioning both candidates are contrast; and ads only mentioning the opposing candidate are negative. The total number of spots for each sponsor is in parentheses.

As is the case in most congressional campaigns, the individual spots aired during the Montana Senate race were overwhelmingly negative: 70 percent made exclusive reference to the candidate opposed by the sponsor. The remaining were almost evenly split between positive (17 percent) and contrast (13 percent) ads.[45] Even though most of the ads attacked Rehberg or Tester, there were important differences in tone between the candidates, parties, and outside groups. The Wisconsin and Wesleyan advertising projects have documented that party and interest group ads are almost exclusively negative.[46] The Montana Senate campaign was no different: 95 percent of interest group ads were negative. Party ads were slightly less negative, with only 82 percent exclusively attacking the opposing candidate and 14 percent contrasting the two candidates. Senator Tester's and Congressman Rehberg's ads, alternatively, had a more even tone distribution. Almost half of Tester's ads were positive spots focusing on the senator and his accomplishments, and only slightly more than a third were negative. The balance contrasted him with Rehberg. Nearly half of Rehberg's ads were contrast spots, with 26 percent of spots attacking Tester exclusively and 26 percent discussing the Congressman. Rehberg's contrast ads typically balanced attacking Tester on issues while either contrasting Rehberg's stance on the same issues or defending Rehberg from charges made in ads sponsored either by Tester or Democratic-allied groups.

It is unusual for candidates to identify their party in their television advertisements, particularly in a general election campaign.[47] Neither Tester nor Rehberg embraced their parties by name in campaign advertisements. Instead, both candidates aired advertisements stressing party independence: with Rehberg bucking President Bush to support the Children's Health Insurance Program (CHIP) and Tester fighting Obama on wolves and EPA dust regulations. Yet the issues discussed and how they were framed played into the issue reputations and strengths well-established by both parties. Political scientist John Petrocik claims that voters associate parties with particular issues that they "own."[48] Republicans tend to "own" fiscal prudence and lower taxes, while Democrats are seen as a party strong on protecting entitlements (Social Security, Medicare, and the like) and the environment. I show elsewhere how campaign advertisements by the parties and congressional candidates help reinforce these issue strengths with voters during the 2000 campaign cycle and demonstrate the advantages these party reputations can provide candidates, particularly when candidates attempt to co-opt the issue strength of the opposing party.[49]

More than half (56 percent) of all advertising spots in the Senate race mentioned in some combination spending, deficits, debt, or taxes. Another 24 percent discussed Social Security, Medicare, or Medicaid—core entitlement programs associated positively with the Democratic Party. Another 28 percent mentioned healthcare, with most of the discussion centering on the Affordable Care Act (or Obamacare). And President Obama appeared in the ads almost as much as the Senate candidates, with 65 percent of all pro-Rehberg ads referencing the President or displaying an image of him.[50]

What each side emphasized in terms of issues underscores what political scientists know about issue ownership and reinforces the fundamental strategies the candidates chose to pursue in the earliest days of the campaign. Both sides focused on issues associated with their party brands. Of all the spots aired by Rehberg, the Republican Party, and outside organizations supporting Rehberg, 63 percent discussed deficits, the debt, or spending (see Table 8.2). The Democratic

## TABLE 8.2
Issue Content of Ads in Montana Senate Race by Ad Sponsor

| Sponsor | Obama | Entitlement | Taxes/Spending/Deficit | Healthcare | 95% | Land | Personality Issues | Total Spots |
|---|---|---|---|---|---|---|---|---|
| **Tester** | **5%** | **31%** | **67%** | **14%** | **0%** | **43%** | **19%** | |
| *Total Tester Ads* | *(1)* | *(7)* | *(14)* | *(3)* | *(0)* | *(9)* | *(4)* | *(21)* |
| Democratic IG | 0% | 48% | 31% | 7% | 0% | 34% | 38% | |
| *Total Democrats IG Ads* | *(0)* | *(14)* | *(9)* | *(2)* | *(0)* | *(9)* | *(4)* | *(29)* |
| Democratic Party | 0% | 9% | 55% | 0% | 0% | 0% | 82% | |
| *Total Democratic Party Ads* | *(0)* | *(1)* | *(6)* | *(0)* | *(0)* | *(0)* | *(9)* | *(11)* |
| All Pro-Tester | 2% | 33% | 48% | 8% | 0% | 31% | 39% | |
| *Total Pro-Tester Ads* | *(1)* | *(20)* | *(30)* | *(5)* | *(0)* | *(19)* | *(24)* | *(61)* |
| **Rehberg** | **74%** | **13%** | **43%** | **30%** | **30%** | **43%** | **22%** | |
| *Total Rehberg Ads* | *(17)* | *(3)* | *(10)* | *(7)* | *(7)* | *(10)* | *(5)* | *(23)* |
| Republican IG | 57% | 18% | 79% | 71% | 14% | 7% | 18% | |
| *Total Republican IG Ads* | *(16)* | *(5)* | *(22)* | *(20)* | *(4)* | *(2)* | *(5)* | *(28)* |
| Republican Party | 64% | 9% | 64% | 18% | 45% | 55% | 36% | |
| *Total Republican Party Ads* | *(7)* | *(1)* | *(7)* | *(2)* | *(5)* | *(6)* | *(4)* | *(11)* |
| All Pro-Rehberg | 65% | 15% | 63% | 47% | 26% | 29% | 23% | |
| *Total Pro-Rehberg Ads* | *(40)* | *(9)* | *(39)* | *(29)* | *(16)* | *(18)* | *(14)* | *(62)* |
| **All Ads** | **33%** | **24%** | **56%** | **28%** | **13%** | **30%** | **31%** | |
| **Total Ads** | **(41)** | **(29)** | **(69)** | **(34)** | **(16)** | **(37)** | **(38)** | **(123)** |

*Source:* Advertisements collected during the campaign by the author. Ads mentioning only favored candidate are positive, ads mentioning both candidates are contrast, and ads only mentioning the opposing candidate are negative. The total number of spots for each sponsor is in parentheses.

campaign also stressed taxes and spending more than any one issue, with 48 percent of spots making mention of these issues—evidence of co-opting. How each side talked about taxes and spending, however, was very different. Republican ads blamed Jon Tester for supporting higher taxes, reckless spending, and America's crushing debt load. Democratic ads most frequently referred to Congressman Rehberg as voting for tax breaks for millionaires and lobbyists. Democrats stressed fairness in the tax code, Republicans emphasized freedom from government.

Entitlements were the second most frequent subject mentioned in Tester's ads, accounting for nearly 33 percent of aired spots. Like other congressional races and the presidential campaign, protecting these entitlements was key—the question was who was best positioned to do so? Democratic advertisements blasted Rehberg for remarks—often presented from the grainy video footage from a 1996 debate between Rehberg and Senator Baucus during Rehberg's first run for the office—made about the future of Social Security. Rehberg said during the debate, "When I talk about ending Social Security as we know it, I do mean that."[51] Democrats and the Tester campaign linked these remarks to previous votes Rehberg had made as a congressman which, they claimed, demonstrated support for privatization of the program. Rehberg's ads on entitlements pushed back, claiming that he had voted to protect Social Security and Medicare (for example, by voting *no* on the Ryan Budget in April 2011 and again in March of 2012).[52] Other ads, notably from the 60 Plus Association and U.S. Chamber of Commerce, made the oft-heard (and much disputed) claim that the Affordable Care Act represented a $500 to $700 million cut in the Medicare program.[53] All told, however, only 15 percent of advertisements aired by Republicans and supporting groups mentioned entitlement programs.

In both instances, the Democratic and Republican campaigns played to their issue strengths: Republicans on taxes and spending, Democrats on entitlement spending. Republicans hoped to attract Montanans weary of federal taxation, mandates, and deficit spending—particularly when many saw not only a balanced budget but a surplus in Helena. Democrats reached out to the considerable number of senior citizens relying upon Social Security and Medicare programs in a relatively old and poor state.

Just as interesting, however, is how both sides also attempted to co-opt the other parties' brand. Tester's ads, in particular, emphasized the need to cut government waste and his votes for a balanced budget amendment in Washington. Relatively speaking, however, it was Rehberg and the Republicans that spent considerable effort co-opting the Democratic issue of Medicare *with* their discussion of healthcare. Health, as an issue, was essentially ignored in Democratic ads, with only eight percent of spots discussing healthcare. Discussion of the Affordable Care Act—even its popular provisions—simply did not happen during the campaign in Tester's or his allies' ads. Healthcare, when it appeared at all, did so in the context of access to community health care centers, reproductive rights, or veterans' benefits.

Groups like Crossroads GPS, 60 Plus Association, Concerned Women of America, and the National Republican Senatorial Committee (NRSC)—along with Rehberg himself—made the healthcare law a centerpiece of their claims that Tester had betrayed Montanans and their trust. "Take the healthcare law. The people didn't want it. Yet Senator Jon Tester cast the deciding vote, forcing it on Montana," says one narrator gravely in an U.S. Chamber of Commerce ad.[54] Crucial were claims that Republicans and their plans provided the best defense of senior citizens and Medicare. Congressman Rehberg would vote to repeal Obamacare because it threatened Medicare with fiscal insolvency and cut hospital and insurer reimbursement rates.[55] In short, Rehberg and Republicans positioned themselves as champions of an entitlement program representing the big government they often derided—a program, it should be noted, signed into law by President Lyndon Baines Johnson, the architect of liberal social engineering! The attention paid to Medicare reflected a key problem faced by the Republicans nationally and in Montana: The public may generally trust them better on issues of taxation, but at the same time, fear efforts to change the social programs they have come to rely upon and expect. Given Montana's begrudging reliance upon many of these and other federally funded programs, Republicans needed to ensure that senior citizens in particular trusted them with their stewardship. Democrats knew this was a weakness, which is why their ads emphasized Rehberg's remarks about Social Security *ad nauseam*.

As Table 8.2 demonstrates, Republican advertisements during the campaign appeared to be more narrowly focused on taxes, spending, and healthcare. And, as Rehberg tried to do from his announcement speech forward, the ads relentlessly reminded Tester of his support of Barack Obama. More Republican ads mentioned President Obama (65 percent) than even mentioned government spending and taxes. The 95 percent number was mentioned explicitly in 26 percent of pro-Rehberg spots, most frequently in Rehberg's own campaign ads. Without a doubt, Republicans hoped that Montanans would view the Senate election as a mandate on President Obama and his policies.

Democratic ads, however, lacked as clear an issue focus. Why? Recall that Rehberg's campaign never spent time developing a personal narrative about him. Make no mistake, there were some advertisements that focused on Rehberg the person, but they were sporadic and did not represent the bulk of the Rehberg advertising effort. Republican outside groups stuck to issues with none focusing on Rehberg's job as a congressman or his family story. This was not the case on the Democratic side. Tester spent considerable effort reintroducing himself in the spring to voters, as already discussed. Even in the summer and fall, he continued to air some positive spots reminding voters of his "responsible" leadership, featuring him talking to the camera from throughout the state. More important, however, was the number of spots devoted to attacking Rehberg as an "irresponsible" person. Nearly 40 percent of all spots derisively called Rehberg a millionaire or a lobbyist who looked out after his own interests when he accepted congressional pay raises and sued the Billings fire department. Most of these spots were aired either by the Democratic Senatorial Campaign Committee (DSCC) or outside groups like the Majority PAC or the Association of Federal, State, County, and Municipal Employees (AFSCME). At first, the attacks stressed Rehberg's wealth, but as summer turned into fall, the ads got more aggressive. In September, the DSCC, Patriot Majority, and Majority PAC launched three separate attacks specifically on the firefighter lawsuit, only to be joined by a firefighter ad from Tester's campaign that had been prepared and in the can, waiting for the right moment. Images of fire and Rehberg's lawsuit blanketed the airwaves during the last six weeks of the campaign.

The Rehberg campaign and outside groups did try to make Tester seem personally undesirable, but their attacks did not have the sharp edge of the Democratic-led efforts against Rehberg. They generally accused Tester of false attacks and suggested he had gone Washington with his support of the President and his agenda. Perhaps the harshest allegations levied were made by American Crossroads suggesting that Senator Tester's support for legislation delaying a cap on swipe fees charged by banks brought millions in campaign donations from Wall Street banks, implying a *quid pro quo*. Another series of allegations purported that Tester supported increasing the so-called "death tax" or the federal inheritance tax, which often puts farmers and ranchers in financial difficulties upon the death of a family member. It was this same tax that Rehberg had credited with greatly reducing his family's ranch holdings in the 1970s. Christie Roberts thought this last charge was the most effective, as evidenced by the campaign's rapid 24-hour response ad entitled "Surprised."[56] The ad has Tester speaking to the camera, "I know that Montanans are too smart to fall for their bull," referencing the NRSC's giving his left hand three additional fingers and a female narrator reminding voters about Rehberg's support for middle-class increases.

Tester's campaign had begun by framing this as a choice between responsible leadership and irresponsible decision making. Tester's allies ran with it. The emergence of the firefighter lawsuit in the final weeks was particularly troubling for Rehberg to overcome—especially in his home county of Yellowstone. One Democratic consultant said that the lawsuit "was a tactical error [on Rehberg's part]. . . . Legally, for their business it might have been the right thing for them to do, but politically it was a disaster."[57] The potency of the ad, from the perspective of the Tester camp, is illustrated by their decision to hold off as long as possible on using it—only adding it to their scheduled rotation once their hand had been forced by the outside groups.[58] Lopach said to me on a busy Friday afternoon after the campaign, "I think the firefighter lawsuit reminded all Montanans about [Rehberg's] values. He does not value the people who put their lives on the line saving us. [Firefighters] are there to help us. My first reaction, the reaction of most Montanans to people who help you, is gratitude. Not 'how can I get money out of them?'"[59]

The key for the Tester campaign was to remind Montanans that they may not always agree with Jon Tester, but they liked and respected him. For the Rehberg campaign, it was to remind Montanans that on issues like taxes, spending, and the Affordable Care Act, Rehberg was closer to them. Which message would resonate? One of the problems Tester and Democrats faced was an advertising disadvantage in the campaign's closing months. The effectiveness of advertising tends to be greatest in the closing days of a campaign when one side has a relative informational advantage. The Republicans and Congressman Rehberg had both on his side as he and his allies aired almost 60,000 separate ads in the last three months of the campaign, or 53 percent of all the spots aired in the first week of August through the first week of November. Perhaps resonance was unnecessary after all.

Clearly, Montanans had ample opportunity to learn more about the candidates and their position on issues from television ads, although at times it was hard to discern clearly some of those positions given the contradictory claims made in some ads. Newspaper coverage of the candidates and campaigns also increased in volume, and the candidates engaged in a series of four debates—three of which were televised. Newspaper coverage also provides an opportunity to see what voters could learn from the ongoing campaign narratives and, as is sometimes forgotten, the official work both Rehberg and Tester still did as incumbent members of Congress.

According to my analysis of candidate coverage in the *Billings Gazette,* 302 articles mentioned Rehberg or Tester in 2011, with a monthly average of 25 articles. In the first ten months of 2012, 474 articles featured either Rehberg or Tester for an average of 40 articles per month, or a 38 percent increase in articles. I classified articles as either positive, neutral, or negative using the following standard: Would the candidate find the article's tone helpful in terms of how the public viewed them? The coverage in the paper of both the congressman and senator was overwhelmingly neutral: about 80 percent of articles mentioning either candidate were balanced in terms of overall tone. Five percent of articles about Rehberg were negative, and two percent of articles about Tester were negative.

The overall tone of the coverage obscures an important difference in how the *Billings Gazette* reported about the two candidates. Most of the coverage of Tester and Rehberg was not about their campaign activities but about their official duties. Of the articles mentioning Rehberg and Tester in 2012, only 26 percent mentioned their campaign for the Senate. Three-quarters discussed their official duties, and Tester was mentioned in almost 60 percent of those articles. In terms of tone, these articles were overwhelmingly neutral but Tester had the edge in positive tone: 26 percent versus 17 percent. Few were negative. Compared to the campaign coverage which was relatively balanced both in the number of articles mentioning Rehberg or Tester (93 versus 94) and tone (12 versus 13 positive in tone, with 13 percent negative for Rehberg and 18 percent negative for Tester), a reader of the *Billings Gazette* could learn more about what Tester was doing as a senator for Montana than Rehberg was doing as a congressman. The impression they got about Tester, on balance, was more favorable. Tester had an informational edge in coverage in the state's largest newspaper that he lacked in the closing months of the campaign on television. In fact, this edge persisted throughout the entire year, even in the last three months of the campaign. If Rehberg and the Republicans were pounding their message with paid advertising, Tester was winning with free media coverage generated by his official press office.

All told, the candidates, parties, and outside groups spent $31 million on television advertising during the race according to advertising invoices and contracts I obtained from Montana's television stations.[60] Millions more were spent on radio, mail, and voter outreach via phone banks and canvassing. And there were the efforts made by the candidates and their official press operations to spread the good word of their doings in Washington. Was all this money and effort wasted, or did the voters actually learn something during the campaign? If so, how did this affect their impressions of the Senate candidates? Causal relationships are difficult to disentangle, especially under real world conditions where it is nearly impossible to control for a host of intervening variables. Add to this the fact that I did not conduct my own surveys of Montana voters during the campaign, and I did not have access to advertising spot data showing which specific ads aired when, with what frequency, and in which markets during the campaign.[61] These types of data would provide the best test of how campaign ads affect voter learning. Any claims of causality made here are made cautiously.

I do, however, have available data on which groups aired advertisements when, the advertisements themselves, and a general idea of when specific ads aired. I also have cross-sectional surveys taken throughout the campaign by Public Policy Polling (PPP) and Team Rehberg, and some information gleaned from tracking polls done for the Rehberg campaign in the closing weeks of the race. Using these cross-sectional surveys over time, we can see what and how voters learned as the campaign intensified. This allows us to draw some tentative conclusions about the effectiveness of each campaign and speak to whether voters moved their candidate preferences in line with their underlying beliefs as the theory of enlightened preferences presupposes.

PPP's brief polls were episodic throughout 2011 and 2012. They do report the job approval ratings of the candidates and provide some cross tabs allowing cursory analyses of how certain groups changed their views of the candidates as the campaign progressed. A comparison also can be made with other competitive Senate races, which PPP also polled throughout 2011 and 2012.

Not much can be discerned from looking at polling on voting intentions. Every single public poll save one—a Public Opinion Strategies poll released in January of 2012—showed the race within the margin of error.[62] The stability in the race is consistent with Rehberg's own polling, which showed Tester only once with a lead just outside the margin of error in late April of 2012. Tester's internals never showed a statistically discernible lead in the last two years.[63] Neither candidate could break the critical 50 percent barrier.

Other metrics show that voters learned about the candidates and updated their impressions as newspaper and paid media efforts intensified. Figure 8.3 charts the job approval ratings of both candidates starting in November 2010 through November 3, 2012—three days before the election. Although both candidates were viewed less favorably over time, Rehberg suffered the most in his job approval rating. Beginning the race tied with Tester, his job approval rating slid inexorably. By the end of the campaign, 54 percent of Montana voters disapproved of the job Rehberg was doing in Congress with only 37 voicing approval. This is a shift of 12 percentage points. Tester ended the campaign at 47 percent approval—a decline of only three percentage points from November 2010.

These results are consistent with Rehberg's internal polling on the favorability rating of both candidates. Given the intensity and negativity of the campaign, it is not surprising to see both candidates lose favorability with voters as the campaign progressed. In April 2011, both Tester and Rehberg had net favorable ratings, with only 35 percent expressing an unfavorable opinion of the congressman—essentially tied with Tester's 34 percent. Tester's unfavorability rating climbed to 41 percent by Bob Moore's September 10th poll in 2012—an increase of seven percentage points. Rehberg, however, went from 35 to 47 percent unfavorability, an increase of 12 points. The negative campaign took a decided toll particularly on how Montanans viewed Rehberg.

Both the PPP and Moore polls uncover a troubling story for the congressman. PPP broke out the job approval ratings for Tester and Rehberg by simple partisan identification (Democrat, Republican, and Independent/Other). One of the chief functions of any campaign is to remind voters of their existing commitments—to

## FIGURE 8.3

*The Job Approval of Montana's Senate Candidates, November 2010 to November 2012*

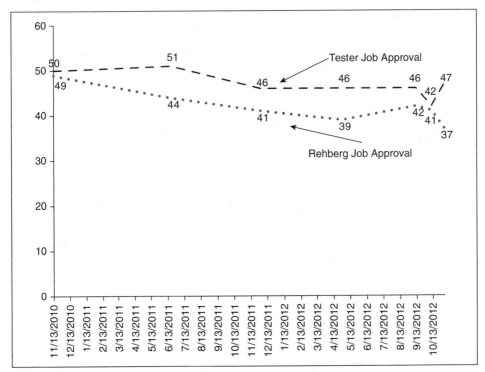

*Source*: Job Approval Ratings obtained from polls conducted in Montana by Public Policy Polling. Polls were conducted on November 10–13, 2010; June 16–19, 2011; November 29–30, 2011; April 26–29, 2012; September 10–11, 2012; October 8–10, 2012; and November 2–3, 2012. All data obtained from PPP's website at: http://www.publicpolicypolling.com/main/. The margin of error ranges from a low of +/- 2.4 percent in the November 2010 poll and as high as 3.8 percent in the September 10–11, 2012 poll.

bring partisans "back home." PPP polls indicate that Democrats never wavered in their support of Senator Tester (see Table 8.3): 87 gave Tester a positive approval rating in November of 2010 and 89 percent did so two years later. Rehberg, however, began a full nine points behind in his approval ratings among his base. Only 78 percent of Republicans approved of Rehberg's job in the House in late 2010 and this fell to 69 percent in November 2012, a drop of nine points. Approval ratings among Independents for both candidates were always lower than among partisans, but again, Tester had a consistent edge. In PPP's first poll, he had an eight-point edge over Rehberg. This ballooned to 18 percentage points in June 2011 and closed at ten percentage points higher just a few days before the election.

**TABLE 8.3**

*Positive Job Approval Ratings for Senator Tester and Congressman Rehberg by Partisan Identification, November 2010 to November 2012*

| | Nov. 10–13, 2010 | June 16–19, 2011 | Nov. 29–30, 2011 | April 26–29, 2012 | Sept. 10–11, 2012 | Oct. 8–10, 2012 | Nov. 2–3, 2012 |
|---|---|---|---|---|---|---|---|
| Republicans (Rehberg) | 78% | 74% | 76% | 64% | 82% | 74% | 69% |
| Democrats (Tester) | 87% | 89% | 80% | 85% | 85% | 82% | 89% |
| Indpts. (Rehberg) | 46% | 35% | 30% | 34% | 32% | 32% | 31% |
| Indpts. (Tester) | 54% | 53% | 46% | 46% | 46% | 44% | 47% |
| Total Sample Size | (1,176) | (819) | (1,625) | (934) | (656) | (737) | (836) |

*Source:* Cells include the percentage of respondents reporting having a favorable job approval rating of Senator Tester or Congressman Rehberg. The sample size of the poll is included in parentheses. See caption of Figure 8.3 for additional information.

## TABLE 8.4
*Favorable Impressions of Congressman Rehberg by Party Identification, February 2012 to September 2012*

|  | Feb 12–14 | April 29–30 | June 10–11 | July 9–11 | Aug 6–7 | Aug 19–20 | Sept 10–11 | Sept 25–26 |
|---|---|---|---|---|---|---|---|---|
| Republicans | 74% | 70% | 75% | 83% | 70% | 80% | 78% | 77% |
|  | (107) | (81) | (86) | (132) | (98) | (116) | (107) | (117) |
| Democrats | 16% | 22% | 12% | 9% | 7% | 3% | 6% | 1% |
|  | (19) | (19) | (12) | (13) | (8) | (4) | (7) | (2) |
| Independents | 41% | 43% | 48% | 47% | 35% | 39% | 40% | 38% |
|  | (82) | (71) | (83) | (78) | (87) | (89) | (94) | (72) |
| Total Republicans | (144) | (116) | 113 | (159) | (140) | (146) | (137) | (151) |
| Total Democrats | (121) | (89) | (100) | (138) | (114) | (125) | (125) | (133) |
| Total Independents | (198) | (165) | (174) | (165) | (246) | (230) | (230) | (188) |
| Total | 463 | 370 | 387 | 462 | 500 | 501 | 492 | 472 |

*Source:* Cell entries indicate the percentage of respondents reporting either a very favorable or somewhat favorable impression of Congressman Rehberg. The number of respondents is indicated in parentheses. Data obtained from Bob Moore of Moore Information with the permission of Congressman Rehberg. Margin of error for the full samples for the April and June polls is +/- 4.9 percent, for all other polls is +/- 4.4 percent.

Moore's polls for Congressman Rehberg also show that Rehberg began with lower favorability ratings at the start of the campaign and, as the campaign progressed, he suffered more in the eyes of Montanans. In February 2012, 74 percent of Republicans expressed a favorable impression of Rehberg (see Table 8.4). This climbed to a high of 83 percent in the July 9 through 11, 2012 poll, falling to 77 percent by late September. In the campaign's final two weeks of tracking, Rehberg's favorability rating for the whole period among Republicans recovered by two points to 79 percent. Among independent voters and Democrats, favorable impressions of the congressman faded throughout 2012. In February, 16 percent of Democrats had a favorable impression of Congressman Rehberg. This fell to one percent (!) in the September poll, recovering to an average of six percent in tracking polls. Only 41 percent of Independents in February had a favorable view of the congressman, and that impression remained fairly stable with only a two-percentage-point drop in the final tracking polls conducted by the campaign.

As the campaign progressed, Republicans did not alter their impressions of Tester and Rehberg all that much. Independents expressed increasingly less approval of both candidates, but by comparison, they expressed more disapproval and less favorability of Rehberg as the campaign wore on. The campaign did not change Democratic impressions of Tester, but their disapproval of Rehberg increased markedly—making Tester's relative advantage among his partisan base even more impressive when juxtaposed against Rehberg's. Republican voters had reservations about Rehberg that the campaign did not resolve. And although I do not possess similar data splitting Tester's favorability ratings by partisan identification, Bob Moore confirmed that Tester's favorability/unfavorability rating "among Democrats was consistently higher than Rehberg's fav/unfav among GOP voters" during the course of the entire campaign.[64]

The effect of the campaign on voter impressions becomes clearer when looking at Rehberg's polling on what respondents heard, saw, or read about the two candidates and how that affected their voting intentions (see Table 8.5A). Recall that 56 percent of voters indicated they had encountered some recent information about Congressman Rehberg in the April 2011 poll; 57 percent volunteered the same about Senator Tester. By early September, both candidates had become ubiquitous fixtures in the news and on television: 85 percent said they had read, heard, or seen something about Tester and 79 percent said the same about Rehberg. Two things are notable: Tester maintained a lead in the recall question throughout the entire campaign, perhaps a function of his information edge in the newspapers.

Second, respondents were asked whether what they had learned about either candidate affected how they would vote. Again, on this question, Tester had an

**TABLE 8.5**

*Recalling the Candidates and its Effect on Vote Choice, April 2011 to September 2012*

Part A: Recall?

| | April | Feb 12–14 | April 29–30 | June 10–11 | July 9–11 | Aug 6–7 | Aug 19–20 | Sept 10–11 |
|---|---|---|---|---|---|---|---|---|
| Rehberg | 56% | 50% | 55% | 65% | 72% | 74% | 71% | 79% |
| Tester | 57% | 58% | 71% | 72% | 77% | 77% | 75% | 85% |
| Tester Advantage | 1% | 8% | 16% | 7% | 5% | 3% | 4% | 6% |

Part B: Recall Affect Vote?

| | April | Feb 12–14 | April 29–30 | June 10–11 | July 9–11 | Aug 6–7 | Aug 19–20 | Sept 10–11 |
|---|---|---|---|---|---|---|---|---|
| Rehberg-More Likely | N/A | 40% | 31% | 34% | 31% | 30% | 32% | 32% |
| Rehberg-Less Likely | N/A | 43% | 42% | 40% | 42% | 46% | 43% | 48% |
| Tester-More Likely | N/A | 42% | 39% | 41% | 38% | 36% | 41% | 36% |
| Tester-Less Likely | N/A | 39% | 35% | 32% | 38% | 38% | 33% | 44% |
| Tester Advantage (More Likely) | N/A | 2% | 8% | 7% | 7% | 6% | 9% | 4% |

*Source:* Cell entries in Part A report the percentage of respondents who had heard, seen, or read something about Senator Tester or Congressman Rehberg recently. Entries in Part B report percentage of respondents indicating how that information would affect or not their vote choice in the Senate race. All information obtained from Moore Information with the permission of Congressman Rehberg. Number of respondents is not reported as the data were not available in the topline polling reports.

advantage which grew relative to Rehberg throughout the course of the campaign (see Table 8.5B). In the table, I calculated the difference between whether the information recalled made respondents more or less likely to vote for each candidate. This yields a recall advantage or disadvantage score. A positive value for each candidate indicates that the information the voters recalled made them on balance more likely to support the candidates, negative values less likely. I then subtracted Tester's recall advantage score from Rehberg's to create a relative recall advantage score. The size and sign of this relative recall advantage score indicates whether Tester has an informational advantage compared to Rehberg in what voters learned about them. Although by the final poll what voters had encountered about the candidates made them less likely to vote for either of them, Tester always fared better than Rehberg. His relative recall advantage score ranged from a low of six in February 2012 to a high of 19 in August of 2012. By early September, Tester's advantage had retreated to eight percentage points.

Data from the likes/dislikes questions asked in the same polls bolster the notion that the campaign hurt Rehberg's favorability relative to Tester's. Comments made about Rehberg on personal matters climbed throughout the campaign from 31 percent in February 2012 to 60 percent in September 2012. Personal comments made by respondents about Tester remained stable throughout at about a third of all likes and dislikes. More striking is the tone of the comments made about both candidates. Again, only about a third of personal comments about Tester were negative and this fell during the campaign from a high of 69 percent in February to only 27 percent in September 2012. Rehberg, on the other hand, averaged more than three quarters negative personal comments throughout—a number that rose to as high as 95 percent in the summer of 2012.

The Democratic-led efforts to make Congressman Rehberg personally unacceptable to Montanans drew blood. Despite spending more and airing more television spots in the final six weeks of the race, Rehberg's favorability and job approval ratings took hits while Tester seemed immune from continued attacks focused on spending, the debt, the inheritance tax, and his receipt of lobbyist money.

This difference suggests three tentative conclusions: First, the message mattered. The emphasis on personal unsavoriness spoke more to voters than advertising centered on issues even if the policy claims might resonate more with the preexisting partisan commitments of the Montana electorate. As the campaign progressed, Tester became increasingly well-liked relative to Rehberg, whose image suffered from repeated mention of his wealth, the firefighter lawsuit, and his willingness to take those awful pay raises.

Second, the enlightened voter theory posits that as campaigns unfold, voters weigh fundamental variables such as gender, race, ideology, and partisanship more heavily in their voting decisions. Although I do not have the data for a robust test, what voters learned during the Montana Senate campaign gives some pause about the pull of at least one fundamental variable on voter impressions of both Tester and Rehberg: partisanship. Partisanship should exhibit a greater influence on a voter's support for the two candidates as the informational environment becomes filled with data consistent with each voter's established commitments.[65] Republicans outnumber Democrats in Montana, and Independents lean conservative, so the Rehberg effort to document Tester's support for the Obama administration should have yielded, if not a victory, at least movement among those conservatives and Republicans to him. Unless, of course, that information was either not being received, or those same voters weighed other information more heavily—such as the personalities and images of the two candidates—than information consistent with the fundamentals.

But voters *did learn* from the Rehberg and Republican campaign's efforts to tie Tester to the Obama administration and its policies. And polling indicated that they remained receptive to this information. In February 2012, 23 percent of respondents in Rehberg's polls said that Tester voted with President Obama more than 90 percent of the time.[66] In September, this doubled to 46 percent—with another 24 percent saying he did so at least three-quarters of the time.[67] Among those voters who reported knowing this, 58 percent viewed Rehberg favorably, but 34 percent still viewed him unfavorably.[68] The Rehberg campaign fielded a poll to fine-tune their closing message during the first two days in October. The campaign seemed poised to return to the same theme that helped Senator Burns recover ground in the fall of 2006: taxes. Moore asked 13 separate questions about specific taxes, asking whether support for the tax would make the respondent more or less likely to vote for a public official. In every instance save one, 73 percent or more of respondents said less likely.[69] Yet, despite a bevy of Republican and Rehberg ads centering on taxes in October and airing 55 percent of all the spots in the campaign's final five weeks, Rehberg remained less favorably viewed than Tester.

Maybe some other campaign dynamic prevented Rehberg's television advertising from blowing up Tester's support. Perhaps Tester's early advertising emphasizing his personal virtues and Tester's willingness to balance his advertising efforts with positive campaign ads (even in the late summer and fall) helped blunt the negative information inundating Montana voters. But another factor must be noted here and more fully developed in the next chapter: At the same time that the air wars escalated, so too did grassroots mobilization on the part of the campaigns and outside groups. Impressionistically, and confirmed by interviews, the Democratic ground game outstripped the Republican effort in

Montana—an impression which is consistent with observations made about the presidential campaign and other congressional races during the 2012 cycle.[70] The ground game may have had as much of an effect on keeping Democrats solid for Tester and increasing independent skepticism of the congressman's personal attributes as did the consistent barrage of negative television ads. I show in the final chapter why this is a plausible explanation for Rehberg's inability to translate his paid advertising advantage into votes despite an advantage in the fundamentals among Montana voters giving Republicans an edge in statewide contests.

## THE FINAL STRETCH

During the last week of the campaign, I returned to the trail with Senator Tester and Congressman Rehberg as they made their closing pitch to Montanans. One week before Election Day, I drove in the predawn hours to Billings to attend a press conference with Senator Tester and Lieutenant Governor John Bohlinger. The conference centered on claims that Rehberg supported privatizing Medicare and replacing it with a series of vouchers— again, an example of how Tester and the Democrats stuck to their party's brand reputation in much of their communication efforts. The event kicked off a week-long bus tour for Tester, who would touch nearly every corner of the state with the other statewide Democratic candidates. I followed the Democratic caravan from Billings as they held "feeds" at the Crow and Northern Cheyenne Indian Reservation in southeastern Montana. By early evening, they would arrive in Miles City for a rally before ending the long day in Glendive—about 45 minutes from North Dakota.

Between the Crow Agency feed and the rally in Lame Deer, Tester ate a few slices of pizza while we chatted about the past 20 months and the closing days of the race. Unlike previous visits, the campaign team looked confident. Tester expressed no regrets about the campaign when asked, and said he believed the campaign had unfolded pretty much as he had expected. He had referenced our first conversation in August 2011, saying "that they're going to try to paint me as something I'm not, then maybe they can beat that guy. And that's what they've tried to do and you know, we've held up pretty well. . . . I think we're in good shape to win the thing."[71] Despite, he acknowledged, the millions of dollars in outside money flooding into the state and onto the airwaves. Tester knew there was an informational disadvantage headed into the final weeks, but if there was a concern, it wasn't that. "Make no mistake about it," he said between bites of pepperoni pizza. "This race is going to depend upon turnout and if we don't get the folks out, we could easily lose it. . . . And he's faced with the same thing by the way. And so this is just a matter of making sure that everybody that can vote does vote."[72] Persuasion and reminding had been done. Now mobilization was key.

Tester expressed regret about the length of the campaign and the constant barrage of ads. Montanans, he fretted, "get tired and they get disenfranchised and say 'The hell with it, I'm not even going to vote.' . . . That's why we're running around the state right now trying to get folks fired up, get them talking to their neighbors, making sure they know that their vote counts and it's important to get their votes."[73] Tester and the Democrats were determined to do everything they could to uncover every last vote throughout the state.

I asked him about the 95 percent number used by Rehberg in his ads and how that affected his campaign. Tester took umbrage with the number and pointed out all the ways in which he had been independent from the Obama administration—many ways that the numbers don't capture. Look at the "XL pipeline, the farm dust, child labor regulations, all the work that we've done with the FDIC and FCC on making sure that the regulations of community banks, credit unions, are applied in a common sense way. I mean none of that's in [the 95 percent number] at all. And then, quite frankly, all the work we've done to try to get Race to the Top to work for rural America, and we've not been successful in that, but we've been beating the crap out of the Department of Education on that. So it's very, very flawed."[74] He had done his best, he believed, with the tough hand he and the nation had been dealt during his six years in office.

As we concluded our final interview before Election Day, I asked the senator if there was anything I should have asked or if there was anything I needed to know. As we sat in the parked car outside a casino on the Northern Cheyenne reservation, he looked off into the distance as he considered his reply. "Shit, I don't know," he began with a frankness I now expected.[75] "I mean, this has been a long, old slog . . . It's been a hard campaign and it's been a lot harder on my wife and my kids and especially my grandkids than it has been on me. I'm . . . These guys can throw anything they want at me. I know who the hell I am. It don't matter."[76]

Tester was comfortable with who he was, and he believed that Montanans still saw him as the farmer with the big belly who worked the land in Big Sandy. He also believed that they would see Rehberg as he did—as an irresponsible tool of lobbyists who had done little for Montana during his career in Congress. "They can make their claims on lobbyists. They can make their claims on Obama. I know what I've done. I know what's gone through. The problem is that they know that's the only way they can win. They ain't going to win talking about Dennis Rehberg's record, I'll tell you that. Ain't going to happen."[77]

Jon Tester knew he had made some tough decisions during an extraordinarily difficult time for the nation. He was comfortable with those choices even if, as he admitted, they weren't perfect. And his central complaint about Rehberg—his campaign's entire message—was that Rehberg wouldn't make the tough calls, would not advance a positive agenda, and was entirely self-serving during his time in Washington. He—Jon Tester—would win because he was better liked and respected. And if it didn't turn out that way, it was fine by him. "I had a job before I got this one and I'll have a job when I get done with this one."[78] With that, he got out of the car and went onto the next rally.

Congressman Rehberg in his campaign RV, looking like Montana's next Senator on the Thursday before the election.

Photo Credit: The author.

I joined Rehberg two days later, also in Billings. One of Rehberg's supporters had donated his time as the driver and drove his RV to the campaign to transport volunteers and congressional staffers taking vacation to help on the campaign. I rode much of the day in the RV, chatting with Rehberg's staffers. Everyone helped themselves to the fridge, stocked with Subway™ sandwiches and soft drinks to energize the team as they stopped throughout the day to leaflet doors in the small towns and hamlets we passed on the way to three campaign rallies in Red Lodge, Big Timber, and Harlowton—all small towns in rural communities that based their livelihoods on energy extraction, agriculture, and—particularly Big Timber and Red Lodge—tourism. These were Republican counties where Rehberg needed a strong turnout on Election Day if he was to counter the Democratic advantage on the reservations and in Montana's urban areas.

Congressman Rehberg after a meeting with supporters in Harlowton, Montana, less than a week before the election.

Photo Credit: The author.

I asked Rehberg what concerned him most in the remaining days. He said exhaustion and slipping up, perhaps because he had seen how two other recent Senate races had veered horribly off track because of ill-considered comments about abortion. "Candidates have a tendency at this point to make mistakes because you're tired. You might say something in shorthand that you've said a hundred times but when you said it in shorthand it may not come out the right way or be interpreted in the right way. And you'll have said something you just can't suck back in."[79] For him, staying rested and careful were the most important things he could do in a close race—a race that was stuck at 48/48 according to the most recent polls at that time.

A tie, by the way, Rehberg thought would go to him in the end. "I have always said," he reminded, "if this thing is tied on Election Day, I win." Why? "It doesn't take a real smart political scientist to know that if Jon Tester can't grow his support beyond 44 or whatever percent it is, then he has to do something to drag my support down and that is supporting a third party candidacy."[80] Rehberg again came back to the outside groups propping up the Libertarian candidate's efforts, as he described it. It was the effort he blamed, in part, for his loss to Max Baucus in 1996, and it still concerned him in 2012.

Why might he prevail on Election Day, I asked, and why might he lose? Rehberg, ever a student of elections, had ready answers. "The point is we're right on the issues. Montana is right of center. . . . They know, as a campaign, they cannot beat me on the issues. And so they have to work over my character. They know that. I call it the 'squirrel theory.' I'll say, 'Jon, the stimulus was a wasted trillion dollars.' . . . And Jon will say, 'Look Squirrel.'" . . . He's doing everything he can to divert the attention away from the issues that the people of Montana are talking about."[81] Rehberg, ultimately, believed that if Montanans voted on issues, he would win. He would only lose if "Jon Tester and the Democrats were successful in diverting attention away from the real issues and made it about me rather than about America and the future."[82]

We got out of the car at the Thirsty Turtle in Big Timber for the penultimate rally. Not many people were in the room—15, 20 tops. Rehberg gave a version of the stump speech he gave in Red Lodge, reminding voters that Jon Tester votes with Barack Obama 95 percent of the time, supports the president's healthcare bill, and had cast his ballot in favor of the "failed" stimulus act. It was standard "rally around the flag" fare for his copartisans, including the all-but-required invocation of Ronald Reagan's "If it moves, tax it. If it keeps moving, regulate it. And if it stops moving, subsidize it" depiction of government. He asked them for their support in the closing days, thanked them, and then took questions from the audience.

An older gentleman, who sat silently during Rehberg's presentation, raised his hand. Denny pointed to him. The man got up, saying he was a Republican and had supported Denny in the past. But, the man went on, he was also a veteran, and Tester had done a tremendous amount for veterans. What had Denny done for veterans?

Rehberg said he had done plenty for veterans, and listed some accomplishments. But, most tellingly, he also said that he was hamstrung in his veteran efforts because he didn't have the resources that Tester did. Tester had four or five staff members devoted to veterans; Rehberg only had one because he had half Tester's staff. Tester had eight offices scattered throughout the state to help with veteran casework, and Rehberg had only four.

When I left Rehberg in Harlowton for the drive back to Billings, he appeared confident and ready to win. But what I saw at the Thirsty Turtle made me wonder if enough Republicans would come home on Election Day to make him Montana's newest United States senator.

## CONCLUSION

Political science has largely concluded that campaigns matter more when they generate informational asymmetries. Research also suggests that campaign advertising efforts have the greatest effect in the waning days of the campaign because the effectiveness of campaign advertisements on voter impressions rapidly decay. Finally, the enlightened preference model of voter learning indicates that fundamental factors such as partisanship should become more important over the course of the campaign as voters receive information bolstering their initial proclivities. In all three respects, the experiences of Senator Tester and Congressman Rehberg in their 2012 campaign suggest problems with this conventional wisdom. The Tester campaign's early advertising advantage yielded positive benefits which persisted throughout the summer and fall; Republican voters stubbornly refused to rally to Rehberg; the Republican advertising advantage in the campaign's final weeks did not move voters toward Rehberg or increase his favorability among them. Part of the reason Rehberg had trouble relative to Tester stemmed, in part, from his campaign's unwillingness to emphasize his accomplishments as an appropriator, which allowed the Tester campaign to emphasize Rehberg's ineffectiveness in combination with his lack of "one of us-ness" with Montanans. Finally, Rehberg—as a House member representing the same geographic constituency as a senator—faced an official resource and press attention deficit relative to Tester that did not do him any favors. At the end of the day, the governing styles and representational relationships both candidates had established during their respective careers echoed in the minds of Montanans and had consequences for the election's eventual outcome.

# NOTES

1. Andrew Gelman and Gary King, "Why are American Presidential Campaign Polls so Variable When Votes are so Predictable?" *British Journal of Political Science* 23, no. 4 (1993), 409–451. See also Steven J. Rosenstone, *Forecasting Presidential Elections* (New Haven, CT: Yale University Press, 1983); Michael S. Lewis-Beck and Tom W. Rice, *Forecasting Elections* (Washington, DC: Congressional Quarterly Press, 1992); Larry M. Bartels and John Zaller, "Presidential Vote Models: A Recount," *PS: Political Science & Politics,* (March 2001), 9–20.

2. Gelman and King, "Why are American Presidential Campaign Polls so Variable When Votes are so Predictable?," 435.

3. Ibid., 433.

4. Based upon spot data collected from advertising contracts and invoices collected by author from Montana's television stations. See Chapter 6, Footnote 54.

5. Devin Dwyer, Emily Friedman, and Christina Ng, "Election 2012: The Campaigns by the Numbers," *ABC News,* November 6, 2012, http://abcnews.go.com/Politics/OTUS/election-2012-campaigns-numbers/story?id=17647443.

6. Jacobson, *The Politics of Congressional Elections,* 99; Paul S. Herrnson. *Congressional Elections: Campaigning at Home and in Washington,* 5th ed. (Washington, DC: CQ Press, 2008), 84–85; More than half of the Tester and Rehberg budgets were devoted to media expenditures. See OpenSecrets.org. Erik Iverson, Rehberg's campaign manager, said that the vast bulk of their advertising budget went to TV. Interview with author, January 24, 2013. Ridout and Franz, *The Persuasive Power of Campaign Advertising,* compellingly argue that despite other methods of communicating with voters, television ads have never been as popular as they are now.

7. See Iyengar, *Is Anyone Responsible?;* Lynn Vavreck, *The Message Matters: The Economy and Presidential Campaigns.* (Princeton, CT: Princeton University Press, 2009); Daron R. Shaw, "The Effect of TV Ads and Candidate Appearances on Statewide Presidential Votes, 1988–96," *American Political Science Review* 93, no. 2, (1999), 345–361; D. Sunshine Hillygus and Simon Jackman, "Voter Decision Making in Election 2000: Campaign Effects, Partisan Activation, and the Clinton Legacy," *American Journal of Political Science* 47, no. 4 (2003), 553–596; Donald P. Green and Alan S. Gerberg, "Recent Advances in the Science of Voter Mobilization," *The Annals of the American Academy of Political and Social Science* 601, no. 6, (2005), 6–9; Green and Gerber, *Get Out the Vote.*

8. Jacobson, *The Politics of Congressional Elections,* 99.

9. Paul F. Lazarsfeld, Bernard Berelson, and Hazel Gaudet, *The People's Choice: How the Voter Makes up His Mind in a Presidential Campaign.* (New York, NY: Columbia University Press, 1948); Berelson, Lazarsfeld, and McPhee, *Voting;* Campbell et al 1960, *The American Voter.*

10. Franz and Ridout, *The Persuasive Power of Campaign Advertising,* location 211. Indeed, political ads should have the greatest effect on the hardest to reach. See Nicholas A. Valentino, Vincent L. Hutchings, and Dimitri Williams, "The Impact of Political Advertising on Knowledge, Internet Information Seeking, and Candidate

Preference," *Journal of Communication* 54, no. 2, (2004), 337–354; Michael Franz, Paul Freedman, Kenneth M. Goldstein, and Travis N. Ridout, *Campaign Advertising and American Democracy.* (Philadelphia, PA: Temple University Press, 2007). But see Druckman, "Priming the Vote, Krosnick and Brannon, "The Media and the Foundations of Presidential Support"; Joanne M. Miller and Jon A. Krosnick, "News Media Impact on the Ingredients of Presidential Evaluations: Politically Knowledgeable Citizens are Guided by a Trusted Source," *American Journal of Political Science* 44, no. 2 (2000), 301–315.

11.   Carol Tavris and Elliot Aronson, *Mistakes Were Made (but not by me)* (New York, NY: Houghton Mifflin Harcourt, 2007).

12.   See also Franz and Ridout, *The Persuasive Power of Campaign Advertising,* location 69.

13.   Ibid; Hillygus and Shields, *The Persuadable Voter.*

14.   Sides and Vavreck, *The Gamble;* Zaller, *The Nature and Origins of Mass Opinion;* Franz and Ridout, *The Persuasive Power of Campaign Advertising,* location 400.

15.   Zaller, *The Nature and Origins of Mass Opinion;* Daron R. Shaw, *The Race to 270: The Electoral College and the Campaign Strategies of 2000 and 2004.* (Chicago, IL: University of Chicago Press, 2006).

16.   Alan S. Gerber, James G. Gimpel, Donald P. Green, and Daron R. Shaw, "How Large and Long-lasting are the Persuasive Effects of Televised Campaign Ads?" *American Political Science Review* 105, no. 1, (2011), 135–150; Seth J. Hill, James Lo, Lynn Vavreck, and John Zaller, "How Quickly We Forget: The Duration of Persuasion Effects from Mass Communication," *Political Communication* 30, no. 4, 521–547.

17.   But Franz and Ridout provide some evidence that early advertising matters.

18.   Richard R. Lau and Ivy Brown Rovner, "Negative Campaigning," *Annual Review of Political Science* 12 (2009), 285–306.

19.   Stephen Ansolabehere and Shanto Iyengar, *Going Negative: How Political Advertising Shrinks and Polarizes the Electorate.* (New York, NY: Press, 1995); Franz, Freedman, Goldstein, and Ridout, *Campaign Advertising and American Democracy.*

20.   Richard R. Lau and Gerald M. Pomper, *Negative Campaigning: An Analysis of U.S. Senate Elections.* (Lanham, MD: Rowman and Littlefield, 2004); Kim L. Fridkin and Patrick J. Kenney, "The Impact of Negativity on Citizens' Evaluations of Candidates," *American Politics Research* 32, no. 5 (2004): 570–605.

21.   For example, Fridkin and Kenney find that ads that engage in "mudslinging" can have a backlash effect on the sponsor. See also Gina M. Garramone, "Voter Responses to Negative Political Ads," *Journalism Quarterly* 61, no. 2, (1984), 250–259; James B. Lemert, Wayne Wanta, and Tien-Tsung Lee, "Party Identification and Negative Advertising in a U.S. Senate Election," *Journal of Communication* 49, no. 2, (1999), 123–134; Richard Lau, Lee Sigelman, and Ivy Brown Rovner, "The Effects of Negative Political Advertising: A Meta-Analytic Reassessment," *Journal of Politics* 69, no. 4, (2007), 1176–1209.

22.   Lau, Sigelman, and Rovner, "The Effects of Negative Political Advertising."

23.   Rehberg, interview, April 4, 2012.

24.   Ibid.

25.   Ad in author's possession. http://www.youtube.com/watch?v=yAkBr5VAF9Q.

26. E-mail to reporters from Aaron Murphy, December 8, 2011; E-mail to reporters from Aaron Murphy, February 2, 2012. Tester mentioned Rehberg's pay increases in his Mansfield-Metcalf remarks about a year before the CSS ads aired.

27. Rehberg, interview, November 1, 2012.

28. Ida. A. Brudnick, "Salaries of Members of Congress: Recent Actions and Historical Tables," *Congressional Research Service*, November 4, 2013, p. 2; David C.W. Parker, "The Montana Senate Race and Why Cutting Congressional Pay May Not be the Best Idea," *Big Sky Political Analysis*, March 14, 2012, http://bigskypolitics.blogspot.com/2012/03/montana-senate-race-and-why-cutting.html; Richard L. Hall and Robert P. Van Houweling, "Avarice and Ambition in Congress: Representatives' Decision to Run or Retire from the U.S. House," *American Political Science Review*, 89, no. 1, (1995), 121–136.

29. Hibbing and Theiss-Morse, *Congress as Public Enemy: Public Attitudes Toward American Political Institutions*. (New York, NY: Cambridge University Press, 1995), 69–80.

30. Pay raises and perks are frequent attack lines used against incumbents suggesting they are out of touch and take advantage of taxpayers. Congressional pay is more complicated than these commercials claim. See Parker, "The Montana Senate Race and Why Cutting Congressional Pay May Not be the Best Idea."

31. Roberts, interview.

32. Press releases in author's possession. I included only press releases sent by the campaign for the express purpose of public release and not e-mails sent to reporters by Communications Director Aaron Murphy.

33. E. Iverson, interview.

34. See Chapter 7.

35. Glendive is the nation's smallest media market and covers only a few counties in sparsely populated eastern Montana. Erik Iverson felt that money spent on ads in Glendive was generally wasted. By contrast, Tester aired nearly 800 spots in the Glendive market during March, April, and May.

36. "Honest," http://www.youtube.com/watch?v=TU_KrJJTDLM.

37. E. Iverson, interview, January 24, 2013.

38. Rehberg, interview, January 3, 2013.

39. E. Iverson, interview, January 24, 2013.

40. "America Back on Track," Patriot Majority USA, http://www.patriotmajority.org/about.

41. This September lead for Tester may not be as great as the graph suggests only because AFSCME introduced ads in both the Senate and Governor's race at the same time. I disentangled the spots and amounts spent as a best I could from the advertising contracts.

42. Using the Sunlight Foundation's "Track the Unlimited Money Tool" (http://reporting.sunlightfoundation.com/outside-spending-2012/super-pacs/), I identified a group called the Now or Never PAC that spent money on broadcast advertising, but I could not find advertising contracts or invoices in the records of television stations even though I found the ad online. I only found a few contracts for Fair Share Action and the Freedom Fund, even though they had more substantial buys than the contracts suggested. Now or Never and the Freedom Fund sponsored ads attacking Tester, and Fair Share

Action attacked Rehberg . All the expenditures were in the final two weeks of the campaign, but including these numbers does not appear to change the fact that the Republicans had the advertising advantage in the final weeks. Finally, the American Bridge to the 21st Century launched an Internet ad attacking Rehberg for the incident on Flathead Lake that is not included in this analysis.

43. Review their coding protocols for television at http://wiscadproject.wisc.edu/download.php and http://mediaproject.wesleyan.edu/about/.

44. The Wesleyan Media Project will release their advertising data in November 2014.

45. Numbers do not add to 100 percent because of rounding.

46. Erika Franklin Fowler and Travis N. Ridout, "Negative, Angry and Ubiquitous: Political Advertising in 2012," *The Forum* 10, no. 4, (2013), 51–61.

47. Jacob R. Neiheisel and Sarah Niebler, "The Use of Party Brand Labels in Congressional Election Campaigns," *Legislative Studies Quarterly* 38, no. 3, (2013), 377–403.

48. John R. Petrocik, "Issue Ownership in Presidential Elections, with a 1980 Case Study." *American Journal of Political Science*, 1996, 40(3): 825–50.

49. Parker, *The Power of Money in Congressional Campaigns*.

50. Unsurprisingly, only two percent of pro-Tester ads mentioned Obama, and when they did, Tester said how he had opposed him.

51. Watch the debate on C-SPAN: http://www.c-spanvideo.org/program/MontanaS.

52. Sean Sullivan, "Rehberg Votes Against the Ryan Budget . . . Again," *National Journal,* March 29, 2012.

53. Gazette State Bureau, "Ad Watch: Pat Boone takes Tester to task on health care," *Billings Gazette,* March 25, 2012.

54. "Not the Kind of Leader Montana Needs," ad in author's possession.

55. Republicans across the country, including Governor Romney, claimed that the Affordable Care Act hurt Medicare's future viability. Sarah Kliff, "Romney's Right: Obamacare Cuts Medicare by $716 Billion. Here's How," Wonkblog, *Washington Post,* August 14, 2012, http://www.washingtonpost.com/blogs/wonkblog/wp/2012/08/14/romneys-right-obamacare-cuts-medicare-by-716-billion-heres-how/. This also became part of the argument made that the Affordable Care Act would lead to seniors losing doctors who would no longer accept Medicare Patients due to lower reimbursement rates.

56. Ad in author's possession.

57. Montana Democratic Operative, interview.

58. Elliot, interview, December 20, 2012.

59. Lopach, interview, November 30, 2012.

60. See discussion in Chapter 6, Footnote 54. Dollar amounts calculated directly from contracts, invoices, and reports run for me by sales managers at various television stations.

61. The Wesleyan Media Project gets real time data on campaign advertising from the Cantor Media Analysis Group (CMAG), but at the time of this writing, the data have not been released to the general public. According to the Wesleyan Media Project's website, "CMAG gathers such data by using a market-based tracking system, deploying 'Ad Detectors' in each media market in the U.S." (http://mediaproject.wesleyan.edu/about/).

Even with the sophisticated advertising tracking technology available to the Wesleyan Media Project, ads can be missed especially in small market states like Montana. The first advertisement aired in Montana was not identified by Wesleyan because it did not air in the state's discovery market of Billings. According to an e-mail exchange with co-director Mike Franz, advertisements that air first in so-called "non-discovery" markets can be missed by their data collection efforts. As a result, the number of ads aired in Montana from the data I have amassed is greater than the early estimates produced by the Wesleyan Media Project. According to my data, just under 139,000 television ads aired by media market in Montana between June 2012 and the first week of November. Wesleyan's estimated nearly 111,000 ads. See Fowler and Ridout, (2013). The difference may also be related to the fact that contracts can be changed and some of the numbers collected are from contracts but not final invoices.

62. "Montana: Romney vs. Obama," *Real Clear Politics,* http://www.realclearpolitics .com/epolls/2012/president/mt/montana_romney_vs_obama-1780.html#polls.

63. Although I was told by Lopach and Murphy that the earliest poll conducted in 2010 showed Tester down by eight (a Rehberg lead outside the margin of error given the likely sample size).

64. E-mail correspondence with Bob Moore and the author, January 10, 2014.

65. Look at other competitive races polled by PPP during 2012, and you see the pull of partisanship on favorability and job approval ratings throughout the campaign. In Massachusetts, Ohio, Nevada, and Florida, as challengers became known, their favorability ratings moved steadily upward among partisans. The exception is Missouri, where the abortion comments halted Todd Akin's momentum. Rehberg and Akin's ratings are the only ones to decline considerably during the campaign. Interesting, among incumbents in these races, Tester's favorability rating was the only one remaining essentially flat throughout the course of the campaign among copartisans. Every other incumbent saw their job approval ratings improve. It is important to note that Tester's approval was the highest on average among the six incumbent senators facing tough reelection bids. Analysis available from author.

66. Moore Information Poll of 500 Montana voters conducted February 12–14, 2012, in author's possession.

67. Moore Information Poll of 500 Montana voters conducted September 10–11, 2012, in author's possession.

68. Ibid.

69. Moore Information Poll of 400 Montana Voters conducted October 2, 2012, in author's possession.

70. Sides and Vavreck, *The Gamble,* 216–220; Seth E. Masket, "Did Obama's Ground Game Matter? The Influence of Local Field Offices during the 2008 Presidential Election," *Public Opinion Quarterly* 73, no. 5, 1023–1039.

71. Tester, interview, October 30, 2012.

72. Ibid.

73. Ibid.

74. Ibid.

75. Ibid.
76. Ibid.
77. Ibid.
78. Ibid.
79. Rehberg, interview, November 1, 2012.
80. Ibid.
81. Ibid.
82. Ibid.

# The End Game

The final public poll of the campaign, conducted by Public Policy Polling (PPP) showed the race at 48 percent Tester, 46 percent Rehberg—within the margin of error.[1] Rehberg's combined tracking sample from the last two weeks of October gave Tester a five-point lead, with Libertarian Dan Cox pulling almost six percent. If Rehberg and Erik Iverson were right, Republicans would come home at the very end and propel Rehberg to victory. If the Tester campaign was right, just enough Republicans would stay with Tester to give him a narrow win. Either way, we likely wouldn't know it until the wee hours of the morning after. I joined the Tester campaign in Great Falls at their election night celebration because, at the end of the day, I had decided Tester was the incumbent and the story began and ended with him. Rehberg held his event in his hometown of Billings.

Outside the hotel ballroom, Team Tester commandeered a room for the press and another for the campaign's operation center—manned by Communications Director Aaron Murphy, Deputy Campaign Manager Dayna Swanson, Tester's Washington Chief of Staff Tom Lopach, and State Director Bill Lombardi. Campaign Manager Preston Elliot and Research Director Christie Roberts staffed the campaign's war room back in Billings where they directed last minute get out the vote operations, compiled vote totals, and responded to any Election Day shenanigans. They were also ready to handle a recount should one be required.

Reports throughout the day indicated strong turnout, and as the polls closed at 8 p.m., Yellowstone, Missoula, and Gallatin Counties remained jammed with hundreds of voters still waiting to register and vote. The crush of voters and the confusing consolidation of multiple precincts in Yellowstone County guaranteed a late night for election workers, reporters, and the candidates.

The first hints of trouble for Rehberg came shortly after the polls closed and national news agencies released their exit poll data. Using a sample of precincts, interviewers grab voters as they leave the polls according to some selection criteria (usually every $n$th voter). Exit pollsters also contact voters who cast ballots early by phone. Exit polls help observers explore the factors explaining how folks voted. Or, using the language of Gelman and King, they help us determine whether fundamentals behaved as anticipated with respect to voting decisions.

At 8:05 p.m., Rehberg's trouble was senior citizens. In 2006, Conrad Burns had bested Tester among older voters by four points and lost. In 2010, when the

Republicans took control of the House of Representatives in the Tea Party-led tsunami, 59 percent of voters 65 and over voted for Republican House candidates.[2] Senior citizens vote reliably and tend to be conservative—particularly older white men, a demographic group representing about 14 percent of Montana's population.[3] Rehberg had to win this group to have a chance against Tester. Exit polls showed Tester barely besting Rehberg among voters over 65: 49 to 48 percent. National exit polls for House races showed 55 percent of these voters cast ballots for Republican candidates in 2012.[4] Rehberg was losing a critical demographic to Tester.

As the night wore on, more signs pointed to a Tester win. Turnout in the state's urban counties was high, and Tester was besting his 2006 performance. Although Rehberg did better in critically important Ravalli and Flathead counties than Burns had in 2006, Tester also increased his vote totals from these fast-growing conservative areas. In rural communities, Rehberg struggled to do as well as Burns in 2006. Although Tester did not improve on his performance in Montana's rural areas, he did not lose much ground relative to 2006.

Tester greeted supporters less than 90 minutes after the polls closed. Early results looked promising. Lewis and Clark County, home to Montana's state capitol Helena, was in by 8:30 and propelled Tester to an early lead. By 10 p.m.,

Election Night at Tester's Headquarters in Great Falls.

Photo Credit: Hilary M.W. Parker.

Tester had 54 percent of the vote with 17 percent of the returns tallied. And yet much of state's largest urban areas, places where Tester expected to do well, hadn't reported. This included Cascade, Gallatin, and Missoula Counties. The early lead boded well for Tester. When political reporter Marneé Banks went live for Montana's CBS-affiliated stations at 10, the crowd was excited. The presidential race had been called for Obama, and Democrats had already picked up two Senate seats in Massachusetts and Indiana.[5]

Results trickled in slowly but surely, and Tester's lead mounted. By 11:30 p.m., one-third of the votes had been counted and the senator's lead had expanded to 20,000 votes. Political reporter Mike Dennison cautioned on

Twitter that many rural areas, places where Rehberg expected to do well, had yet to report.[6] Tester addressed reporters right before the 11 o'clock news, saying things looked good. He had been circulating throughout the night sharing quips with friends, while a series of visiting dignitaries like Senator Baucus kept the crowd pumped. By 12:30 a.m. some people began to drift away. The outcome would not be known for many hours still.

When Cascade County, home of Great Falls and Malmstrom Air Force Base, reported before midnight, it was the beginning of the end. The county, which Tester had narrowly won in 2006, fell squarely for Tester. Tester bested his 2006 vote totals by almost 2,100, while Rehberg lost nearly 500 votes relative to Conrad Burns's 2006 performance. Rehberg had invested heavily in Cascade, stressing that Tester's support for the START Treaty would cost Malmstrom jobs. Cascade County also happens be the home of the state's highest percentage of veterans, and it is likely that Tester's veterans work made a substantial difference.

At 2 a.m., Montana's senior Senator Max Baucus hit the stage to "I Gotta Feeling" by the Black Eyed Peas to introduce Tester. "We're going to make it. There's no question about it, but sometimes in life, you have to wait for good things to happen" said Baucus to laughter from the 75 or so supporters left. Tester took the stage, thanking everyone for sticking with him through the campaign and the long evening. "Yes, it is two a.m. in the morning and you guys have hung in there very, very well. It means a lot to me," he said, adding that unfortunately "we don't have a victory to announce tonight." He told his supporters to get a couple of hours of sleep, and that the campaign would keep in touch. Some of the largest counties in the state, including Flathead, Ravalli, Yellowstone, Missoula, and Silver Bow had only reported partial results with just two-thirds of the votes counted. Tester's lead shrank a bit as the night wore on, but not by much. Dennison reported at 2:30 a.m. that Rehberg was still 16,000 votes behind. Early returns from Yellowstone County, which had been plagued by long lines and three-hour waits to vote, showed a narrow Tester lead. Rehberg was losing in his own backyard. But the race was still up in the air when I hit the sack at four.

At 6:30 a.m., I woke to update my analysis of key precincts in swing counties. That analysis showed that Rehberg was underperforming in areas where Burns had done well in 2006, in particular in strong Republican precincts in Gallatin and Flathead counties. Little had changed during the night: the *Associated Press* (*AP*) had still not called the race, and few additional precincts had reported results on the Secretary of State's website. Dennison had tweeted that Tester's lead actually increased by 1,000 votes, but there were still 75,000 votes outstanding from Butte, Kalispell, Hamilton, and Billings. Tester's campaign was frustrated because they believed the numbers simply could not yield a Rehberg win. Much as they had in 2006, they scheduled a press conference at 9:30 a.m. to claim victory with or without the *AP*'s imprimatur. In preparation for the press conference, I made my way to the hotel restaurant for a bagel, some coffee, and an electrical outlet to charge my phone.

As I was getting ready to leave, Tester and his family came into the dining room. Tester spied me at the cash register, shouted "Parker!" and waved me over, inviting me to sit with him and his family. We reminisced about the events over the previous 24 hours and agreed that this campaign would be remembered not only for its expense but for how *Citizens United* had shaped electioneering. It would be a case study in how congressional candidates adapted to the new resource realities.

As breakfast began to wrap up in anticipation of the press conference, Aaron Murphy hurried over to Tester with his cell phone. Murphy had the *AP* on the line, and they were calling the race for Tester. Tester took the phone, spoke briefly to *AP* reporter Matt Gouras, gave him some remarks, and as he ended the call, the scene erupted in tears and hugs. Tester's phone began to ring. First, it was Majority Leader Harry Reid, and then Senator Chuck Schumer, calling to congratulate Tester. Unlike 2006, Senate control no longer hung in the balance because Republican Senator Scott Brown had lost in Massachusetts, and Republicans had failed to beat Missouri Senator Claire McCaskill. They had also lost Indiana's Senate seat. All told, not only did the Democrats hold the Senate, with Tester's win they had gained two seats.

As Tester and his family took to the podium in the ballroom, the crowd erupted in chants of "Six more years!" The senator's son, Shon, introduced his family and parents to the assembled reporters and supporters. Both Christine and the Testers' adopted daughter, Melodee, spoke about what their dad meant to them and how despite all the outside money, he had prevailed because of who he was. "Outside groups spent a lot of money trying to turn my dad into someone he's not," said Christine in her soft voice. "You can't do that with Jon Tester. You can't do that with someone who raised a family like ours. You can't do that with someone who values accountability, responsibility, and freedom." Again, even in the final days of the campaign, the juxtaposition with Rehberg is there: Jon Tester exhibits the Montana values that Congressman Rehberg does not.

When Tester took the microphone, he spoke briefly. "I've been waiting a long time to say this: It is over," he said to applause from the crowd. Tester first thanked "his rock," Sharla, before acknowledging the long hours and days put in by the countless volunteers and staff that made victory possible. He thanked the people of Montana who were sending a "Montana farmer, with Montana values, back to the United States Senate." He made mention of the thousands of television ads and the millions of dollars spent in the race. "This victory is our victory" and it "proves that neither corporations nor millions can buy the state of

Montana." After taking this final jab at the Supreme Court and its *Citizens United* decision, he thanked Congressman Rehberg and his family for their effort and service over the past 12 years. Tester called upon Montanans to come together to face the nation's tough challengers. In acknowledging Congressman Rehberg's career, he—perhaps for the first time since I had covered him—called him "Denny" rather than Dennis. It was now time to heal.

After the *AP* called the election, Chris Bond released Rehberg's concession fourteen minutes before Tester's press conference started. "Jan and I are tremendously and eternally grateful for the support, kind words, and prayers we have received from countless Montanans," it read. "It has been an honor to serve the people of Montana. The voters of our state have spoken, and I respect their decision. Senator Tester and I share an abiding love for Montana and America, a value which transcends political party or disagreements on matters of policy. I congratulate Jon on his victory in this hard-fought campaign."[7] According to Tester, Rehberg never called to congratulate him. Rehberg, a man proud of his political acumen, was likely shocked. In the end, Rehberg lost by 3.7 percentage points and a little more than 18,000 votes—a margin about five times Tester's margin over Burns in 2006. The only consolation for Rehberg, perhaps, was the fact that he held Tester yet again to less than 50 percent of the vote—in fact, Tester's vote share had declined by half a percentage point from his 2006 performance.

Sharla Tester, relieved the race is over, hugs Bill Lombardi, Jon Tester's State Director.

Photo Credit: Hilary M.W. Parker.

## HOW THE CAMPAIGN MATTERED

If campaigns provide voters with information to help them weigh fundamental variables like partisanship and ideology in the final vote decision, how do we account for a result at variance with these underlying fundamentals in Montana? Montana voters consciously went against the grain when they cast their ballots for the Senate—and most of Montana's statewide elected offices in 2012. At the same time Mitt Romney beat President Barack Obama with almost 55 percent of the vote, Montanans elected Democrats to the United States Senate and the Governor's mansion. They voted for a Democratic Secretary of State, Auditor, and State Superintendent of Education. In only the open Attorney General and House races did Montanans elect Republicans. Clearly, Tester and the Democrats in the state had convinced Montanans to weigh partisanship differently.

Before explaining how the campaign mattered and what factors likely added up to Tester beating Rehberg, it is worth considering the facts. At one level, little had changed between 2006 and 2012. In 2006, Jon Tester won only 15 counties in his campaign against Senator Conrad Burns, but he won almost all of the largest and fastest-growing ones. In 2012, Tester won every single county he had won six years before, adding only his home county of Chouteau, which he had lost narrowly in 2006. Otherwise, Tester's victory looked identical to the one that had initially sent him to Washington.

What seems at first blush as static is anything but. The aggregate numbers obscure important shifts in support that in almost every case helped Tester win by a larger margin over Rehberg. These shifts reveal that Rehberg did run a strong campaign, but that Tester ran a better one. A political operative who had worked on multiple Democratic campaigns and for the Democratic Senatorial Campaign Committee (DSCC) during the 2012 cycle confirmed this. "Overall, I think they both, you know, ran good campaigns" she told me during a January trip to Washington after the election. "I just feel like Tester . . . ran it a slight bit better and had more to use on Rehberg."[8]

The urban counties that Democrats must dominate to win statewide show that Rehberg's team had, in fact, made important gains relative to Burns's performance in 2006. In 35 counties, Rehberg gained votes relative to Burns, while losing votes in 24 counties. In the ten largest counties, Rehberg received 16,371 more votes than Senator Burns had. Only in Silver Bow and Cascade Counties did Rehberg lose votes relative to Burns. In the Republican strongholds of Flathead and Ravalli Counties, Rehberg picked up an additional 6,200 votes. Even in heavily Democratic and liberal Missoula County, Rehberg won 2,000 more votes than Conrad Burns had in 2006.

Tester's campaign, however, improved his vote totals dramatically over 2006 in the state's fastest-growing and urban counties. Tester pulled 28,647 more votes from the ten largest counties alone, about 10,000 more than his final margin of victory. In every urban county, Tester added votes to his 2006 totals, including Ravalli and Flathead. Most impressive were Tester's gains in Gallatin County, which he narrowly lost to Burns in 2006. In 2012, the turnabout was seismic. Tester pulled 7,500 votes more than he had in 2006, winning the county handily with 52 percent of the vote. He also increased his vote share by 5,200 votes in

Missoula and nearly 4,200 in Yellowstone County, the state's largest. This provides tentative support for the hypothesis that the Tester campaign's sophisticated get out the vote (GOTV) operation—mirroring the national Democratic Party's—had been responsible in part for Tester's win. More on that later.

Looking at the rural, less-populated areas of the state shows that Rehberg did not improve upon Burns's performance. In Montana's ten least populated counties, Rehberg pulled a grand total of eleven additional votes out of the 6,935 cast. Tester lost 153 votes relative to his performance six years ago. In essence, the campaign in the state's rural area was fought to a draw, which spells doom for a Republican candidate hoping to offset the large, urban gains made by Democrats. And although Tester only improved his vote totals in the three majority-Native American counties in Montana (Big Horn, Glacier, and Roosevelt) by three percent, Rehberg lost more than 1,000 votes in those three counties when compared to Burns's 2006 performance. Rehberg got outperformed and outmatched in nearly every county, even in those areas where he improved substantially upon the Republican performance in 2006.

Exit polls shed light on the electoral coalition both sides built (see Table 9.1). As is the case nationally among Democrats, Tester bested Rehberg with women by nine percentage points—two points better than he did against Burns in 2006. Tester also beat Rehberg among every age group but those between 30 and 44. College graduates and postgraduates voted for Tester, while those with only some college and high school graduates voted for Rehberg—a pattern consistent with 2006. Voters with family incomes less than $50,000—which is about $5,000 greater than the state's median family income—sided with Tester by 12 points. Tester lost voters making more than $50,000—again, a pattern consistent with national trends. Unmarried men and women favored Tester by 11 and 30 points respectively, while married men and women favored Rehberg by 15 and three points, respectively. Voters *seemed* to move as the fundamentals would suggest: higher-income voters, men, and those with less education supported Rehberg, while college and postgraduate professionals, women, and the less-economically secure supported Tester. The main surprises were older voters, who tend to be conservative, and the high rate of defections among Republicans relative to Democratic voters.

## THE DEMOCRATIC BRAND

In 2012, Democrats successfully stressed protection of the social safety net against Republican plans to alter Social Security and Medicare for future generations. The "Ryan plan," developed by House Budget Chairman Paul Ryan of Wisconsin, was featured negatively in Democratic congressional ads across the

## TABLE 9.1
*Exit Polls from the 2012 Montana Senate Race*

| A. Gender | | Tester | Cox | Rehberg | Difference btw. Tester and Rehberg | Percent of Sample |
|---|---|---|---|---|---|---|
| | Men | 45% | 6% | 49% | –4% | 48% |
| | Women | 51% | 7% | 42% | 9% | 52% |

| B. Age | | Tester | Cox | Rehberg | Difference btw. Tester and Rehberg | Percent of Sample |
|---|---|---|---|---|---|---|
| | 18–29 | 47% | 14% | 39% | 8% | 15% |
| | 30–44 | 47% | 5% | 48% | –1% | 24% |
| | 45–64 | 49% | 7% | 44% | 5% | 41% |
| | 65+ | 49% | 3% | 48% | 1% | 21% |

| C. Education | | Tester | Cox | Rehberg | Difference btw. Tester and Rehberg | Percent of Sample |
|---|---|---|---|---|---|---|
| | High School Grad | 42% | 8% | 50% | –8% | 21% |
| | Some College | 45% | 7% | 48% | –3% | 32% |
| | College Grad | 46% | 9% | 45% | 1% | 29% |
| | Post-Grad | 63% | 3% | 34% | 29% | 16% |

| D. Income | | Tester | Cox | Rehberg | Difference btw. Tester and Rehberg | Percent of Sample |
|---|---|---|---|---|---|---|
| | Less than 50,000 | 52% | 8% | 40% | 12% | 46% |
| | 50–100,000 | 43% | 9% | 48% | –5% | 37% |
| | 100,000 + | 48% | 2% | 50% | –2% | 17% |

| E. Gender and Marital Status | | Tester | Cox | Rehberg | Difference btw. Tester and Rehberg | Percent of Sample |
|---|---|---|---|---|---|---|
| | Married Men | 40% | 5% | 55% | –15% | 29% |
| | Married Women | 47% | 3% | 50% | –3% | 33% |
| | Unmarried Men | 51% | 9% | 40% | 11% | 19% |
| | Unmarried Women | 59% | 12% | 29% | 30% | 19% |

*Source*: Exit Polls conducted by Edison Research on Election Day. Data obtained from CNN's 2012 Election Coverage, http://www.cnn.com/election/2012/results/state/ MT/senate.

country. Democrats claimed that the Ryan plan endangered the safety of Social Security and Medicare, even if the plan and Ryan resolutely stated that the terms for those already receiving benefits or close to retirement would not change. Nevertheless, the merest whiff of support for the plan by Republican candidates meant advertisements would be aired charging them with the eventual annihilation of the federal social safety net.

Rehberg felt the sting of such ads even though he was one of only four Republican House incumbents to vote against the Ryan plan.[9] No matter. Earlier votes were used to demonstrate Rehberg's support for turning Medicare into a voucher program or to change Social Security. Rehberg believed that changes in both programs were indeed necessary for them to survive in some form in ensuing years given the impending difficulties both faced financially. Democrats, of course, preferred to keep both programs in their current form but wanted to find ways to increase revenues to pay for these programs, including the possible indexing of both benefits based upon income.

The emphasis on the Democratic Party's bread and butter certainly hurt Rehberg among older voters, where he lost considerable support to Tester. This was definitely a place where the Tester campaign and outside groups' decision to focus on Medicare and Social Security yielded benefits for the Democrats. I asked both Andrew Maxfield, Senator Tester's pollster, and Christie Roberts, the campaign's research director, about where Tester stood with older voters at the beginning of the campaign. "We weren't doing as well among the over-sixties," Maxfield admitted. Roberts expressed surprise about voters' lack of skepticism about Rehberg concerning entitlements. "Certainly, [Rehberg] got a lot of press over voting against the Ryan plan the first time around, and it was pretty early in his Senate campaign and I think that helped him," said Roberts. It was this vote, she believed, that provided Rehberg with some protection with voters on the issues. Maxfield stressed the need to compare and contrast the two candidates on these issues: "That's why we wanted to talk some about Medicare and Social Security because they needed to hear what was gonna happen to those programs [and about the] . . . starkly different positions on those programs [held by the two candidates]."[10]

The campaign's unearthed footage of Rehberg's debate with Baucus in 1996, with his infamous quote about Social Security, became the centerpiece of the larger argument about the social welfare safety net and Republican efforts to change it. The quote is taken out of its fuller context, as Rehberg continued to say: "But not for those who are entirely dependent on it or have a reasonable anticipation it will be there."[11] To be fair, Republicans have long argued for changes in the cost of living adjustment (COLA) for Social Security, a change which Democrats have always called a benefit cut.

The Rehberg campaign was furious about the clip and accused the Tester campaign of distorting his position. "**In reality, Rehberg is a strong supporter of Social Security**, who has supported changes needed to strengthen and preserve the program for current beneficiaries and future generations," wrote Chris Bond in a campaign press release.[12] Rehberg told me how he flew with President Bush to Great Falls where Bush unveiled his plan to privatize Social Security in 2005. Rehberg says he pleaded with the President to not go through with it because it would go over like a lead balloon. Nevertheless, Roberts noted that Rehberg's record on Social Security and Medicare was inconsistent. "Rehberg is on both sides," she alleged. "When he ran for Congress . . . he proposed the partial privatization of Social Security, young people being allowed to invest their money in the stock market, and then back peddled when Bush brought it forward in 2005. . . . Same with the Ryan Plan, with voucherizing Medicare. In 2009 he voted . . . to make Medicare into a voucher system."[13] At least, when compared to a Democrat, Rehberg did not appear as consistent in his support for the social safety net.

This was an important issue for Tester to win. First, about 20 percent of Montanans received some kind of Social Security benefit in 2012, higher than the national average.[14] Second, the issue helped them with women. Maxfield said it's a common misperception that women care more about a set of so-called "women's issues." Rather they are a bit "more concerned on average than men with programs like Social Security and Medicare and so those things might have mattered a little more to them at the end than it did initially."[15] It certainly mattered to unions engaged in voter mobilization, as they focused much of their member outreach efforts on pay and benefits, according to union organizer Lenny Williams, who served as the political registrar for his local chapter of the International Brotherhood of Electrical Workers (IBEW) in Butte, Montana.[16] According to a national survey conducted by Lake Research for the National Committee to Preserve Social Security and Medicare, those who said Medicare and Social Security were important to their vote favored Democratic candidates for Congress and "overwhelmingly" preferred the Democratic plan to the Ryan plan.[17] In this respect, the emphasis placed by the Democratic candidates in Montana on preserving existing entitlement benefits for retirees and future beneficiaries echoed party strategy elsewhere. It yielded the anticipated benefits and likely contributed to Tester's win.

## IT'S THE ECONOMY, STUPID?

Another important factor is the emphasis Rehberg and Republicans placed on jobs and the economy. The campaign blamed much of the slow economic recovery on the president, his healthcare plan, and the failed stimulus. Montanans were certainly pessimistic about the national economy: Exit polls showed that on Election Day, only 16 percent of Montanans had a good view of national economic conditions. Conversely, 81 percent agreed that the economy was either not so good or poor.[18]

It is less clear, however, that this affected personal economic outlooks and feelings about the direction of Montana's economy.[19] In fact, compared to the rest of the nation, Montana had fared well during the Great Recession. While unemployment skyrocketed to a high of ten percent nationally, and other states with competitive elections like Nevada fared much worse, Montana's unemployment never got higher than 6.8 percent—well below the national average.[20] In fact, by the fall of 2012, Montana's economy was firmly recovered and the state's gross domestic product expanding.[21] The state's budget showed a surplus of $457.1 million (above estimates), and Montanans felt good about their state.[22] Only 18 percent told Election Day pollsters that their family's financial situation had gotten worse, and of those who believed that, three-quarters voted for Congressman Rehberg; 42 percent said their personal finances were about the same, and 23 percent had said they had gotten better. In both cases, a majority of respondents who believed their family was doing well financially voted for Tester. Even in the early days of the campaign, Tester's pollster had noted the distinction between how Montanans saw the direction of the state versus the national government. "You know, 'the right direction, wrong track' on the state of Montana was fairly reasonable. It wasn't great, but it was reasonable. And in positive territory. But in terms of the nation and the economy and prospects for the future, people were concerned."[23]

A Montana Chamber of Commerce poll taken in December 2011 illustrates the differences. Only 30 percent believed that Montana's economy was moving in the wrong direction, but 66 percent felt that way about the nation.[24] If people focused more on their own personal situation as some political science research suggests they do, it would be difficult for the Republicans to gain much traction when blaming Tester for the nation's economic malaise. In fact, Maxfield felt strongly that the message wouldn't work because voters, in this case, were more sophisticated in casting blame. "They appreciated that they'd just come out of a major crisis in 2008," replied Maxfield to my question about the role of the economy in the election, taking a long pull on his Styrofoam coffee cup. "They knew that President Bush had run up spending, and the deficit was partially his doing," he said. But Republicans and Rehberg "made a big bet early on that the economy and voters' dissatisfaction of the economy and their attribution of blame would drive the race. And clearly it didn't."[25]

Another way of thinking about how the economy played a role in the campaign is to consider how campaigns generally talk about economic issues. The economy was improving, but it is difficult to claim that it was growing robustly. There were still concerns that the sluggish national growth would turn south, and unemployment numbers remained historically high relative to growth in the national gross domestic product. Lynn Vavreck claims that "insurgent" candidates—those not advantaged by economic conditions (such as Senate Democrats in 2012)—need to find an issue on which they are closer to the voters in order to blunt the effect of economic considerations on vote choice.[26] The Tester campaign did exactly that, stressing entitlement programs, Rehberg's unlikeability, and most importantly, Jon Tester's considerable personal assets.

## "RESPONSIBLE" DECISION MAKING: THE POLITICS OF REPRESENTATIONAL STYLE

The series of attacks made on Rehberg and Tester throughout the campaign suggested a bigger underlying theme: Neither candidate truly represented Montana, nor were "one of us." The critical distinction between the attacks on both candidates, however, centered on their fundamental believability from the perspective of voters. Voters already questioned Rehberg's character, his willingness to look out for the interests of others, and an apparent lack of accomplishments during his 12 years as the state's congressman. The Democratic attack lines reminded voters of preexisting doubts. Voters could believe that a millionaire would line his pockets with pay raises, and they could imagine someone who filed a lawsuit against firefighters may not look out for them. The charges that Tester was in the pocket of lobbyists and took their cash for his own campaign, however, had trouble sticking. Why?

Part of the answer lies, perhaps, in the ability of Tester to reestablish himself with voters through a series of positive advertisements—advertisements that dominated the airwaves in the spring of 2012. This suggests that early advertising might not be a wasted effort, particularly when it provides an informational advantage for a candidate. But as important was how the campaigns strove to express their candidates' authenticity through connections to the land. The images of Montana landscapes are in nearly every ad they sponsored, and the notion of the land—either the people who make their living from it (ranchers, farmers), or how that land should be used (protected or employed for extractive purposes) is often highlighted. More than 40 percent of both Tester's and Rehberg's own ads made some mention of public land use or used imagery to make a connection with the state's dramatic landscape. Outside groups, however, focused on land and land use in only 21 percent of their televised ads. Both campaigns believed, it seems, that demonstrating a connection and sense of place with the land was important to building support among Montanans who feel this connection deeply.

Tester and his campaign simply did a better job of making Montana a central part of his paid and unpaid media efforts. Tester's ads always began with a shot of him saying he approved the message on his farm with his near-universally recognized red barn in the background—and his ads often featured him walking the farm, doing farm chores, or simply in a pastoral setting. Even his campaign press releases begin with "Montana farmer Jon Tester."[27] Rehberg's ads—while they often began with him along the fence line in a flannel shirt—did not show him on his ranch, physically working the land. One ad showed him driving around Washington, DC, in his jeep with his personalized Montana license plate "MT Rancher." But that's a far cry from the dirty, stained shirts worn by Tester as he fixes his combine. Team Tester exploited this aggressively by intimating that Rehberg was "all hat and no cattle." They pointed out that Rehberg hadn't registered livestock with the Department of Livestock, Inspection, and Sales since 2000, when he went to Congress, and that he, in fact, had become a wealthy real estate developer.[28] In his closing remarks at the first debate in Big Sky, Tester said that "Building houses and mansion-ranchin' is not ranchin'."[29] Rehberg, who closed last, was thrown off balance by Tester's stinging rebuke to his ranching heritage. "I have a herding operation, and I guess someone doesn't understand the difference between farming and ranching," he rebutted. "Because if you do ranchin,' you have livestock, and guess what? They eat every day. . . . I didn't have the luxury of having anyone take over the ranch for me."[30] (Rehberg told me during our first trip together that ranching is about resource management, understanding what parts of the land you preserve and what parts from which you making a living to pay the bills. He saw subdividing some of his ranch for development as part of that process. "We carved out 800 acres," he said in our last interview. "There's 6,400 acres still available for ranching."[31] Tester's comment still bothered him because he saw ranching as the root of his identity and a lens through which he saw the world.)

Because Tester more successfully evoked a connection to the land and to the state's dominant industry not only through imagery but by virtue of the fact that he continued to farm, Montanans found it difficult to believe the harsh attacks levied against him. The guy with the dirty shirt and the flattop certainly didn't appear to benefit from lobbyist cash. In 2006, there was evidence that Conrad Burns's staff had made questionable ethical choices, that trips and dinners had been plied on them, and hence the allegations of a *quid pro quo* were believable. The guy working 2,000 acres in Big Sandy could not be benefiting personally from lobbyist connections. Rehberg, who had foregone his role as an active rancher, who subdivided his land for development, and who drove a Jeep (read:

not a pickup) and wore nicely tooled leather boots looked to some exactly like the kind of person who would look out for himself at public expense—regardless of the merits of the charges. Perception became reality. Jon Tester, at the end of the day, seemed more Montanan, and that made him immune from some of the worst of the negative advertising.

Both Jake Eaton and Erik Iverson from Rehberg's campaign expressed frustration that, despite all the evidence from their polling, they could not gain traction against Tester. "We had issues that we tested against [Tester] that were 60, 70, 81 percent less likely to vote for him once they knew about this. . . . These issues were off the chart, and it wasn't just one or two, there was like six to eight of them. But Montana voters didn't really give a shit. They are like, 'We don't care, we know he is wrong on the issues. We just don't like the other guy.'"[32] Eaton, whom I interviewed only a few weeks after the campaign had concluded, was angry. "The real lesson for me is don't talk about issues. People don't give a shit about issues. It's all about personality. And until Republicans learn that, they're doomed."[33]

The toughest charges levelled against Tester concerned the possibility of a *quid pro quo* from the banking industry on the debit swipe fee issue. I asked a Montana Democratic political operative not involved in this race why the charges didn't stick. "They didn't believe he was taking it [lobbyist money] to enrich himself. . . . The thing with Jon is he never did anything for those guys. What's the old line . . . you can't eat their steaks, drink their whiskey, screw their women and vote against them . . . right? He never did anything for them."[34] They didn't stick because Jon didn't take anything from lobbyists other than completely legal and above board campaign contributions; no whiskey, steaks, or . . . you get the point.

Rehberg could have proceeded differently. He could have emphasized his personality and rehabilitated his image among Montanans. Another Montana political operative, who had worked for Conrad Burns, said as much: "Denny could have introduced himself on radio. He could have done some basic stuff. He didn't have to go negative right away. I think that probably would have helped him [had he] gone up with two or three media spots."[35] A Republican consultant not involved in the campaign agreed. Looking across the races in 2012, he asserted that "empathy mattered a lot. I don't know if it mattered more this year because there was a greater amount of angst, or there was some long term buildup of pessimism or fatigue or discouragement. . . . But I think that was a significant element to a lot of these, at least in the Senate races."[36]

How would he have run Rehberg's campaign had he been calling the shots, knowing that Rehberg had higher negatives from the get-go versus Tester? "The [path]. . . is to figure out what it is that my guy does well, or has to talk about, or has for assets to establish that he is a person of good character. And I run right at it, a long time, not unlike running the football. You have to establish it." Add other people who can speak to the candidate's basic goodness. "If I have time and my guy or gal is at all credible on the tube, talking directly to people," he continued, "I have them do that. I weave in family. I find other people who can vouch for that candidate. I just think it critical to have that personal credibility."

Rehberg did have some ads that did that, but they were few. The campaign used both Rehberg's mom and his wife Jan in ads, not to establish the congressman as a great guy but to respond to charges levelled by the Tester campaign and outside groups. The best ad created by the Rehberg campaign never actually aired on television, appearing only on YouTube in the closing days of the campaign.[37] And it used family, as the Republican consultant recommended, to establish the kinder, gentler Denny I had witnessed on the campaign trail. The spot featured Rehberg's youngest daughter, Elsie, who was a high school freshman at Billings West in 2012. Elsie speaks directly to the camera about her dad, his hard work, and his determination to be there for his family. It closes with vintage footage of Rehberg holding Elsie's hand, walking away from the camera, when she was only two. It is the footage from Rehberg's House ad from his 2000 campaign, a touching reminder of Rehberg's fondness for children and his involvement in raising his daughter. The advertisement humanizes Rehberg, showing a personal side of him few Montanans saw. Rehberg is smart, can be incredibly charming, and is often funny. Maybe if he had shown this side more often to constituents or had made an effort to communicate it consistently in his advertisements, he could have halted the erosion of his favorability.

Without a doubt, the lawsuit against the City of Billings created the biggest headache for the Rehberg campaign. Certainly, outside groups and the Tester campaign thought it was important for voters to remember, as the lawsuit dominated the airwaves in the last six weeks. They also turned the lawsuit into an attack on firefighters more generally. Preston Elliott said that it was always the campaign's intention to hold the firefighter spots to the end, and that their polling showed that the firefighter lawsuit really moved numbers in the closing weeks.[38] It was the final nail in the personality coffin and showed that Rehberg's "irresponsible" decisions had severely negative consequences for Montana, costing the City of Billings $26,000 in legal fees alone. That was tough to reconcile with Rehberg's penchant for keeping government lean and mean fiscally.

## DAN COX: SPOILER?

Perhaps the single greatest reason offered for Tester's victory—especially among Republicans—was Libertarian Dan Cox's candidacy and efforts made by Montana Hunters and Anglers to promote him to disaffected Republicans. Rehberg and his staff repeatedly charged that Montana Hunters and Anglers was a front group set up by former Baucus staffers, taking a page directly from Jim Messina's book, who in 1996 had used the Reform Party candidacy of Becky Shaw to draw votes from Rehberg when he ran against Baucus.[39] They argued that Democrats aggressively sought out Libertarian candidates to pull votes that otherwise would go to Republican candidates. Certainly, Montana Hunters and Anglers aggressively attacked Rehberg on issues of concern to Libertarian-minded voters, stressing his support for HR 1505, a bill they claimed was a land grab that greatly expanded the power of the Department of Homeland Security. Citizens for Strength and Security built on this theme in the spring and summer of 2012, claiming that Rehberg supported using drones to spy on Montanans. In the fall, Montana Hunters and Anglers even aired an ad showing a father and his son out on a hunting trip, the son pointing out a camera in the trees tracking their every move. The father got his gun and shot the camera. The ad ends with the tagline "Vote for Cox: The Real Conservative."[40]

Erik Iverson had repeatedly stressed that for Rehberg to win, Cox had to be held to three or four percent. Cox drew nearly seven percent of the vote cast in the Senate election, more than the margin separating Tester and Rehberg. Of course, became the oft-repeated logic, Cox spoiled Rehberg's party. It is the same story that long had been levied against third party candidates, including Ralph Nader who supposedly was responsible for Al Gore's loss in Florida during the 2000 election.

Cox's presence on the ballot certainly drew votes from Rehberg, of that there is little doubt. Did he draw enough for Rehberg to lose? Three pieces of evidence suggest that absent a Libertarian candidate on the ballot, Rehberg still would have lost a close race to Tester.

Consider first Rehberg's loss in 1996 to Max Baucus. During that campaign, Rehberg lost a considerable share of Republican supporters—many of whom cast their ballots for Democratic Senator Max Baucus and not the Reform Party candidate. Rehberg consistently found it difficult to rally his base during the campaign and underperformed among that base relative to Tester's support among Democrats. Exit polls conducted by the Edison Research Group show that 95 percent of self-identified Democrats voted for Tester, with only four percent defecting to Rehberg. Republicans were more than twice as likely to defect from Rehberg as Democrats were to vote for either Rehberg or Cox: Only 87 percent of Republicans reported voting for Rehberg. Those votes, however, did not go to Cox: Only three percent of Republicans voted for the Libertarian candidate. Fully ten percent of self-identified Republicans voted for Tester. Dan Cox drew support disproportionately from Independents: Ten percent voted for Cox while 48 percent voted for Tester. Rehberg managed to attract the votes of only 38 percent of Independents, ten percentage points less than Tester.[41]

Which Republicans voted for Tester? It's hard to say with any precision because the sample of Republicans casting ballots for Tester is too small from which to draw any statistical inferences. We have some hints, however, from Rehberg's tracking polls. Republican voters who described themselves as only "somewhat" conservative viewed Rehberg less favorably than very conservative Republicans (86 percent of very conservative Republicans saw Rehberg favorably while only 77 percent of somewhat conservative voters did).

Who were these Republicans? Again, hard to say. They were likely older women, who viewed Rehberg slightly less favorably than Republican men. Among all respondents, women over the age of 55 had the least favorable impressions of the congressman: 53 percent viewed him unfavorably, compared to 48 percent of women between the ages of 18 and 54 and 46 percent of men over the age of 55. Montana Democrats certainly picked up the national narrative accusing Republicans of waging a war against women but emphasized access to healthcare and cuts to community health centers over reproductive rights. Healthcare, Medicare, and Social Security were important among this demographic group that had either retired or was nearing retirement. This is the same age group facing mammograms and increased risk for breast cancer, an issue that the Tester campaign and Democrats hit hard throughout the race but especially in the summer with their Lisa Jones spot accusing Rehberg of cutting funds for mammograms and cancer research.[42]

Another way to look at whether Libertarian Cox stole the election from Rehberg is to compare the performance of the Senate candidates to their presidential candidates by examining vote totals at the level of individual precincts. Campaigns not only target individuals but particular geographic areas thick with strongly motivated copartisans. Precinct targeting allows for the efficient allocation of scarce volunteer manpower. To identify strong Republican and Democratic precincts, I simply averaged the vote totals for President Obama and Governor Romney at the precinct level. This overestimates Romney's support; Democratic voters are more efficiently distributed into densely populated urban areas. Romney's vote average across precincts was 58 percent and Obama's was 39 percent. I identified precincts where Romney and Obama performed one standard deviation above their mean precinct performance. Precincts where voters gave Romney more than 77 percent of the vote I classified as strong Republican precincts. Precincts where Obama received more than 58 percent of the vote I categorized as strong Democratic precincts. In addition, I coded districts where Romney received between 47 and 53 percent of the vote as "swing." I then computed the total vote cast in these precincts in the Montana Senate race. The results are reported in Table 9.2.

## TABLE 9.2
*Vote Performance by Precinct in the 2012 Montana Senate Race*

| | Percentage of Total Vote Cast | | | |
| --- | --- | --- | --- | --- |
| | Tester | Cox | Rehberg | Total |
| Strong Democratic Precincts | 75% | 5% | 20% | 126 |
| Swing Precincts | 54% | 6% | 40% | 65 |
| Strong Republican Precincts | 23% | 7% | 69% | 102 |

*Source*: Strong Democratic precincts are defined as those where Obama received one standard deviation above his mean precinct. Strong Republican precincts are defined as those where Romney received one standard deviation above his mean precinct performance. Totals may not add to 100 percent due to rounding. Data from Montana's Secretary of State.

Dan Cox did not cost Rehberg the election. In strong Republican precincts, Rehberg received only 69 percent of the total vote cast with Cox drawing 7 percent. Tester received 23 percent of the votes cast. Compare this to the strong Democratic precincts of which there were 126 compared to only 102 strong Republican precincts. Tester averaged 75 percent of the vote, Rehberg 20 percent, and Cox 5 percent. Tester did six points better in the strongest Democratic areas than Rehberg performed in the strongest Republican areas. Most important, however, is the fact that Tester did three percentage points better in Republican precincts than Rehberg did in Democratic precincts. Cox performed only two percentage points better in strong Republican precincts than in strong Democratic precincts. Cox drew nearly as many votes from the state's greatest concentration of Democratic voters as he did in the most Republican areas. Rehberg suffered some defections to Cox, but more importantly, he lost more of his base to Tester than Tester lost to him. Although it is difficult to draw conclusions from aggregate voting patterns of individual-level behavior, the fact that precinct level analysis confirms patterns observed in exit polls allows more confidence in the conclusion that Cox had little effect on the final outcome.

The pattern in swing precincts simply underscores the noneffect of Cox on the final outcome. Cox did almost as well in swing precincts as he did in strong Republican precincts, earning six percent of the votes cast. Tester simply outperformed Rehberg in swing precincts, earning 54 percent of the vote cast compared to only 40 percent for Rehberg. Despite the protestations of the Rehberg campaign, Rehberg did not lose because of Cox. Most likely, he would have lost a closer race to Tester without Cox on the ballot.

The gubernatorial race adds confirmatory evidence. In that race, the Libertarian candidate Ron Vandevender did not receive the benefit of outside groups advertising on his behalf, and he only received four percent of the vote. Democratic

Attorney General Steve Bullock still managed to beat former Congressman Rick Hill for Governor in a tighter race with a margin of only 7,500 votes separating the two candidates.[43] To win the election, Rehberg would have had to draw slightly less than 80 percent of the vote cast for Dan Cox while losing only 20 percent to Tester (assuming, of course, that Cox voters still chose to participate in the election). This is a mighty assumption and very unlikely. A Democratic operative familiar with Montana, but not directly involved in the Tester campaign, agrees. "I think Cox puts a point or two on the board for Jon. I think you remove him from the race, the score is different, but the outcome is the same."[44] Most likely is the fact that Cox's presence on the ballot allowed a number of Democrats, Republicans, and Independents upset by daily onslaught of negative advertising or disappointed in both of the major party candidates to vote "none of the above."

The disparity in turnout in strong Republican versus strong Democratic precincts combined with Tester's stronger showing among Republicans suggests that the Democratic narrative made inroads across the partisan spectrum. "If you're losing ten percent of your base, that's a serious problem," said a Republican consultant succinctly stated when informed of the exit polls from the race.[45] The seasoned Montana Republican operative was harsher in his assessment. It is worth reporting his remarks at length.

> I mean, I used to—and still do—talk to a lot of Montana Republican legislators and activists. And all of them are like "I might vote for Denny, but I'm not happy about it" or "I'm pissed about it." Or "Denny doesn't call me back. Max is always here. Max is always asking what he can do. God damn it, Jon Tester is helping us on veterans' stuff. You never see Denny." . . . And then the firefighter department lawsuit? Not only is it an offense to Billings but it reignited all the nastiness of the Conrad Burns firefighter issue. It just blew that back up. Not only does Denny do the firefighter lawsuit, he hires the meanest, baddest trial lawyer in all of Montana—probably the Northwest—in Cliff Edwards. So it is a major poke in the eye of Billings not coming long after the memory of Conrad Burns pissing off the firefighters. So he just knitted his own narrative.[46]

This is further evidence that representational relationships matter, and the Tester message of responsible decision-making worked. And the Rehberg campaign suspected as much at the end. After the Montana Republican Party and the Rehberg campaign aired some ads stressing Rehberg's independence and willingness to buck the party line, the campaign and the National Republican Senatorial Committee aired—as their closing spots in October—a testimonial from Mitt

Romney asking Montanans to send Rehberg to the United States Senate.[47] Rehberg's personal brand had been tarnished, and they hoped the Republican brand could bring the base home at the very end. It wasn't nearly enough.

## THE DEMOCRATIC GROUND GAME

The ability of Democrats to keep much of their base while increasing their vote totals considerably over Tester's 2006 performance hints at another reason why Tester managed to beat the odds: their ground game. National political observers credited the Obama campaign and the Democrats nationally with an impressive ground game based upon sophisticated targeting of voters with carefully calibrated messages. During the heat of the campaign, *New York Times* reporter Jackie Calmes wrote that,

> For all of the attention to television advertising, the Obama campaign has made an investment likely to reach hundreds of millions of dollars—a gamble, really—in its ground game, with state-of-the-art technology for demographic data mining, consumer marketing, video production and social media, including the campaign's own Dashboard social network to link, motivate and expand the ranks of volunteers.[48]

Not everyone was as impressed. In their political science treatment of the Obama-Romney campaign, Sides and Vavrek report that while national political observers like *Slate* magazine's John Dickerson credited Obama's "much vaunted ground game" for his victory, they estimated at best Obama managed to pull an additional 248,000 votes from his field efforts.[49] Citing other studies of field organization, they argue that "at most, effective mobilization will increase turnout by a single-digit number of percentage points—perhaps as much as 8–9 points, and often less—among those who are contacted."[50] Tester's slim margin of 3,152 in 2006 increased to more than 18,000 in 2012. To gain additional votes based solely on voter contact and mobilization would require the Tester campaign to touch—assuming an increase of nine percent—more than 160,000 voters. Of course, this is a best case scenario that at the same time discounts other efforts to mobilize and engage voters via paid and free media. It also does not account for the competing efforts of other groups and the Rehberg campaign to mobilize and persuade voters in the opposite direction.

It is true that the Democratic Party and its allies seemed to have the edge in using new, sophisticated techniques to reach voters and persuade them with mail and face-to-face contacts. Sasha Issenberg's book *The Victory Lab* details the efforts primarily of Democratic consultants to harness social science research to make more effective fundraising and mobilization pitches to voters and activists. In 2006, "liberal groups looking to coordinate their increasingly ambitious research agendas" created the Analyst Institute.[51] The organization "was founded on a faith in randomized-control experiment" to help develop a series of insights and knowledge that would help Democrats and their allies "decide close races" with the power of carefully calibrated messaging.[52] This included the use of "social pressure" based upon the research of two Yale political scientists, Alan Gerber and Doug Green.[53] By showing the voting histories of neighbors to a voter, there was a statistically significant effect on increasing voter turnout relative to groups receiving no mobilization appeal. Democrats used these and other findings to alter how they communicated throughout the campaign while gathering information from voter contacts to improve future contacts.

From all accounts, Republicans seemed a step behind these efforts nationally.[54] I spoke with a Republican political consultant who had participated in campaigns in Montana but not during the 2012 cycle. He agreed that Republicans had a problem with their GOTV operations. "I think the Democrats were better about targeting and message delivering during the entire four-year arc of the campaign than Republicans were."[55] The issue, he stressed, was demographics. "One of our biggest challenges is that we're running out of ground troops. We don't have young people, we don't have minorities. Our old ladies can't walk very well anymore, so we don't have people that are going door to door very much."[56] And that's a problem because door contacts can be more effective than phones, but you have to have the right people on the doors. Doors are better than phones because they are "three dimensional rather than two dimensional.... [But] when you're talking about voter advocacy, I'm going to listen to somebody that's from my demo," he stressed during our conversation.[57]

In Montana, the Democratic ground game seemed more sophisticated than Republican efforts. Democrats conducted a coordinated campaign funded by the Democratic Party and contributions from statewide candidates.[58] These campaigns used volunteers to ship mail, make phone calls, and run the field operation throughout the state from the top of the ticket down. A national Democratic operative familiar with the DSCC efforts throughout the country, and Montana in particular, said Democrats did a better job building voter models and updating those models with new information throughout the campaign. These models helped the coordinated campaign better target their canvassing, voter registration, and mail efforts. "We had to build the [Montana voter] model ourselves, and then we would revise it throughout the last few months" she told me.[59] This model gives "everyone on the voter file a score. So then you're starting to target within these scores, and you can even sort of drill down to figure out what type of [message works best]. Montana, for example, is not really someplace where you want to go screaming about choice, you know, across the state, but you can do like targeted mailings on choice into what the model says are folks that are likely to be responsive to that message."[60] She stressed that with television airwaves becoming saturated, the ground game becomes more important. "Doing the actual groundwork and talking directly to voters . . . knocking on their doors and having conversations is becoming more important simply because people can so easily tune out the TV ads these days."[61] Even phone calls can be easily screened with nearly ubiquitous caller ID. Face-to-face contacts, she and others highlighted, can make a big difference.

Several outside organizations also conducted get-out-the-vote campaigns, including an effort spearheaded by unions like the American Federation of Labor and Congress of Industrial Organizations (AFL-CIO). The League of Conservation Voters (LCV) and their state affiliate, Montana Conservation Voters (MCV), also engaged in voter outreach efforts. According to data assembled by the Sunlight Foundation, other groups also spent money on mail, phone banks, and voter outreach in Montana, including Worker's Voice, Planned Parenthood, Majority PAC, and VoteVets for the Democrats.[62] Republican groups spent mostly on television, although Americans for Tax Reform, Crossroads GPS, Focus on the Family, Americans for Responsible Leadership, Gun Owners of America, and a group called The Conservative Strikeforce did limited voter outreach primarily via phone and mail.[63]

There are not as consistent data with which to provide a clear analysis of the effect of these efforts as there is for advertising. That said, interviews conducted with participants in voter outreach suggest the breadth and intensity of the effort to get voters engaged and cast ballots for Tester and other Democratic candidates.

According to information provided to me by MCV's Executive Director Theresa Keaveny, the national League of Conservation Voters knocked on "273,643 doors, enroll[ed] 31,186 people to vote by mail, and turn[ed] out an additional 7,648 voters who did not vote in 2006."[64] These efforts to identify and communicate with voters by door, phone, and mail began in September 2011, with the canvass starting in April 2012.[65] The group targeted voters who had been identified as conservation supporters who leaned Democrat in addition to registering voters who had not participated in 2006 or in the 2010 midterm. At the same time, MCV focused their grassroots efforts on getting out the vote for Democratic gubernatorial nominee Steve Bullock in areas where "the League of Conservation Voters was not canvassing for Jon Tester."[66] This meant that the MCV concentrated its efforts in Park, Cascade, and Flathead Counties in addition to some precincts in Bozeman and Billings. The LCV, on the other hand, put its efforts into Missoula, Lewis and Clark, Yellowstone, and Gallatin Counties.

MCV had to focus on Bullock because the MCV is a state, not federal PAC Keaveny noted. Although these efforts focused on Bullock, the voters brought to the polls from this effort were likely Tester voters, too—especially because the state PAC had access to the LCV voter targeting list and would target Tester voters with information on Bullock. The canvassing efforts demonstrate how Democratic groups carefully allocated resources so they didn't duplicate the efforts of other groups in the field. "We knew about another group that was canvassing Great Falls," Keaveny told me, "And we agreed where we would canvass and where we would not."[67] All of this, by the way, is legal. "We leveraged the investment made by the League of Conservation Voters on the ground for our field program for Steve Bullock," she summarized.[68] This is also important because she believes that the best voter intent contacts are made face-to-face, meaning groups doing this kind of work have better data with which to target—thereby increasing the effectiveness of later reminding and persuasive efforts made by mail, the phone, and on the doors.

MCV also worked with the Environmental Defense Fund to pay for the campaign's first ads focusing on Rehberg's votes against stricter regulations on mercury pollution and led the grassroots effort to bring attention to Rehberg's support for HR 1505, the land bill aggressively advertised as a federal land grab by the Montana Conservation Voter's partner, Montana Hunters and Anglers. Keaveny said they physically fenced off Rehberg's congressional office in Missoula after Rehberg's support for the bill was announced, emphasizing the bill would make it harder to access public land.[69] "1505 was a, that was a big deal for some Montanans," said Tester's pollster. "Giving central government that much control over public lands" upset a certain segment of voters, particularly those who owned guns and hunted.[70] Exit polls indicated that 75 percent of respondents owned at least one gun. Rehberg won this group, but Tester drew 42 percent of gun owners going to the polls on Election Day.[71] Perhaps some of these voters were indeed concerned about what they saw as a gross expansion of the Department of Homeland Security's powers.

The nonpolitical arm of the LCV, with which Keaveny could not work or coordinate with since she worked on direct advocacy, sent out a letter to their target universe using social pressure to woo voters. The letter provided the voting history of the recipient's neighbors, using it to exhort the recipient to do their part and to vote. It was a pitch that had been fine-tuned through academic study and the work of practitioners according to Sasha Issenberg, who wrote about the use of social science experimentation on voter mobilization and persuasion in *The Victory Lab*.[72] Keaveny said she did not know about this effort until she herself received the same letter in the mail in the days leading up to the election. She reported her belief that the LCV had worked with the Analyst Institute in developing this flyer, the same group Issenberg reported as in the forefront of using experiments in the practical political world to help improve grassroots organization.[73] Keaveny noted that both the MCV and the Montana Conservation Education Fund had done experiments with the Analyst Institute in every year since 2006 except 2011.[74] Even the scripts used by canvassers had been rigorously tested. It was a window into how Democratic-affiliated groups worked consistently to make their voter contact operations work both more effectively and efficiently. Republican groups may be doing the same type of experimentation and tinkering, but I heard nothing of it in my interviews.

Were the LCV and MCV contacts effective? According to preliminary numbers, 84 percent of those contacted by these groups registered to vote by mail.[75] This is much higher than the statewide average of 59 percent voting by mail. Additionally, the individuals contacted by the LCV and MCV canvass had a higher rate of absentee ballot return. Statewide, 92 percent of those requesting an absentee ballot returned it. Of MCV members, 94 percent requesting an absentee ballot and contacted by MCV returned it, and 93 percent of low-propensity voters identified and targeted by MCV returned their mail ballots.[76] After helping to register voters, LCV and MCV would follow up with voters receiving an absentee ballot, calling or knocking on their door to make sure the ballot was returned. It appeared their efforts worked well. Their effectiveness is especially impressive when considering the fact that the organization expressly included low-propensity voters in its contact universe and had such a high rate of return. By comparison, voter turnout among all registered voters in 2012 was 72 percent, and in strong Democratic precincts, only 64 percent of registered voters did, in fact, vote.[77] Seen in this light, the canvass conducted by the conservation groups likely did help Tester and Democratic candidates bank additional votes in the weeks leading up to Election Day.

I received an unsolicited phone call from a source at the AFL-CIO's national office in the weeks following the campaign and was given information concerning the group's voter outreach in Montana. According to a memo I received via e-mail, 5,000 GOTV doors were knocked on Election Day, and more than 68,277 live phone contacts were made by the AFL-CIO.[78] Even more impressive were the 62,686 doors knocked with a persuasion message in the fall. Only 10,577 of these persuasion efforts were made to active union members—the rest were made to the general public.[79] My source indicated that their own internal analysis demonstrated their persuasive messages developed for canvassing worked even better among members of the general public than they did among their own membership—messages the general public may not have received had unions not been unshackled by *Citizens United* in their political activities.

I spoke with Lenny Williams, a trade electrician and a member of IBEW in Butte, about his work during the 2012 cycle for Democratic candidates. The AFL-CIO had two main efforts ongoing during the campaign, one emphasizing voter identification, mobilization, and persuasion and another focusing on member-to-member communications. Williams spent much of his official time on member-to-member mobilization and then volunteered every weekend starting in July leading up to Election Day for individual campaigns. Campaign efforts focused on voters who were undecided and voters who leaned Democratic. He talked about how he and others calibrated their messages on the doors depending on the audience. Among women, they discussed healthcare and choice. Undecided voters heard about *Citizens United* and outside spending. And Union members heard about the firefighter lawsuit. Interestingly, many of the members of Williams's local union chapter in Butte began the race cool toward Tester. Why? "A lot of our members didn't like Tester's Forest Bills Act. They thought it took away from them."[80] Williams and his fellow canvassers emphasized Tester's work with veterans, because many of the members of the building trades industry were veterans themselves.

Williams stressed how well the firefighter issue worked with union members on the phone and at the doors. "Two things happened," relayed Williams. "One, these guys are union members, and they have an affiliation with [firefighters] that way. The other thing that happens, if you have a firefighter on your shoulder, people are going to like you. People like firefighters. They like them like they like their dad, they look at them like the heroes that they are. That alone was enough to sway several of our members."[81] GOTV efforts complemented the messages in the paid media and increased their effectiveness. Canvassers could relate directly to the concerns of those who answered the door; they were of the same "demo," as the Republican consultant put it.

Looking at the big picture, Republican-allied organizations that spent money in Montana concentrated their efforts on mass advertising with little attention paid to voter contact or outreach. Of independent expenditures over $10,000 spent in the Montana Senate race by groups supporting Tester or opposing Rehberg, 28 percent was spent on mail, phones, or field organization. Only 5 percent from conservative groups was spent on GOTV.[82] This reflected national patterns.

It seemed to me that Republicans in Montana put more emphasis on phones than on face-to-face contacts.[83] I posed the question to the former Burns staffer: Did Republicans rely more on phones for mobilization than doors? He affirmed that suspicion. "That came out of the '03/'04 models, the Karl Rove models, that door knocking was less efficient and less effective than massive amounts of phone calls. And I heard that again this race, call this person who'd already been called ten times. . . . That phone stuff is very much a Republican thing. Because the Democrats tend to cede the phone stuff to Service Employees International Union (SEIU) and the AFL-CIO, the unions tend to pick up that stuff and they also fund the ground game."[84]

Rehberg and Iverson certainly claimed that the inability or unwillingness of Republican groups to invest in a ground game hurt. Rehberg maintained he simply couldn't find a ground game with his limited resources, and that outside groups like Americans for Prosperity or Crossroads GPS might have provided better assistance had they worked to target and drive Republican-leaning voters to the polls. "We were kind of watching and hoping that maybe the Americans for Prosperity were gonna do it. A ground game, voter ID, door-to-door, get-out-the-vote because we didn't have the resources. Tester didn't either, but he didn't have to. They [labor and the environmentalists] did it for him."[85]

At the end of the day, it is hard without concrete data to know how and if the disparate ground game efforts mattered in Montana. One analysis based upon aggregate national data compiled by the Sunlight Foundation indicates that those organizations investing more in voter contact had a higher "return on investment," meaning their candidates won more often than candidates supported by organizations spending more on mass media.[86] This study, however, does not measure precisely which methods of voter contact worked, or how many contacts were required to persuade an individual to vote and to vote for the candidate preferred by the group contacting the voter. At best, I can note the differences in how Republicans and Democrats engaged in mobilization and suggest tentatively that it had perhaps a marginal effect on the outcome.

## A FINAL LOOK

I asked Rehberg why he lost on his last day in office. We sat outside a radio studio in Billings where he had just conducted his last interview as Montana's congressman. I asked him if there was a silver bullet that took him down. Wearing a Carhartt jacket and an open-collared blue oxford (after swearing he'd never wear a blazer again), he said there wasn't. "It was death by a thousand cuts."[87] As Jake Eaton put it, there was "no kill shot" in any of the charges but it was the cumulative weight of them that made the difference.[88]

I asked a Republican political operative not involved in the race the same question. The former Burns staffer said that Tester "didn't create a fireable offense in six years. He voted wrong. Definitely voted outside the mainstream of Montana for six years, as it relates to all the cross tabs. But at the end of the day, he didn't do anything bad."[89] Tester, on the other hand, had out-hustled Rehberg. "'Look at all the stuff I [Tester] have done. Look at the veterans' work I've done for you. Look at the work on ag, look at the Native American work I've done. I'm a regular guy, and by the way, look at the alternative. Look at the choice you're faced with if you take me out. This is a man that's been elected six more years than I have and he's done nothing for you.' . . . And if you can couple that with heavy media and keep that choice, which is what Tester did, he outraised and outspent Denny by a long shot, and with outside money, Denny can't overcome it."[90] In the language of political science, voters looked retrospectively at Tester's and Rehberg's records. They believed that Tester had done more than Rehberg, and as a result, he merited reelection.

Nearly six months after the campaign, I caught up with Tester in Bozeman. We reminisced and chatted about the lessons from the campaign. He went right to *Citizens United,* the decision that he had excoriated during the campaign. I told him that the evidence demonstrated that he benefitted as much if not more from outside money spent in Montana.[91] He continued to insist the system was broken. "It still needs to be transparent," he came back. "If I would have had my way at the very beginning we would have said, 'Hey, let's keep all the outside money out.' In fact, we made that proposal and it got muddy pretty quick. But bottom line is that whether it helped me or helped him or helped both of us evenly or unevenly, I don't think outside money where there's no connection to knowing where it came from is helpful to the political process."[92]

I asked if he would consider a reform that may not change the corporate or labor union piece of the equation but might allow for full transparency. "Sure, I would support anything that would move us toward more transparency. Absolutely," he replied. In fact, Senator Tester introduced a constitutional amendment along with Senator Baucus early in the 113th Congress to repeal *Citizens United.* He would play with the money rules as long as they were in place, but he would fight to change what he felt was a process encouraging negativity and disgust with democracy.

At the end of our interview, I reminded the senator that in 2006, he had won 15 counties and 49.2 percent of the vote. And that six years later, he had won one more county but only 48.5 percent of the vote. He had failed to expand his reelection constituency; in fact, it had contracted. I asked how he would expand his base before 2018. He replied in a very unpolitician kind of way: "I think for me to be successful I don't think you look at it from that perspective. I just don't. Expanding your base. . . . You look at the issues and you try to do what's right to move the country forward. . . . A guy that worked for Lee Metcalf . . . said that you can tell if you're doing anything if it's a close race or not. If you don't do much, you've got a chance of winning a big wide race. If you're doing stuff, it's going to be a close race."[93]

"So doing a good job always means reelection is going to be tough?" I responded.

He turned serious. "Absolutely right. If you're out there affecting change and making things work better for folks, it's always going to be [close]. You know, it doesn't matter what job you are doing. If you don't make any waves, you're liable to have that job a lot longer. If you get in there and work and roll up your sleeves and get after it, it makes you more of a lightning rod."[94] It is exactly the answer I had come to expect from Big Sandy's dirt farmer.

## CONCLUSION

Nate Silver's 2012 Senate predictions missed the mark in Montana and North Dakota. He gave Congressman Rehberg a 66 percent chance of besting Senator Tester. Why was Silver off, and why—if most Senate elections are largely the consequence of fundamental factors such as the state of the national economy, the preexisting partisan inclinations of voters, and the popularity of the president—did Senator Tester eke out a win when all the fundamentals indicated otherwise? In one sense, Congressman Rehberg's explanation was apt; it was "death by a thousand cuts" and it is difficult to say with great confidence that any *one* factor was the reason for Tester's victory.

It is easy, though, to see why Silver and other election forecasters could have been wrong when watching the campaign on the ground. All campaigns begin in a particular place, a geographic constituency, carrying with it a set of representational expectations shaping how members of Congress campaign and later represent that place in office. The story of Montana's Senate race boiled down to a choice between two individuals who had developed representational styles based on place-based connections and affecting a "one of us" presentational style back home. Ultimately, it was Senator Tester who convinced voters that he best represented the "last, best place" as a working farmer tied intimately to the land, a dogged champion of veterans, and as an earnest person interested in seeking legislative solutions to nettlesome problems. Congressman Rehberg's work as an appropriator, his unenviable position of serving the same geographic constituency with half the official resources, and the coolness some voters felt toward him personally served as clear liabilities in a charged political environment. Home style—the presentation of self, the explanation of Washington work, and the allocation of official resources—is difficult to quantify and model. It was that which is the most elusive from afar but apparent up close, home styles, that proved the prognosticators wrong long before the voters cast their ballots on Election Day in Montana.

# NOTES

1.  "Tester, Flake Lead Senate Races, Romney up 7 in Both AZ and MT," *Public Policy Polling*, November 4, 2012, http://www.publicpolicypolling.com/main/2012/11/tester-flake-lead-senate-races-romney-up-7-in-both-az-and-mt.html; Real Clear Politics, http://www.real clearpolitics.com/epolls/2012/senate/mt/montana_senate_rehberg_vs_tester-1826.html.

2.  "Election Center," *CNN*, http://www.cnn.com/ELECTION/2010/results/polls/#USH00p1.

3.  United States Department of Commerce, Census Bureau, "American FactFinder," http://factfinder2.census.gov/faces/nav/jsf/pages/index.xhtml.

4.  "House Exit Polls," *The New York Times*, http://elections.nytimes.com/2012/results/house/exit-polls.

5.  I recreated the events of the night with the help of Marneé Banks and Mike Dennison's Twitter feeds. Marneé tweets with the handle @MarneeBanks and Mike @ mikedennison. Indiana and Massachusetts were called before Montana's polls had officially closed.

6.  Dennison's Twitter feed.

7.  Rehberg Press Shop, "Rehberg Statement on Montana Senate Race," November 7, 2012.

8.  National Democratic operative, interview, January 7, 2013.

9.  David Catanese, "Explaining the Four 'nos' on the Ryan Plan," *Politico*, April 15. 2011,http://www.politico.com/blogs/davidcatanese/0411/Explaining_the_four_nos_on_the_Ryan_plan.html.

10.  Maxfield, interview.

11.  "Montana Senatorial Debate," *C-SPAN*, October 28, 1996, http://www.c-spanvideo.org/program/76280-1.

12.  Press release, Rehberg Press Shop, "Trailing in Polls, Tester Doubles Down on Dishonest Attacks," August 22, 2012, emphasis in the original, in author's possession.

13.  Christie Roberts, interview.

14.  U.S. Social Security Administration, Office of Retirement and Disability Policy, "OASDI Beneficiaries by State and County, 2012," http://www.ssa.gov/policy/docs/statcomps/oasdi_sc/2012/table01.html.

15.  Maxfield, interview.

16.  Lenny Williams, interview with author, February 12, 2013.

17.  "Medicare and Social Security in the 2012 Elections," National Committee to Preserve Social Security and Medicare, November 15, 2012, http://www.ncpssm.org/Portals/0/pdf/post-election-polls.pdf.

18.  "Election Center," *CNN.com*, http://www.cnn.com/election/2012/results/state/MT/senate.

19.  There is an ongoing debate about whether citizens vote their "pocket books" or their perceptions of national economic conditions. See Jean-Francois Godbout and Eric

Belanger, "Economic Voting and Political Sophistication in the United States: A Reassessment," *Political Research Quarterly* 60, no. 3 (2007), 541–554 for a review and for new developments. They claim that political sophistication and campaigns provide an important moderating effect.

20. United States Department of Labor, Bureau of Labor. Statistics, "Local Area Unemployment Statistics," http://www.bls.gov/lau/.

21. Data obtained from the St. Louis Federal Reserve, http://research.stlouisfed.org/fred2.

22. "Montana Budget Surplus $268M above estimates," *Associated Press*, September 14, 2012.

23. Maxfield, interview.

24. "2011 Montana Chamber P-Base Survey Toplines," in author's possession. The survey included a sample of 600 Montana Voters and was conducted November 14–18, 2011.

25. Maxfield, interview.

26. Vavreck, *The Message Matters.*

27. Meredith Shiner,"GOP Gambles on Drought Assistance Bill," *Roll Call,* August 1, 2012.

28. Montanans for Tester, "DEBATE: Rehberg is no longer a rancher,". June 16, 2012, press release.

29. Remarks made at the Big Sky Montana Senate Debate held on June 16, 2012, http://www.youtube.com/watch?v=jN7ZOfPKDoo.

30. In fact, Tester himself had told me they had sold their animals when he got elected to the United States Senate because he couldn't manage them while travelling back and forth to DC. Tester, interview with author, November 11, 2011.

31. Rehberg, interview, January 3, 2013.

32. E. Iverson, interview.

33. Eaton, interview.

34. Democratic operative, interview.

35. Burns staff member, interview.

36. Republican consultant, interview with author, November 26, 2012.

37. E-mail from Elsie Rehberg sent by Montanans for Rehberg, November 5, 2012. See video here: http://www.youtube.com/watch?v=jF73WXo-I5E.

38. Elliot, interview.

39. But my analysis of exit polls suggests otherwise. See Chapter 4.

40. View the ad here: http://www.youtube.com/watch?v=xFzxnWJfTGw.

41. "Senate: Montana," *CNN,* http://www.cnn.com/election/2012/results/state/MT/senate.

42. Press release, Montanans for Tester, "New TV spot holds Rehberg accountable for 'wrong priorities in DC." July 11, 2012, video can be viewed here: http://www.youtube.com/watch?v=uaB_BSaMzQ4.

43. Montana Secretary of State, "Official Election Results," http://sos.mt.gov/elections/2012/2012_General_Canvass.pdf.

44. Montana Democratic operative, interview.

45. Republican consultant, interview.

46. Burns staffer, interview.

47. E-mail sent by Montanans for Rehberg, November 2, 2012. Video can be viewed here: https://www.youtube.com/watch?v=oVSv6lD227Y&list=UUFXtu0-Vggk5iaEa4MsCALA.

48. Jackie Calmes, "Obama Campaign Banks on High-Tech Ground Game to Reach Voters," *The New York Times,* June 26, 2012.

49. Sides and Vavreck, *The Gamble,* 216, 220–222.

50. Ibid., 222.

51. Sasha Issenberg, *The Victory Lab: The Secret Science of Winning Campaigns.* (New York, NY: Crown, 2012), 7.

52. Ibid.

53. Ibid., 6; Green and Gerber, *Get Out the Vote.*

54. See Matt Richtel and Nicholas Confessore, "Republicans Are Wooing the Wired," *The New York Times,* February 8, 2014.

55. Republican consultant, interview.

56. Ibid.

57. Ibid.

58. Democratic National operative, interview.

59. Ibid.

60. Ibid.

61. Ibid.

62. "Follow the Unlimited Money Tracker," *Sunlight Foundation.* See Chapter 8, footnote 42.

63. "Montanans Choose Bullock, Tester in 2012 Election," Montana Conservation Voters Election Report, http://www.mtvoters.org/files/ElectionReport.pdf; Theresa Keaveny, interview with author, December 13, 2012.

64. "Montanans Choose Bullock, Tester in 2012 Election."

65. By comparison, the groups' work against Senator Conrad Burns did not begin until September of 2012. Interview with Keaveny.

66. Ibid.

67. Ibid.

68. Ibid.

69. Ibid.

70. Maxfield, interview.

71. "Election Center," *CNN.com,* http://www.cnn.com/election/2012/results/state/MT/senate.

72. Issenberg, *The Victory Lab.*

73. Keaveny, interview.

74. Ibid.

75. Ibid.

76. E-mail exchange with Theresa Keaveny, February 10, 2014.

77. Voter turnout data available at Montana Secretary of State's website; Turnout in strong Democratic precincts calculated by author.

78. Memorandum, "Review of Total Voter Contact Numbers For." no date, received by author via e-mail on November 9, 2012 and in his possession.

79. Ibid.

80. Lenny Williams, interview with author, February 12, 2013.

81. Ibid.

82. My analysis of independent expenditures of more than $10,000 dollars compiled by the Sunlight Foundation.

83. Steve Daines's House campaign was an exception to this.

84. Montana Republican operative, interview.

85. Rehberg, interview, January 3, 2013.

86. Lindsay Young, "Outside spenders' return on investment," *Sunlight Foundation*, December 18, 2012, http://sunlightfoundation.com/blog/2012/12/17/return_on_investment/.

87. Rehberg, interview, January 3, 2013.

88. Eaton, interview.

89. Montana political operative, interview.

90. Ibid.

91. Kim Barker, "In Montana, Dark Money Helped Democrats Hold a Key Senate Seat." *ProPublica*, December 27, 2012, http://www.propublica.org/article/in-montana-dark-money-helped-democrats-hold-a-key-senate-seat.

92. Tester, interview with author, May 17, 2013.

93. Ibid.

94. Ibid.

# Lessons Learned

**W**hat can be learned from the Montana Senate race and Tester's victory to help us better understand representation and congressional campaigns elsewhere? There are three important lessons for political scientists and professional campaign practitioners. First, campaigning in a new resource environment post-*Citizens United* changes the way candidates, interest groups, and political parties use these new sources of revenue for electioneering. Second, as media environments become increasingly saturated—as was the case in Montana—the message matters as much, if not more, than the message's timing. It also suggests the value of employing other strategies to reach voters. Finally, reputational relationships crafted by members of Congress with constituents may matter more than ever before in an era of decreasing institutional trust in Congress and devolution of campaign control to a myriad of outside organizations encouraged in part by the post-*Citizens United* resource environment.

After the Supreme Court's decision in *Citizens United*, many political observers assumed Republicans would reap huge benefits because they could tap into the bountiful resources of corporations and wealthy individuals to fund their campaigns. Indisputably, more money than ever flowed into the political process in 2010 and 2012, shattering previous records. In the 2012 presidential campaign alone, $2.6 billion was spent, and much of that came from Super PACs that raised money unfettered by the Federal Election Campaign Act.[1] One possible interpretation of the Republican Party's historically impressive victory over the Democrats in the 2010 midterm elections was the ability of conservative organizations to spend Republican challengers into competition with well-heeled incumbents.

That interpretation is flawed: Keeping Republican challengers competitive financially did not yield results in 2012 consistent with the 2010 midterms. In 2012, the shoe was on the other foot—Democratic incumbents won despite facing financially competitive Republican challengers. According to an analysis by the Sunlight Foundation, many Republican organizations spent far more than Democratic organizations and received a far lower return on their investment.[2] Republicans spent a lot of money in 2012 with very little to show for it. And it is mistaken to presume that Democrats kept the Senate simply because two Republican challengers made gaffes in Missouri and Indiana. Why did Republicans and their allies struggle in 2012 after achieving such success in 2010?

One obvious explanation is the difference in the electoral environments: In congressional midterms, the party opposing the president has historically done well. But the experience in Montana hints at other reasons worth additional exploration. Recent political science research indicates that campaigns can affect outcomes when the information environment provides one side with a clear advantage. This suggests that campaigns affect outcomes most readily in noncompetitive elections because rarely does one side achieve a considerable information advantage for any length of time in competitive elections. In competitive elections, then, the fundamentals such as the state of the economy and the electorate's partisanship should yield outcomes consistent with those underlying factors. In the 2012 presidential election, this meant an Obama victory according to forecasting models and the research presented in Sides and Vavreck's *The Gamble*. It is striking, then, that the fundamentals favored Republican Congressman Rehberg in Montana, his campaign enjoyed an informational advantage in the last six weeks of the campaign, and he still *lost*.

*Citizens United* has led to more money pouring into elections and a richer information environment, but Rehberg's loss to Tester suggests that informational advantages in the mass media do not always yield the anticipated benefits. Democrats may have been behind the mass media 8 ball in the closing days of the race, and the partisan fundamentals in Montana did not favor them, but their more effective use of resources may have made the difference.

As Rehberg and his allies unloaded financially in the final weeks of the Senate campaign on television, advertising time became increasingly scarce and more expensive. By the end of the campaign, more than one station manager told me there was no more time for interest groups, political parties, or candidates to buy on television even if someone had money to buy it. Television advertising rates are subject to the laws of supply and demand, and rates rise as demand increases throughout an election season. This means that as more money poured into Montana in the summer and the fall, it purchased fewer television spots. In particular, outside groups and political parties had even less purchasing power because television stations are not obligated to offer them the lowest unit rate under FCC regulations as they are for candidates.[3] Television stations certainly took advantage of that fact and charged outside groups exorbitant rates. The hard dollars spent by candidates simply went further on television throughout the entire campaign.[4] On the other hand, money spent earlier in the election cycle—when advertising costs were much cheaper—could perhaps be used to greater effect. At the very least, it would be easier in such an environment—with less political advertising—to create and sustain a considerable informational advantage in advertising spots.

This relates to another key point. As airwaves become saturated with a plethora of messages from many different organizations, it is harder to break through the clutter. And it is increasingly likely that some people chose to tune out altogether. This reinforces the point that money spent on television early may yield greater electoral benefits and exhibit greater staying power, contrary to recent research by political scientists. Tester's early advertising advantage in the spring—the largest during the whole campaign—may have given him a boost that continued to sustain him through the summer and into the fall. The evidence, while far from conclusive, is certainly worth further investigation.

Maybe Tester's early advertising advantage didn't help him win, but the message he conveyed in the spring and in later advertising in the summer and fall did make a difference. Tester's first ads were distinctive, memorable, and reminded Montanans what they liked most about the man: Him. This message planted the seeds which later blossomed in the fall: They like Tester, and they don't really like Rehberg. As liberal interest groups pounded Rehberg for his pay raises, the firefighter lawsuit, and his personal wealth throughout the fall, voters were also reminded by Tester's own ads that Tester was still the same dirt farmer they had elected in 2012. Going up early may have helped Tester make a deep impression among voters that insulated him when the harsh negative ads came hot and heavy in the fall.

Related to this point is the fact that the Republican outside groups hammered on the same themes throughout the campaign, never deviating from their core message that Tester was in the pocket of Obama and lobbyists. These messages worked to the extent that voters did increasingly learn that Tester voted with Obama 95 percent of the time, but repetition did little to change the fundamental dynamics of the race.[5] Although the information environment provided Rehberg and Republicans an advantage, it did not move votes, likely because the information was neither new nor changed preexisting views. Voters knew Tester was a Democrat, they knew that he had done some things to support the president, but repeating it did not change their impressions of Tester as a person.

Interestingly, the Democratic message—which consisted of showing how Rehberg was not warm and cuddly—did provide new information, or at least helped remind voters of what they already knew. The attacks began with pay raises and the taxpayer-funded SUV, then focused on Denny's riches, and concluded with the firefighter lawsuit. The campaign plan was carefully orchestrated to reveal particular attack lines at particular points, all with the express purpose of building on the groundwork laid in the spring: Tester is a good guy, and you'd rather have a beer with him than Rehberg. Political scientists must delve deeper into the question of advertising timing and the effectiveness of personalities on voter impressions—especially given the new media realities.

Many races in 2012 seemed to turn on the question of which candidate appeared more empathetic, but political science scholarship stresses the importance of partisanship and economic well-being as more central to voter choice. Perhaps this is changing.

Campaign messages matter, and likeability can trump ideological or partisan kinship. An important but perhaps subtler point must also be made. In an increasingly globalized environment which erodes communication barriers, the world has become both smaller and, at the same time, less intimate. Everything has become less personal. We can shop for clothes, do our banking, and even get our news far from home because of the Internet. As we become increasingly globalized, our local economies and communities seem more distant. It is not a stretch to presume that the flood of money on radio and television airwaves feeds this sense of isolation. Why wouldn't constituents feel disconnected from Congress and its members when they are just as likely to be disconnected from their neighbors?

The upshot of increased societal fragmentation and segmentation is that interpersonal relationships—because they are becoming less common—are becoming *more meaningful* and *more effective* as a means of representation and electioneering. They are three-dimensional in an increasingly two-dimensional world, something to which my Republican consultant eluded.[6] Having a person knock on your door and talk politics, or a candidate shake your hand at a coffee shop, provides for a more intimate political experience than an ad watched on YouTube. Democrats excelled in Montana and nationally at the ground game in 2012 and used a sophisticated array of techniques—backed by social science research—to get folks to vote and to vote for their candidates, but they did it the old-fashioned way, person-to-person. Certainly, mass media is subject to diminishing returns, and perhaps that's exactly what happened in Montana. The information advantage Republicans created on television meant little because either voters tuned out (there were nearly 170,000 ads which began back in March 2011, after all) or Democrats countered by reaching voters in more personal ways tailored to the voter's own particular needs and interests. It is instructive that many of the Democratic-allied groups active in Montana—who were outspent on television—used considerable resources for grassroots mobilization.

The lesson that messages matter and grassroots mobilization is a useful tool with which to reach voters seems to have been well-learned in Montana in the aftermath of the 2012 race. As these words are written, Senator Max Baucus has resigned his seat after his appointment to serve as U.S. Ambassador to China. In February of 2014, Congressman Steve Daines—the presumptive Republican nominee—aired his first ad, focusing exclusively on his personal biography and connections to Montana. Newly appointed interim Democratic Senator John Walsh followed the next week with his own spots focusing on his military career. The Montana Republican Party has not stood idly by after losing all but two statewide races in 2012: It has put substantial resources into cleaning up its microtargeting list and developing voter outreach efforts to play catch up with the Democrats.

The final lesson learned from Montana concerns representation and the presentation of self to constituents by members of Congress. Connection to place and a trusting relationship with constituents is essential and can critically undermine other advantages a member might have. Tester had built a stronger relationship with constituents and evoked stronger place connections than had Congressman Rehberg. Part of the story, of course, begins with the fact that Tester had more official resources with which to build that relationship than Rehberg—this allowed him to build a stronger presence in earned media. This is particularly important in smaller states where the senator and congressman are often compared directly. Another important piece is the fact that Tester actually worked the land from which Montanans and Westerners feel such a strong pull. A connection to place—always central to Western politics—may also increase in importance as people grapple with their lost identities in this globalized world. But that's not the whole story, either.

The final part of the story has to do with how the public views Congress and their individual representatives. In general, the public has always held Congress in disdain. Never loved, the public practically hates Congress in the current political environment. As of this writing, Congress has a job approval rating of only 12 percent.[7] On the other hand, the individuals generally approve of the job their own member of Congress does. In November 2013, Tester's job approval rating—while underwater—was considerably better than Congress's at 44 percent.[8]

The public generally trusts collective entities less than individuals. Bankers and doctors fare worse as groups than a person's own banker or doctor, so in this sense, our hatred of Congress and love of our member is part of a more general phenomenon. Political scientists Greg Fleming and Diana Mutz note that people are not as well-equipped psychologically to make judgments about collectives because they are prone to negative perceptual bias; that is, when asked about a collective, the people draw from a biased sample about what they know about the collective and make a negative summary judgment. Likewise, people tend to be positively biased to those close to them because their experiences are more positive. In fact, much of the information one encounters about his or her individual member of Congress in the earned media is likely neutral or positive, so the positive psychological bias gets reinforced.[9]

Given the predisposition to think better about one's own member of Congress, stressing and building positive constituent impressions with close attention to the state or district seems obvious. Tester's ability to build a strong constituent relationship with Montanans—even after putting aside his resource advantage as a senator—yielded tangible benefits that built on the positivity bias of Montanans. Rehberg, unfortunately, did not build that relationship during his time in Congress as effectively and—given that Montanans were more likely to hear and remember negative information about Rehberg personally—may have actually reinforced the negative messages broadcast against him the race. This made it easier to paint Rehberg as "one of them"—as Congress—which put the congressman in a difficult spot. Montanans believed Tester was distinctive from Congress, while they saw Rehberg as indistinguishable from an institution they did not like or respect. The election strategy is not new to Montana; members have always been running for Congress by running against it and tarring incumbents with the institution's baggage. Tester made Rehberg the incumbent, which he was, in a sense. And this may have made the difference in Tester's unexpected victory.

## FUTURE DIRECTIONS

This study answers many questions, but raises others. Three especially are worthy of study in the post-*Citizens United* world of campaigns. First, political scientists have a good sense of how particular modes of engagement affect voters and their perceptions.[10] A clear sense of whether and how different modes of communication work in an information environment saturated by multiple messages from a variety of sources is lacking, however. The experience in Montana suggests that particular messages matter more—that is, messages focused on candidate traits can trump issues. And certain modes of communication—interpersonal and face-to-face—trump mass media. But the Montana experience is only suggestive; more systematic work is necessary to make these conclusions generalizable. The work by Lynn Vavreck and John Sides in their path-breaking study, *The Gamble,* is one recent and notable effort that begins to do just this.

Second, this study indicates the importance of place in representational styles and suggests that place-based connections are important not just in Montana but in the American West more broadly. How do representatives evoke place when they govern and campaign? Is demonstrating a connection to place more important in certain places or is this place-based style of representation widespread? Are evocations of place more important now given the increasing saturation of mass media markets by 501(c)3 organizations and the loss of connection citizens feel in an globalized era? A larger scale study is necessary to develop a clearer picture of the centrality of place as a "one of us" mode of representation.

Finally, if the message matters, this study strongly hints that the messenger matters, too. We know that outside groups are overwhelmingly negative in their mass media efforts, but generally speaking, we know less about sponsorship effects on the willingness of voters to first receive the message and then be persuaded by it. Although it is generally well-known that voters are more willing and able to receive information that supports their preconceptions (and discarding information which does not), does that receptiveness depend on whether the organization, candidate, or party shares a place-based connection with the voter? In other words, are messages sponsored by organizations outside a geographic consistency more likely to be discounted and discarded by voters regardless of the message they communicate to voters? Or can outside organizations adopt messages, frames, and place-based appeals used by candidates to increase the receptivity and effectiveness of their own communication efforts? These questions are important for candidates, organizations, and parties to answer because the answers ultimately affect the campaign strategies they pursue and the ways in which they attempt to engage voters during a campaign.

## CONCLUSION

In closing, it is curious how hard political scientists have searched for campaign effects and have, by and large, come up wanting. Perhaps we are not thinking of the campaign and its effects in quite the right way. Fenno's call to study members of Congress, their home styles, and careers is important because those careers have lasting effects on how members of Congress behave. Recall how the early political careers of Rehberg and Tester laid down important markers for their governing styles and affected the choices they made when they appeared on the national stage as a congressman and senator, respectively. If we begin to view the campaign as a longer sequence of events—as a narrative governed by a place, a career, and representational choices—perhaps the effects of campaigns on election outcomes will become more readily apparent. The stories that campaigns can tell—and how they tell them—begin with the representational styles and choices members of Congress make when they first get to Washington and the lessons learned from their first efforts to explain their Washington work back home. As political science has left the study of home styles behind, we are doing a great disservice to the study of Congress and of campaigns. Fenno's call to leave Washington, to go back to the district to study members of Congress and their explanations of Washington work, rings with greater relevancy and urgency now than when he first issued the challenge nearly four decades ago.

Everyone cites Fenno but nobody does Fenno. Having done it under the Big Sky, I can honestly say that political science is missing a big part of the representational story that simply isn't captured by big *N*, quantitative studies or forecasting models.[11] In particular, we need to pay as much attention to place, context, and timing as we do to measurement. Place shapes the narratives and manners in which candidates aim to connect with constituents. Context precludes certain choices, while recommending and even necessitating others. And timing is even more important in campaign environments increasingly saturated by outside organizations and groups with competing messages. Campaigns have consequences for election outcomes not because they generate game changing moments. Campaigns have consequences because of the way they shape the information environment voters use to make decisions. In Montana in 2012, Senator Tester won because he enjoyed an informational advantage not reflected in the number of ads. He won because he framed the choice for voters that echoed the representational preferences of Montanans and their particular understanding of relationship to place. At the end of the day, Montanans saw Jon Tester as the authentic, consistent representative who had established his good character in his dealings with them. Denny Rehberg might have been all of these things, but his campaign and his representational relationship with Montanans didn't seem to show it.

## NOTES

1. "The Money Behind the Elections," The Center for Responsive Politics, *Opensecrets. org*, https://www.opensecrets.org/bigpicture/.

2. Young, "Outside Spenders' Return on Investment"; Nicholas Confessore and Jess Bidgood, "Little to Show for Cash Flood by Big Donors," *The New York Times,* November 7, 2012; Barker, "In Montana, Dark Money Helped Democrats Hold a Key Senate Seat."

3. See Oxenford, "Political Broadcasting."

4. Some examples from KECI in Missoula demonstrate the point. On September 16, Jon Tester's campaign paid $65 for a spot on the Voice. AFSCME spent $160. On September 18, Rehberg's campaign paid $270 for a spot on the local news at 10. Crossroads GPS aired two spots during the news, paying $315 for one spot and $585 for the other.

5. In Rehberg's February 2012 poll, 23 percent said that Tester voted with Obama more than 90 percent of the time. By his early September 2012 poll, 46 percent said more than 90 percent of the time.

6. Republican consultant, interview.

7. "Congress and the Public," *Gallup*, http://www.gallup.com/poll/1600/congress-public.aspx.

8. "Montana Miscellany," Public Policy Polling, November 21, 2013, http://www.publicpolicypolling.com/main/2013/11/page/2/.

9. R. Douglas Arnold, *Congress, the Press, and Political Accountability.* (Princeton, CT: Princeton University Press, 2004).

10. See Issenberg, *The Victory Lab* for an overview.

11. But see Justin Grimmer, *Representational Style in Congress: What Legislators Say and Why it Matters.* (New York, NY: Cambridge University Press, 2013).